Creating GeoCities Websites

Written by

Ben Sawyer and *Dave Greely*

Creating GeoCities Websites

Library of Congress Catalog Card Number: 99-62143

ISBN: 0-9662889-1-2

5   4   3   2   1

Educational facilities, companies, and organizations interested in multiple copies of this book should contact the publisher for quantity discount information. Training manuals, CD-ROMs, electronic versions, and portions of this book are also available individually or can be tailored for specific needs.

MUSKA&LIPMAN

Muska & Lipman Publishing
9525 Kenwood Road, Suite 16-372
Cincinnati, Ohio 45242
www.muskalipman.com
publisher@muskalipman.com

This book is composed in Melior, Columbia, Helvetica, and Courier typefaces
using QuarkXpress 4.0.4, Adobe PhotoShop 5.0, and Adobe Illustrator 8.0.
Printed in Cincinnati, Ohio in the United States of America

Foreword

The Internet space is truly an amazing place. It is constantly evolving and changing the way we communicate, interact with others, and conduct our daily business.

When we first pulled a Sun Workstation computer out of the box on the living room floor, we had a vision and a belief that as people flocked to the Web, they would want to find a place to call home—a place to thrive in a virtual world. We thought that place needed to have a sense of community—a familiar and user-friendly environment that would provide the tools and technologies to express their values, opinions, and passions with other people of similar interests. We decided to name that place GeoCities.

Today, we have over 3.5 million members living among 41 virtual communities of topical interests called Neighborhoods. We call our members Homesteaders, because the Internet is still kind of a "wild west frontier." A new Homesteader is signing up every six seconds, and with nearly 19 million visitors to the Web sites created by our Homesteaders, it's no wonder that GeoCities has grown to be one of the top five most trafficked sites on the Internet.

GeoCities' tremendous growth and popularity can be attributed to one major component—our Homesteaders and the millions of Web pages they've created. GeoCities would not exist as it is today without our Homesteaders. We take great pride in showcasing the content on their Web pages to millions of visitors from around the world. Throughout our Neighborhoods, you will discover information on every subject imaginable, including polls, forums, chat rooms and advice columns that compliment our members' sites. It's these Neighborhoods, and the people that live in them, that provide the foundation of community—one of the largest and fastest growing on the Internet.

When we learned of this book being published, we jumped at the chance to provide the authors with an inside look into GeoCities and the tools and technologies that drive the success of our content, as well as our member pages. One of those tools is GeoBuilder, our online, easy-to-use, Web page publishing program. This book is a guide devoted to teaching the ins and outs of GeoBuilder, as well as tools that make GeoBuilder one of the most widely-used online Web publishing programs.

You will find examples of some of our most popular member pages and learn what it takes to build and design one of your very own. You'll also learn how to incorporate cool multimedia objects and graphics and how to build an online store and sell products and services directly through your site. The book also reveals secrets on how to build lots of site traffic and other ways of making easy money through GeoCities' Pages That Pay program.

We hope this book and our story will inspire you to join GeoCities to discover the world of personal Web page publishing and our community. As the Internet moves from its phase of novelty to more of a necessary utility, it's only a matter of time before every individual with a computer will have their own personal Web page. We hope you enjoy the book as much as we enjoyed contributing to it. We look forward to seeing you on the Web. Thank you for your interest and support of GeoCities.

David Bohnett and John Rezner
Co-founders, GeoCities

About the Authors

Ben Sawyer

After graduating from New York's Bronx High School of Science, Ben Sawyer attended the City University of New York-Baruch. In 1992 he worked on the campaign staff for Clinton/Gore '92. He later worked on political projects for several major campaigns, as well as a Legislative Reapportionment and on the news analysis staff for then-President Elect Bill Clinton. In 1995, he returned to his home state of Maine and began a career as a high-tech freelance writer for a number of magazines and newsletters.

In 1995, Sawyer wrote his first book—the *Ultimate Game Developer's Sourcebook*—which was published in early 1996. In June 1997, Sawyer and co-founder Dave Greely started Digitalmill, which performs book, research, and periodical work in the computer industry. Sawyer also founded Next Big Thing, which handles public relations, media relations, and Internet marketing for small software companies.

Sawyer has authored or co-authored several books including *Creating Stores on the Web* and the forthcoming *MP3 Power! with Winamp.*

Dave Greely

After graduating from the University of Maine in 1989, Dave Greely worked as a sportswriter for eight years at the *Kennebec Journal,* where he won numerous national, state, and regional awards. In 1996 and 1997, Greely worked with Sawyer on a number of projects, including the *Microsoft Internet Strategy Report* for Jupiter Communications, before founding Digitalmill.

Greely is the co-author of *Creating Stores on the Web* and the forthcoming *MP3 Power! with Winamp.* Greely lives in South Portland, Maine with his wife Liz and his 2-year-old son Cameron.

Dedications

To my friend Amed Khan—as promised.

—Ben Sawyer

This book is dedicated to my parents, David and Janet Greely, who have supported me through the often difficult times of starting a new business and whose parenting gave me the confidence and ability to do it.

—Dave Greely

Acknowledgements

We would like to thank the following for their contributions to this book:

Toni Zuccarini, Mary Millhollon and Stephanie Mabee, all of whom contributed to the book's content. Justine Clegg and Joann Meyer of Digitalmill, both of whom helped keep us in line and on schedule (not an easy task).

Everyone at GeoCities, who kept us on top of the developments and additions to their excellent service. David Rogelberg and Sherry Rogelberg at Studio B, our literary agency. And of course everyone at Muska & Lipman, especially Andy Shafran and Elizabeth Bruns, who took our work and made it better.

Credits

Publishing Manager
Andy Shafran

Editorial Services Manager
Elizabeth A. Bruns

Development Editor
Mark Cierzniak

Copy Editor
Ruth Younger

Technical Editors
GeoCities
    James Glicker
    Steve Horowitz
    John Rezner
    Allison Nussbaum
    Ed Pierce

Proofreader
Audrey Grant

Cover Designer
Dave Abney

Production Manager
Cathie Tibbetts

Production Team
DOV Graphics
    Dave Abney
    Stephanie Archbold
    Michelle Frey
    Linda Worthington

Indexer
Cary Sherman

Printer
C.J. Krehbiel Co.

Contents

Part I GeoCities Basics

Chapter 1

Chapter 2

Chapter 3

Part II Tools & Templates

Chapter 4

Chapter 5

Chapter 6

Chapter 7

Part III Making an Exciting Site

Chapter 8

Chapter 9

Chapter 10

Chapter 11

Chapter 12

Part IV Beyond Homesteading

Chapter 13

Chapter 14

Chapter 15

Chapter 16

Chapter 17

Index

Introduction

Welcome to *Creating GeoCities Websites*! This is the best *and only* book you'll need for creating great-looking and free Websites on GeoCities, the world's largest Web community.

GeoCities is the innovative company that redefined how the world thinks of community on the Internet. Over the past few years, millions of people have flocked to this popular site to create some of the best designed and most popular sites on the Web. Taking a different philosophy than other Web providers, GeoCities gives anyone a free site to call home.

This 350-page, full-color book guides you on a tour of the GeoCities community. It leads you through all of the ins and outs of learning how to use the powerful tools and programs provided by GeoCities. In the next seventeen chapters, you'll learn how to painlessly build sites from scratch, edit and add images, multimedia, and cool special effects, and see dozens of real examples of well-designed GeoCities sites.

This short introduction defines the standard conventions you'll encounter while reading. It also give you a quick overview of the content of this book. Continue on and enjoy *Creating GeoCities Websites*.

What You'll Learn in This Book

This book teaches you how to effectively master GeoCities and create a great looking site. You'll learn how to use the provided tools and programs to create a Website that generates a lot of traffic, achieves your personal goals, and sells items online – all the while having a lot fun. All of the examples, techniques, and most of the sites in this book are practical and usable.

The following are several important concepts that you will learn in reading this book:

► Building a Website doesn't have to be hard or expensive.

► GeoCities provides all the needed tools to build, promote, and energize your site.

► Expert-looking Websites can come from non-experts who have the right knowledge of GeoCities and HTML.

► Creating Websites is all about good design, interesting sites, valuable content, and exciting add-ons.

Readable and Friendly Text

As you read this book, you'll find we don't gloss over difficult subjects nor do we assume you understand all sorts of new terminology. Instead, we give you complete explanations, step-by-step techniques, and comprehensive coverage of all the features found within GeoCities.

We're not going to waste your time by talking about obscure issues such as TCP/IP protocols, Java programming, or other complicated WWW concepts and technology, because those topics aren't the focus of this book. Instead, we're going to provide you with a practical guide to making good Websites on GeoCities. You'll find help in achieving all your site-related goals in these easy-to-understand and fun-to-read chapters. You'll enjoy seeing sensible examples and building content that can complement a variety of different Web pages.

Conventions Used in This Book

As you read, you will find several different conventions that highlight specific types of information that you'll want to keep an eye out for:

► Every chapter will have a Moving On section. This section will tell what you learned in each chapter and how the next few chapters will introduce you to new concepts.

► All URLs are displayed in **boldface.** You can type them into your browser window and go directly to the site referred to.

Besides the above textual conventions, we also use several different icons throughout this book, shown below.

TIP

Text formatted in this manner offers extra information related to the issue being discussed. You'll find personal anecdotes and experiences, specific design techniques, and general information extras in "Tip" boxes.

CAUTION

Actions and commands that could make irreversible changes to your files or potentially cause problems in the future are displayed in this manner, as "Caution" material. Also included are possible security concerns. Make sure you read this text carefully as it could contain important information that directly affects enhancing your Web page.

NOTE

Notes present interesting or useful information that aren't necessarily essential to the discussion, but provide additional material to help you avoid problems. Notes also offer advice relating to a specific topic.

Keeping the Book's Content Current

You made a long-term investment when you purchased this book. To keep your investment paying off, we've developed a companion Website for you. The site contains:

▶ Up-to-date information on the world of GeoCities

▶ Corrections or clarifications to the book's text and images

▶ New resources you can use to stay on the cutting edge

▶ URLs of readers like you who submit their Website

▶ An interactive discussion to talk about GeoCities

▶ Extra chapters and techniques that we couldn't cram in here

Essentially, this up-to-date Web site is your one-stop shop for this book, so take advantage of it!

Stop by at:

http://www.muskalipman.com/geocities

Or, if you'd like to send e-mail to the production staff or authors directly, we'd love to hear from you. Your input and comments are critical to making sure this book covers all the right information in an easy-to-use manner. Send e-mail to **geocities@muskalipman.com.**

Part I
GeoCities Basics

1

GeoCities FAQ

If you are familiar enough with the concept of building a personal home page, you are probably familiar with GeoCities. What you might not understand is what GeoCities has to offer to people with a wide variety of home page-building skills. Everyone from beginners to newcomers can, with the help of GeoCities, make their presence felt on the World Wide Web.

In a short time, the Web has changed the way people work, communicate, share their ideas, and collect information. It is also a great way to express your opinions and your creativity. This chapter covers some basic questions about home page building in general and GeoCities in particular. The rest of the book will continue to answer these questions in far more detail. After reading this book, you will be ready to make a contribution to the community of GeoCities and its millions of members.

NOTE

What is a FAQ?

FAQ stands for *Frequently Asked Questions*. A FAQ is a list of common questions and their answers. This chapter contains a series of common GeoCities-related questions that many individuals have when joining the GeoCities community, along with their answers.

Basic GeoCities Questions

What is GeoCities?

GeoCities (**www.geocities.com**) is both the number one free home page service on the Web and is one of the most vibrant Web communities. GeoCities members—called Homesteaders—can share their knowledge, opinions, interests, and more with the three million other GeoCities members and with 100 million people who are connected to the World Wide Web.

Figure 1.1
The GeoCities home page.

NOTE

Member=Homesteader

Members of the GeoCities set of services aren't simply customers; they're Homesteaders. Because GeoCities is more a community than simply a place to store a few Web pages, the goal is to make all members feel at home.

Throughout this book, we'll refer to GeoCities members as Homesteaders.

GeoCities offers a diverse set of Web communities organized around participants' interests. Homesteaders post messages, chat, and interact with one another to pursue friendships, commerce, and the sharing of thoughts and ideas. In many ways, GeoCities lets you do many of the things you would do in a real city. You move in, build a home (your free home page), meet and interact with other people, shop, do business, and have fun—all online.

How was GeoCities started?

GeoCities was originally founded in 1994 by David Bohnett and John Rezner. At the time, the company was known as Beverly Hills Internet and was—like many companies at that point—a provider of Web access, hosting, and development. Shortly thereafter, the company decided to offer customers the ability to develop free home pages that are organized in online communities such as SiliconValley (**www.geocities.com/SiliconValley/**) for technology buffs; CapitolHill (**www.geocities.com/CapitolHill**) for political junkies; and SunsetStrip (**www.geocities.com/SunsetStrip/**) for rock music fans.

By December 1995, the company was signing up thousands of users and it had 14 specific interactive communities. The founders then decided that the free home page community movement would be its focus. The company changed its name to GeoCities and focused on building membership for its free home page service. By 1996, more than 250,000 Homesteaders had built Web sites.

By June 1997, GeoCities was the fifth most popular site on the Web, and by October 1997 the company had its one millionth Homesteader. In April 1998, as the company rocketed toward two million members, the company hired Tom Evans as its new CEO and prepared for a public offering in the stock market. Founder David Bohnett became Chairman of the Board, where he works today, helping to guide the long-term vision for the company he founded.

GeoCities went public on August 11, 1998, and today boasts more than three million unique Homesteaders who periodically update their Web sites. It is consistently one of the five most-accessed sites on the entire Internet.

What is a home page?

A home page is your own personal spot on the Internet where you can list information about yourself, your family, your pets, your business, or anything else that interests you. Simply put, a home page is your addition to the collective information found on the Internet. A home page includes information in the form of text, pictures, graphics, multimedia content and more. It is a way for you to share your thoughts, knowledge, opinions, interests, and creativity with the world.

Your GeoCities home page can be about anything as long as it does not violate the GeoCities guidelines against content such as pornography or hateful material. You can build the world's definitive resource on anything from Ultimate Frisbee, synchronized swimming, or Leonardo DiCaprio movies to Web page building, carpentry, or model airplanes.

A home page allows you to do things such as post pictures from your most recent trip, post favorite recipes, share your passions and knowledge, meet people who share your interests, make money, and more.

If you're not interested in starting a small niche interest page like the examples above, you can certainly interact with others interested in broad subjects such as health and fitness, business and money, and others that GeoCities has already organized.

Why should I put my page on GeoCities?

Many Internet Service Providers (ISPs) can provide you with a place to build your own home page. Usually, however, you must pay ISPs monthly fees to connect to the Internet and also to host your Web site—and then you don't even get all the great benefits that GeoCities Homesteaders receive. Many people have free Internet access at school or work, so they can use GeoCities and never have to worry about ISP charges. Listed below are a few of the reasons to place your home page on GeoCities:

- ▶ **Home page building tools.** GeoCities provides a number of excellent home page-building tools, such as free graphics and software, to help you develop your own pages.

- ▶ **Topic-oriented communities.** GeoCities provides a community of members who might be sharing and building pages about topics similar to yours. For example, an entire section of pages is devoted to the X-Files, which you can easily join if that is the focus of your Web site.

- ▶ **Publicity and promotion tools.** Numerous built-in publicity and promotion tools increase the number of visitors who stop by and take a view.

- ▶ **Free services.** GeoCities will always have a free level of service. This means that schools, small businesses, and millions of individuals can count on having an economical way to publish information about themselves.GeoCities may not be the only place to make your home on the Web, but it may well be the best.

GeoCities Membership Questions

How do I become a member of GeoCities?

Chapter 2, "Getting Started with GeoCities," covers the entire signup process in detail. Essentially, you go to **http://www.geocities.com** and click on the button labeled **Join Now**. You will be asked a number of questions that will place you in the most appropriate neighborhood—the one that best matches your personal interests. Once you have completed the registration process, you can start building your page. It's that easy.

What do I get when I join GeoCities?

You will receive access to your free home page space, which totals 11 megabytes (enough for 1,400 pages of text).

You will also have access to GeoCities' chat rooms and message boards and will be enrolled in the GeoPoints program, which lets you earn discounts and free merchandise on GeoCities. GeoCities also offers discounts on software and other special offers. In addition, you will be eligible for weekly prize drawings and can access special page-building tools like the GeoCities image library and multimedia special effects such as the PhotoCube and ThingMaker.

GeoCities also offers a free e-mail account and a free image library (**www.geocities.com/members/tools/clipart/**) that helps you dress up your site.

Do I have to build a page to become a member of GeoCities?

No. In fact, GeoCities is one of the most visited sites on the Internet. That's because some of the best sites in the world are built on GeoCities. Each day millions of Web surfers visit sites that have been built on GeoCities by Homesteaders. But you can sign on as a member and never build much of a page—instead you might just use the e-mail or visit the discussion forums and chat rooms.

However, while GeoCities is about much more than just building home pages, becoming a GeoCities Homesteader is the biggest reason to join GeoCities.

How good does my GeoCities site have to be?

With over three million completely different sites, you'll run across a wide variety of site topics and qualities. What's most important is that you build your own site about your own specific topics. A site about your favorite local band, your small business, or sailing the San Francisco Bay Area may be of interest to more people than you think.

A good site should be easy to comprehend and should contain content (pictures, text, video, music, and so on) of interest to someone else. Your site should matter to you, of course. Otherwise why build it? However, no ultimate judge decides what's a good-looking site and what isn't.

People who create attractive and informative pages do have an edge. While your site may have an uninteresting design, it can be lifted to the level of excellence by compelling writing, gorgeous photos, or exclusive information. Just because a site looks like it was built by a Web design expert doesn't make it a "good" site.

If you do build a site that's interesting to you, chances are others will find it worth visiting. Your goal need not be to make your site the most visited on the Web. Just make it the best site for *you* and let those who share your interests do the rest.

GeoCities Policies and Procedures

Will GeoCities help me build my site?

No one from GeoCities will personally help you build your site. However, the company offers extensive help through materials and forums devoted to building pages. GeoCities also offers BluePrint (**www.geocities.com/main/help/Blueprint/**), an online magazine devoted to building great home pages. Many members have also designed pages devoted to teaching you how to build pages on GeoCities.

GeoCities also has Community Leaders who volunteer to help their neighbors. Community Leaders are experienced and dedicated Homesteaders who have been trained to help other members with just about any problem they encounter. For more information on Community Leaders, go to **www.geocities.com/main/help/qna/guide_leaders.html**.

You can also take advantage of the help from this book and all the free built-in tools you'll find in GeoCities. All these aids will enable you to find the answers to your specific questions and any support you may need while building your own site.

Who owns the content on my site?

If you have personally created the material on your site, you own it. GeoCities doesn't ever own your material, but merely provides the means for you to post it. Accordingly, you are responsible for the content on your site, which includes complying with the terms of service and content guidelines of GeoCities, following laws or copyrights that exist, and making sure your site doesn't contain illegal or libelous material. If you break any laws or GeoCities' guidelines, your site may be taken down.

Does GeoCities protect my site?

GeoCities works hard to ensure the security of your site's backend—the files you create that become your home page.

However, if you use a poorly selected password (such as the word "password") or if you give your password out, you can jeopardize your site. Never share your password with anyone, even if the person claims to be from GeoCities.

Some people might try to imitate your design, graphics, text, or other content by simply cutting and pasting from their browser to their own machine. Make sure you place copyright (©) information on your site to warn people that your site's content is not to be copied without permission. Fortunately, most people would rather link to your original work than steal it.

On the other hand, if you have some good writing or an image that you don't mind sharing, let people know that they can post it on their site by requesting your permission and giving you proper credit. You will frequently see postings, on GeoCities and the Web in general, that are courtesy of someone else. Giving others permission to use your material is a great way to build promotion and links back to your site.

You should also never post material on your site that is copyrighted, such as a cartoon of Bart Simpson or an article from a newspaper, without obtaining permission from the owner.

What about privacy?

GeoCities is a member of the TRUSTe privacy program. TRUSTe is an independent, nonprofit initiative whose mission is to build users' trust and confidence in the Internet by promoting the principles of disclosure and informed consent. In an effort to demonstrate commitment to its members, GeoCities has agreed to disclose all GeoCities' information practices and to have its privacy practices reviewed and audited for compliance by TRUSTe. In general, when you visit a Web site displaying the TRUSTe mark, you can expect to be notified of the following:

▶ What information the site gathers/tracks about you (for example, mailing address, age, pages visited, etc.);

▶ What the site does with the information it gathers/tracks. (Is it used to sell products to you?);

▶ Does the site share the information it gathers/tracks with others? (Does it pass your information on to other organization without your consent?);

▶ The site's opt-out policy. (Can you ask to be kept off all mailing lists?);

▶ The site's policy on correcting and updating personally identifiable information;

▶ The site's policy on deleting or deactivating your name from GeoCities' database.

For more information about GeoCities' privacy practices, visit **http://geocities.com/main/info/company/privacy.html** and click on the questions that are relevant to you. GeoCities also strives to provide a clear and concise application form requesting only pertinent information and to continually serve its members in a secure and responsible manner.

What about the safety of children on GeoCities?

GeoCities protects the privacy of all its members and has special policies particularly focused for children. In addition to the previously mentioned privacy question, GeoCities provides an entire Kids-only community— EnchantedForest. At the EnchantedForest community home page, the warning states:

> "Kids: Remember! Always be careful who you talk to and what you tell strangers about yourself online. Use a nickname in chat and forums (even on your Web page), and **never** tell anyone your real name, e-mail, telephone number, or any other personal information."

Not meant to scare parents away from the Internet or GeoCities, this policy reminds you to always use common sense when meeting new people online.

Why are ads served every time someone visits my page?

GeoCities requires an ad to be placed on every page. You may choose between an advertising banner called the GeoGuide or a separate pop-up ad that appears periodically as visitors navigate through your site.

The GeoGuide is a customizable navigation guide that helps visitors communicate with you about your page and helps them navigate GeoCities. It also contains a built-in banner.

The pop-up ads are never served alongside a page that has a GeoGuide.

GeoCities' primary source of revenue is the advertising that is sold on its members' sites. These advertisements are what allow GeoCities to provide you with 11 megabytes of free space, technical support, tools, and other GeoCities services. GeoCities does offer an enhanced level of service, which costs $4.95 a month, does not require ads on your pages, and has several other benefits – which we cover in Chapter 16, "Enhanced Service: GeoPlus."

What is the GeoCities Watermark?

The GeoCities Watermark is a special graphic (the GeoCities logo) that constantly displays itself in the lower right-hand corner of your Web page. It displays only in version 4.0 Web browsers from Netscape and Microsoft. You cannot destroy or change the appearance of the GeoCities Watermark and it appears on all pages of your Web site.

GeoCities uses the rather inconspicuous Watermark for several reasons. Clicking on the Watermark takes members to sites on GeoCities that deal with topics similar to yours. The Watermark also serves to inform surfers that your site is on GeoCities.

When a visitor clicks on the Watermark, a pop-up box with links to Avenue pages appears. These links give the visitor the chance to discover more Homesteads with similar content. GeoCities will continue to upgrade the Watermark based on member feedback.

Will GeoCities ever remove my pages?

If you violate the accepted user policies, such as including hate speech or pornography on your site, or displaying otherwise inappropriate or copyrighted material, GeoCities will remove your site. Otherwise, you can expect your page to remain on GeoCities for as long as you wish.

For more on GeoCities' guidelines, go to **www.geocities.com/members/guidelines/**.

Technical Questions & Specifications

Can I use my own page-building tools and FTP tools with GeoCities?

Yes. While GeoCities provides the GeoCities File Manager, the GeoCities QuickPage Builder, the GeoCities PageBuilder, and the extensive GeoStudio program (all of which are discussed in detail in this book) to help you manage your files and build your pages, you needn't use these programs. GeoCities is compatible with all major page-building tools— freeware, shareware, or professional. This flexibility lets you design and build your page however you want.

GeoCities also lets you use your own File Transfer Protocol (FTP) program. Don't worry if you are not familiar with either a page-building program or an FTP program; we cover how to use your own FTP program in this book. Most of the popular Web page-building tools list further resources—books and manuals—to help you.

Can I use Microsoft FrontPage with GeoCities?

The most popular HTML tool in the world, Microsoft FrontPage, can easily be used to build and maintain your GeoCities sites. In fact, FrontPage integrates well with GeoCities and is used by thousands of Homesteaders. But, GeoCities does not support the proprietary FrontPage extensions that allow you to use some special interactive features. Components such as Themes, Bots, and some advanced tools require special FrontPage servers, which are not available on GeoCities.

FrontPage will let you know when you upload a page that requires these special extensions, which will help you build a site that will work on the GeoCities servers.

Do I have to know HTML or JavaScript in order to build my GeoCities site?

Knowledge of HTML is helpful but not absolutely necessary. In general, the more you know about the languages of the Web (HTML, JavaScript, Dynamic HTML, etc.), the better your pages will be. However, you'll find plenty of programs that don't require any HTML knowledge.

This book has a basic HTML reference guide and we've provided sample bits of code throughout the book. If you want to learn more about HTML, we suggest you check out some of the useful books on HTML such as:

> *HTML 4 for the World Wide Web: Visual QuickStart Guide*
> by Elizabeth Castro
> Peachpit Press, 1997
> ISBN: 0201696967

Does GeoCities support Java, CGI Scripts, Forms, Dynamic HTML, and VBScript?

GeoCities supports putting Java applets on your system, although applets that have server side extensions or that try to write back to the site won't work. GeoCities only supports the pre-approved CGI Scripts that it offers to all users. These include:

▶ **Home page-building tools.** GeoCities provides a number of excellent home page building tools to help you develop your own pages. These tools include free graphics and software, just to name a few.

▶ **Form/e-mail integration.** With its forms remailer, GeoCities offers extensive support for Web forms. Chapter 11, "Adding Multimedia to Your GeoCities Site," of this book covers everything you need to know in order to add interactive Web forms to your site.

▶ **Page counter.** You can easily follow the traffic created by visitors to your site by counting visitors. Chapter 10, "Adding Special Effects to Your Pages," shows how to use the Page counter in more detail.

▶ **Site guestbook.** Visitors can leave messages for you and future visitors by signing an online guestbook. Chapter 10 shows how to use this cool feature.

▶ **ESPN News Wire.** The ESPN News Wire allows you to include current headlines and continuously updated scores on your site.

Finally, you can use any downloadable technology that can be processed by a Web browser (including JavaScript, Dynamic HTML, VBScript, etc.) on GeoCities.

Does GeoCities offer personal chat rooms, RealAudio, RealVideo, or Netshow?

GeoCities currently offers community chat rooms but not personal chat rooms. Although this could change in the future, you are currently forbidden from putting a personal chat room on your site if it sends advertisements. Since most of the third-party chat rooms available require that you distribute advertising, adding a personal chat room at this time is difficult. If chatting is absolutely imperative, you are allowed to include your ICQ chat address on your Web site so visitors can page you if you're online.

GeoCities does support RealAudio, RealVideo, and Netshow, although it doesn't offer the specialized servers that let you send out audio or video to hundreds or thousands of simultaneous users. (You'll have to find somewhere else to deliver that live concert of your band.) However, you can offer downloadable or HTTP streaming versions of these file types. Either one works very well for personal small audience use. VivoActive is another video format that works especially well for lower-end sites that offer streaming video. There's also room to offer high-quality MP3 files. All these tools and technologies are mentioned in depth later in this book.

Business on GeoCities

Can I build a store on GeoCities?

You can build two types of stores—associate stores and GeoShops— on GeoCities.

Associate stores can be set up with any of the GeoCities–sanctioned associate partners. With an associate store, you recommend products to your site's visitors that are part of the Pages That Pay program. You then provide links from your site to the particular service or Web store. Through the embedding of information, the store can determine if the customer was referred from your site. If you send enough customers to a particular Web store, you can receive store credit or cash.

Associate stores are a great way to sell things and earn money without any risk. However, some people want to sell more than the associate programs will allow—and they want to sell their own items from their own store. For these people, GeoCities offers a program called GeoShops (for a fair monthly fee) that lets you develop and run a completely Web-based store. GeoShops includes a virtual URL such as **www.your-company.com**, up to 25 megabytes of space, secure payment acceptance and more.

Chapter 17, "GeoShops: E-Commerce Made Easy," covers the ins and outs of creating a GeoShop.

You can't actively sell products on GeoCities unless you are either part of the GeoShops program or an approved associate program.

Can I put information about my business on GeoCities?

GeoCities doesn't mind if people offer information about their business on a free site unless they are engaging in overt commerce, such as selling, posting a catalog with prices, or soliciting funds. You are welcome to post information about your items that your business produces, services that you render, and ways to contact you (such as an e-mail address or a telephone number) for further information.

What will bring people to your business site is not your business itself. It will be the content and information you put up about your area of business. If people are impressed by the information, they may contact you in search of additional help or to use your services.

How can I get millions of people to visit my GeoCities page?

Promote your site as much as you can. As many new members discover, building a page can often be the easy part; getting people to visit your site is the hard part. For more on promoting your site, see Chapter 13, "Promoting Your GeoCities Home Page."

What if I need more space for my Web site?

Since you can't sign up for and build multiple GeoCities sites, you have two options if you need more space. You can either wait for GeoCities to hand out more space (they've upgraded several times during the life of the service) or purchase the GeoPlus service which, for a small monthly fee, offers twice as much room as a free site.

What is GeoPlus and how is it different from my free GeoCities service?

GeoPlus is an extension to GeoCities' free home page service that offers a number of advantages over the free service. If you build an incredible site and find the need to graduate to something more, the GeoPlus service might be for you. In addition to extra space, some other benefits are a personal URL and additional CGI Scripts. Also, GeoPlus members are exempt from having advertisements on their pages. The cost of the basic GeoPlus package is $4.95 per month. For more on GeoPlus, see Chapter 16, "Enhanced Service: GeoPlus."

Is there anything else I should know?

When it comes to building home pages, you can never know enough. GeoCities is also a growing service that will constantly offer more options, special services, and other benefits as it grows. However, this book covers the heart and soul of building home pages on GeoCities. We'll point out sites you'll want to visit, books to read, and tools to use along the way. Even if you consider yourself a GeoCities expert, you can learn more here. And if you're not an expert now, you will be when you finish this book.

2

Getting Started with GeoCities

Now that we have answered some basic questions about GeoCities and everything it has to offer, let's get started working with GeoCities and taking those first steps toward building a home page. This chapter explains some common GeoCities terminology, walks you through the sign-up process and gives a quick run-down of some of the aspects of GeoCities that will help make your stay in this community a long and enjoyable one.

Understanding GeoCities Components

Before you create your site, let's take a moment to get familiar with the important areas and sites on GeoCities where you'll spend a lot of time. This section helps you understand the difference between Avenues, Marketplaces, Neighborhoods, Members' Area, and GeoCities reference information. Later on in this chapter, we take a GeoTour to make sure you know how to navigate around GeoCities.

NOTE

GeoCities Terminology

Homesteader: Homesteaders are GeoCities members who have built their own set of pages online.

Community Leader: Community Leaders are volunteers dedicated to a specific area of GeoCities. They can teach you the ropes and answer questions about starting your Website, and they are available for technical and moral support when you design your pages. All Community Leaders are experienced Homesteaders who have created their own Web pages and can share their expertise with you. To become a Community Leader, you must have a site that is focused on that community's topic. Simply fill out an application at the community in which you are interested.

GeoAvenues

Avenues are collections of news stories, articles, member home pages, and columns that relate to a specific topic. Each Avenue is geared towards collecting the best set of GeoCities content for its topic, such as medicine, art, and so on. Figure 2.1 shows how Avenues are listed on the GeoCities home page.

Figure 2.1
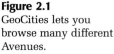
GeoCities lets you browse many different Avenues.

Avenues are the quickest way to find GeoCities-based information in a specific topic area. For example, in the Family Avenue, you'll find online articles about family issues, an area specifically geared toward kids entertainment, links to pertinent chat areas, and references to current news articles.

Visitors vote on GeoCities Websites to help classify the sites into the right Avenues. Avenues also help you to settle into the right Neighborhood and to build your own Website.

Neighborhoods

Neighborhoods are the logical system through which GeoCities lets members place their Websites. More than 40 different Neighborhoods are available for you to visit, explore, and join—each with its own theme. Each Neighborhood is further divided into several suburbs that help you locate even more specific information. GeoCities guides new members into joining Neighborhoods that match the topics of their pages. For example, you can expect to find many X-Files sites in the Area51 Neighborhood, while a poetry club might set up shop in the SoHo Neighborhood. Figure 2.2 shows the GeoCities' listing of the SoHo Neighborhood.

Figure 2.2
This Neighborhood
focuses on artists,
writers, and poets.

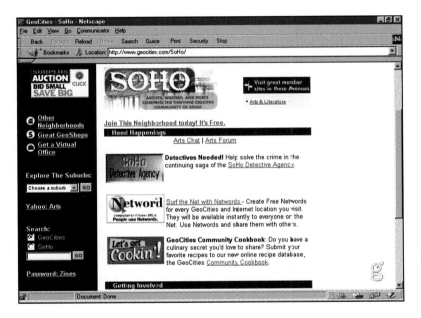

Marketplace

The Marketplace (**http://www.geocities.com/marketplace/**) is where you can learn about GeoCities commerce partners and opportunities. This site shows you how to enable your site for electronic commerce with GeoCities online partners, place classified ads, and purchase GeoCities-related merchandise from the GeoStore.

Electronic commerce and online purchasing are discussed in more depth in Chapter 13, "Promoting Your GeoCities Home Page." You'll learn how to commerce-enable your site and how to use some of these more advanced services. Figure 2.3 shows the Marketplace ready to do business.

Figure 2.3
Learn how to buy and sell CDs, books, and more from your Website.

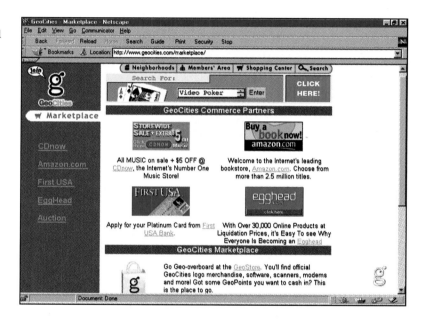

Members' Area

The Members' Area (**http://www.geocities.com/members/**) is the starting point for the millions of people who belong to GeoCities and use its services. This site contains references to GeoCities tools, online magazines, and communities, as well as provides answers to common questions and solutions to technical problems. The Members' Area, shown in Figure 2.4, is your main point of operations as a GeoCities member.

Figure 2.4
Visit this site often to learn about new and updated GeoCities services and references.

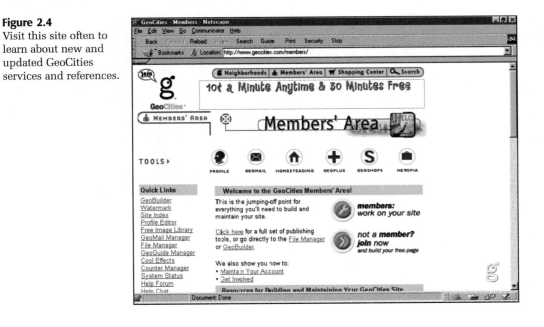

Information about GeoCities

The GeoCities Information site (**http://www.geocities.com/main/info/**) describes information about GeoCities as a company, gives technical descriptions of the service, and provides links to news releases about GeoCities from around the world. In addition, you'll find official policy statements, technical support guides, and tips for engaging in chat sessions online.

Searching GeoCities

The GeoCities Search Site (**http://www.geocities.com/search/**) allows you to find specific members, pages, and sites on a specific topic. You can search all of GeoCities or look for a specific member's site. Figure 2.5 shows the GeoCities Search page.

Figure 2.5
Search GeoCities when you want to quickly find a specific page or set of pages on a topic.

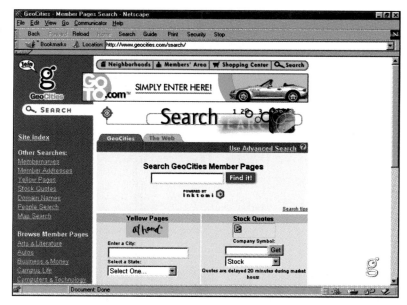

In addition, several links to other Internet-wide search services make it easy for you to find what you're looking for.

Taking a GeoTour

GeoCities is a dynamic and large service. New members often enjoy taking a quick tour around the entire set of GeoCities services before they join. To take a GeoTour, visit **http://www.geocities.com/main/help/geotour.** Here you can read about everything from the GeoCities community to membership opportunities to the guidelines that are set for all members. See Figure 2.6 for the start of the GeoTour.

If you don't feel the need to read over every last detail, you can always leave the GeoTour and begin the registration process by clicking on **Join** at the bottom of the opening GeoTour page.

Figure 2.6
Starting the GeoTour.

Joining GeoCities

Now that you are familiar with some terms and components used on GeoCities, it's time to sign up and start building your site, a relatively quick process. Click on the **Join** button on any of GeoCities main pages or visit **http://www.geocities.com/join/** directly in your browser (Figure 2.7).

Figure 2.7
Here's where you begin the process of signing up for your account.

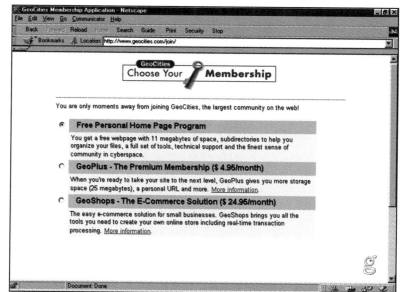

You can choose from four different types of memberships, which offer specialized services.

▶ **Free Personal Home Page Program**—This is the most popular GeoCities service because of its price and amenities. You get access to 11 megabytes of diskspace, all the GeoCities tools, and the chance to join your favorite GeoCities Neighborhood. This membership level requires that an advertisement be included on your Web pages.

▶ **GeoPlus–The Premium Membership**—For only $4.95 a month, you get a personalized URL, more disk space, and an ad-free Website. Many GeoCities members switch to this service level once their site is up and running successfully. For more on GeoPlus, see Chapter 16, "Enhanced Service: GeoPlus."

▶ **GeoShops–The E-Commerce Solution**—Priced at $24.95 a month, GeoShops lets you set up a fully commerce-enabled Website. Sell items and process credit cards with your GeoShop. For more on GeoShops, see Chapter 17, "GeoShops: E-Commerce Made Easy."

You'll have to decide which service level is right for you. All services allow you to participate in GeoCities chats and Neighborhoods, and to use the built-in Web tools. We cover all of the available services in this book, focusing for the next few chapters on helping you build your free personal home page.

Once you select your Member Service level, click the **Join** button at the bottom of the page. GeoCities steps you into a New Member Application (see Figure 2.8).

Figure 2.8
GeoCities needs to know the standard sign-up information.

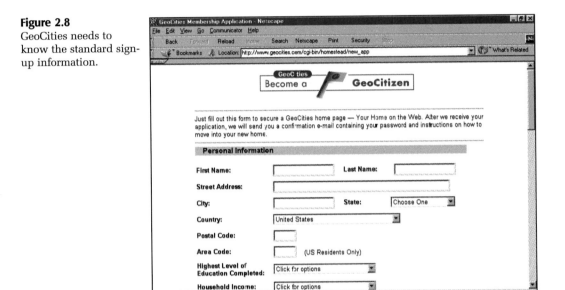

Type in pertinent information—such as your name, address, e-mail address, and desired page theme (this information can be updated later). At the bottom of the New Member Application page, GeoCities lists its "Content Guidelines and Member Terms of Service." This section describes the major rules around hosting your site on GeoCities. For example, no nudity or pornography is allowed on any GeoCities page.

CAUTION
Know the Rules

Ignoring the guidelines can lead to your membership being revoked and your pages being removed without warning. GeoCities is a fun, family-oriented environment. Following the guidelines helps to ensure that the community remains positive and friendly.

TIP

Recheck that E-mail Address!

The single most important piece of information you provide is your valid e-mail address. Make sure you type it in correctly, or you won't be able to fully create your site and will have to re-register. GeoCities sends welcome and confirmation messages to this e-mail address once you join!

Click on the button labeled **I Agree** to continue. The next screen shows a series of special offers geared specifically toward GeoCities members. These offers, which are always changing, let you sign up for personalized news delivery services and show you how to sell books and CDs online. Sign up for the special offers that interest you, then click on the **Submit** button at the bottom of the screen. (You can always adjust your settings to these offers later.)

Your next step in the sign-up process is selecting your Neighborhood (Figure 2.9). GeoCities provides you with a list of Avenues—topics of interest into which they classify member sites. Select an Avenue and click the **Continue** button.

Figure 2.9
Find the right spot for your new Website.

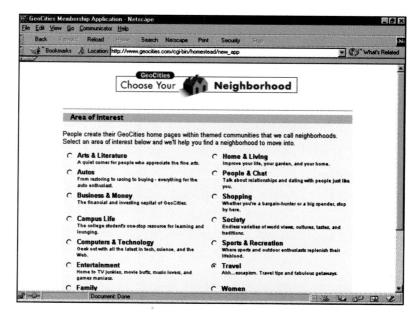

GeoCities then shows you a list of Neighborhoods that are related to the topic area you selected. The goal behind this exercise is to help you find the best spot to place your Website. People can find your site more easily when it's grouped with related member sites. Select a specific

Neighborhood to join and click on the **Continue** button. GeoCities returns with a list of available vacancies into which you can move, as shown in Figure 2.10.

Figure 2.10
Which GeoCities Block should you live on?

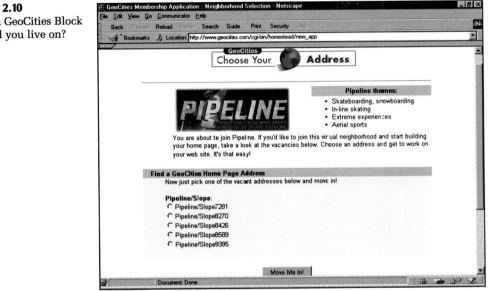

Select a vacancy and click on the **Move Me In!** button. Congratulations, you are now a member of GeoCities (Figure 2.11).

Figure 2.11
Your membership sign-up is complete.

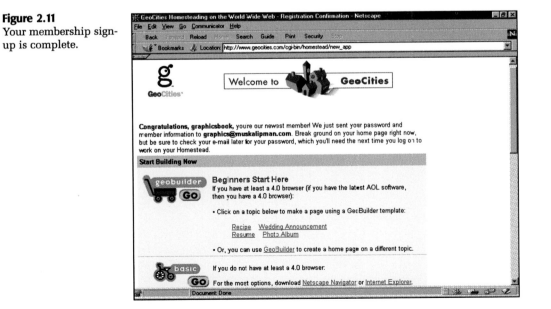

GeoCities has moved you in and you now have an area where you can build your Website. You can start building a page now using the three different caliber of site generators (for beginning, experienced, and expert individuals at building Websites). Or, you can visit **http://www.geocities.com/members/** to learn more about various online resources available for building your site. The rest of this book steps you through building and enhancing your Website!

All your confirmation information—including your URL, membership name, and initial instructions—will be sent to you via e-mail. The e-mail will also include your password, which you'll need to make any changes or updates to your Website. Hold on to this e-mail because it is an important resource as you move forward with construction of your Website.

Figure 2.12 shows our site as it is right now—not much so far.

Figure 2.12
This is what your initial page will look like.

Members' Services

Now that you've joined GeoCities and received your password information by mail, let's take a look at the Members' Services Area. This is your main center of operations for learning about and using GeoCities when you're online. It includes links to valuable GeoCities tools and resources, allows you to update your personal profile and password, and links you directly to the GeoCities File Manager!

Changing Your Password and Other Information

You can always change your password to something easier to remember by going to the Profile Editor page. Click on the **Profile Tools** link from your Members' Area home page (**http://www.geocities.com/members/tools/profile_editor.html**). First, you are prompted to log on as shown in Figure 2.13. The Profile Editor steps you through the process of changing your password. Enter your member name and the password that GeoCities has provided. (Note: The logon is case–sensitive.) Click on the **Submit** button.

Figure 2.13
Modify your personal information on the Profile Editor page.

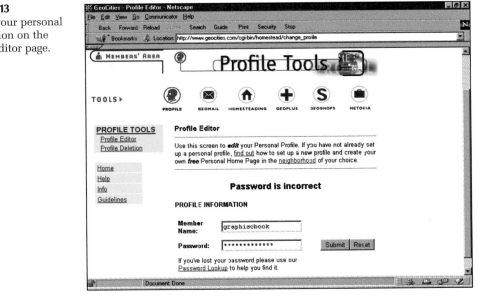

Read all the information on this page. Changing your member name changes your GeoCities e-mail address, and changing your e-mail address changes your password. Figure 2.14 shows the Profile Editor Page, which allows you to make modifications to your personal information and your interest in special offers. You can change any of the information you originally entered when you registered. Once you have made the desired changes, click the **Submit Changes** button at the bottom of the page.

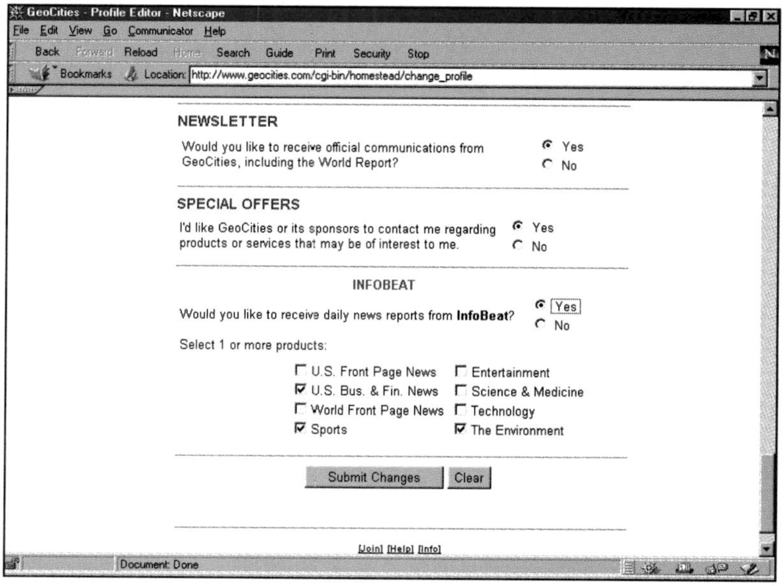

Figure 2.14
Change your password or profile information here.

Part I   GeoCities Basics

Read *Blueprint*—The Online GeoCities 'Zine

Blueprint (**http://www.geocities.com/main/help/Blueprint/**) is GeoCities' official online help 'zine. It is geared towards helping new, intermediate and even advanced home page builders get the most out of the Web. Written entirely by Homesteaders, *Blueprint* features GeoCities' "build" tutorials, help resource tools, free "takeaway" elements and regular columns about content, technical problems, and more.

Core columns include Hey TechMan (a technical Q&A), Stripdown (the code behind design issues), Free Farm (fresh page design and free elements) and Content Workshop (covering page content issues). There are also featured columns that cover things such as GeoCities events and home page news and views.

Figure 2.15
The *Blueprint* home page is a good place to begin your search for page-building tips and tricks.

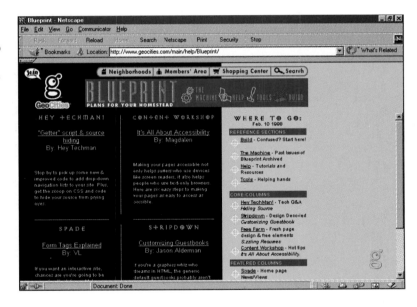

Manage Your GeoMail

In Chapter 14, there is ample information on how to receive your GeoCities mail. However, the GeoMail Manager page (see Figure 2.16) lets you decide specifically how you want your GeoMail account to work.

Your GeoMail e-mail address is always **membername@geocities.com**. However on the GeoMail Manager page, you can choose to shut it off (you still keep your page). You can also choose to merely have all e-mail to that account forward to a different e-mail account (such as the one you actively used before signing on with GeoCities). Just type that e-mail address into the forwarding address field at the bottom of the page.

If you choose to keep your GeoMail account active and not forward it, you will need to configure your favorite e-mail package to work with this account. Chapter 14 covers this in detail for all the major e-mail packages.

Figure 2.16
Use the GeoMail Manager to configure how you want your GeoCities e-mail address to operate.

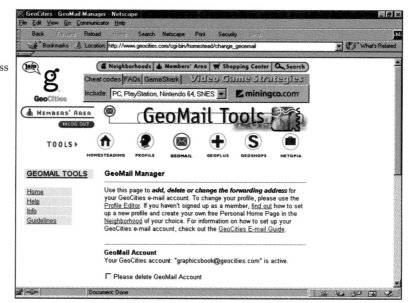

Moving On

Now that you know the basic GeoCities terminology, how to move around the site, and where to go to sign up and get help, there's no reason to just sit there. Let's get moving! The Web requests your presence.

3

Creating Your
Initial Home Page

Chapters 1 and 2 introduce you to GeoCities basics and familiarize you with the tools and resources provided. Future chapters focus on using specific parts of GeoCities (banners, ads, and stores, for example) and adding individual items to your site (graphics, sounds, and video, for example). This chapter is short and solution-focused—it guides you through actually building a good-looking GeoCities Website from scratch.

In this chapter, you read a case study about a friend who creates a Website with the GeoBuilder Editor that will showcase her personal interests (independent music and film). (The GeoBuilder is covered in more detail in Chapter 6. You can build a site catered to your interests. Before reading this chapter, it's assumed you've already joined GeoCities and looked around the system.

Away We Go

The first step in this chapter requires you to log on to your GeoCities account and go to the **Homesteading** section of the **Members' Area** (Figure 3.1). From here you can decide which tools to use to build your site quickly. GeoCities provides several page-building tools (as described in Chapters 4 and 6), but you use the GeoBuilder graphical editor for this example.

Figure 3.1
Start your Website here.

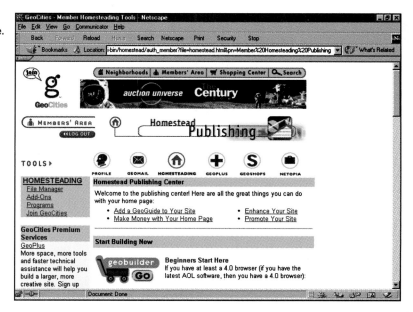

GeoBuilder works directly inside your Web browser, making it a breeze to use. Click on the text labeled **GeoBuilder** to launch this graphical editor and you are ready to go (Figure 3.2).

Figure 3.2
GeoBuilder is a usable and understandable Web-building tool.

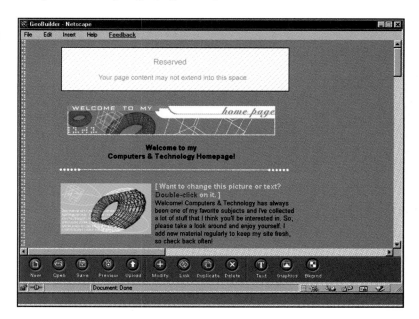

As mentioned, this chapter illustrates how easily you can build a page with GeoBuilder by showing you what happened when we turned someone with absolutely no Web-page building experience loose with

GeoBuilder. Our guinea pig made sure she explored all the options provided.

Our user didn't want the initial template—a Computers and Technology home page. She clicked on the **New** button and chose a different template. For variety, she chose Entertainment.

Again, this template is similar to the others—with a spot for a photo, introductory text, a section for links, a place to include something about yourself, and a footer so that visitors can e-mail you. Pretty basic, but it is a start.

Basic Page Editing

GeoCities doesn't expect you'll use the text it provides, but rather offers it as both example and placeholder. Our neophyte decided to change the header, which read "Welcome to my Entertainment Home Page." Since she wanted her page dedicated to independent music and film, she changed it to read "IndieWorld: Junk-free music and film."

Changing Words and Style

To change the heading, she double-clicked on the existing text, which brought up the Text Editor (Figure 6.3). You can also open the Text Editor by clicking the **Text** button.

Figure 3.3
GeoBuilder allows you to change not only the words, but the characteristics of selected text.

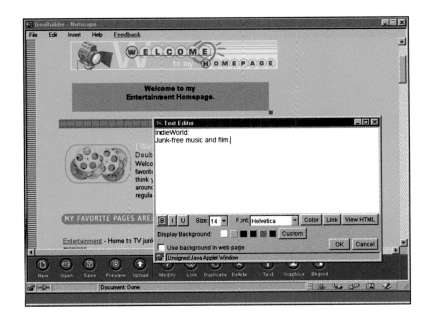

Our novice user wanted to change her header's characteristics as well as its words. After typing in the desired phrase, she played with it in the Text Editor. Across the bottom of the Editor, a number of available features will help her change the format of her text:

▶ **Font Attributes**
   You can make the text bold (B), italic (I), or underlined (U) by clicking those toggle buttons.

▶ **Font Size**
   You can select from seven different font sizes, ranging from 10 to 48 points.

▶ **Font Type**
   Fonts include Helvetica, Times Roman, and Courier. Much like standard word-processing software, you can highlight a piece of text and compare the various font options.

▶ **Font Color**
   You can also change the text color from basic black by clicking on **Color** and working with the Color Picker. The Color Picker lets you select from a wide variety of colors and then fine-tune them by sliding the three arrows back and forth. A Preview window shows you what you have done so far. Knowing she would eventually change her background color from the screaming green in the template to white, our beginner searched for a dark shade of red for the text headline.

With a nice color selected, she changed her page title to 48-point, italics, Helvetica. She also decided to change the look of her slogan ("Junk-free music and film") to 18-point, bold, italics, and Courier. Don't forget to click on the **OK** button to apply your changes.

TIP
View the Code

After you set your text and font attributes—before you click on the OK button—choose View HTML for fun. You'll see all the tags and codes that are functioning behind all of the changes you are making to the text. Don't be completely confused by the mysterious code. You can quickly return by clicking on **View WYSIWYG**.

Resizing and Moving Text Boxes

After clicking **OK**, our volunteer couldn't see the second line of text in her header. She rectified that problem by clicking on the text and dragging the small red box in the lower-right corner of the highlighted text, so that the box also encompassed her second line.

Adjusting Graphics Elements

The next thing she wanted to do was tweak the divider, which when first presented, looks like a strip of film. By clicking and dragging, she squeezed the film divider to a very thin strip, shortened it, and centered it under the heading.

Upon further review, she decided she didn't like the banner—"Welcome to My Home Page"—above the header. She clicked on it, hit the **Delete** button, and—poof!—it disappeared.

Unfortunately that left a gaping green hole above her header. To move the header and the film divider up to fill the space, she first clicked on the text and dragged it toward the GeoGuide placeholder; she then did the same with the divider. Figure 3.4 shows the revised page with the text and graphical changes made.

Figure 3.4
You can drag text and graphic elements around on your page.

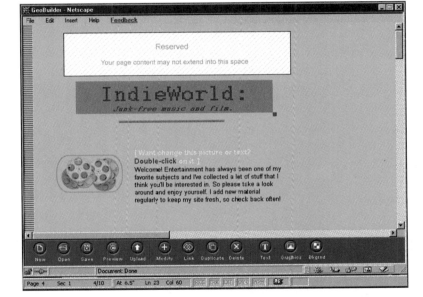

Adding and Deleting Images

With her header set, she decided to add two photos, one on top of the other, and some text to the right of the photos under the header. She knew she didn't want to use the film rolls GeoCities provides in the template. If it were up to our volunteer, she would have liked to use a photo of the punk band Fugazi (a representative of independent music) and a picture from the movie *Suburbia* (an example of an independent film). Because she had neither immediately at her disposal (and since this chapter deals exclusively with GeoBuilder), she went digging through the GeoBuilder Clip-Art Library.

She needed two photos, so she moved the film rolls up by clicking and dragging. With the film roll graphic still highlighted, she clicked on the **Duplicate** button. GeoBuilder stores a duplicate image in the top-left corner for later use. It was already highlighted, so she dragged it below the first graphic.

She also wanted two blocks of text, so used the **Duplicate** button in the same way on the text block next to the film roll graphics (Figure 3.5).

Figure 3.5
The Duplicate button makes it easy to copy text and graphics.

Duplicate Button

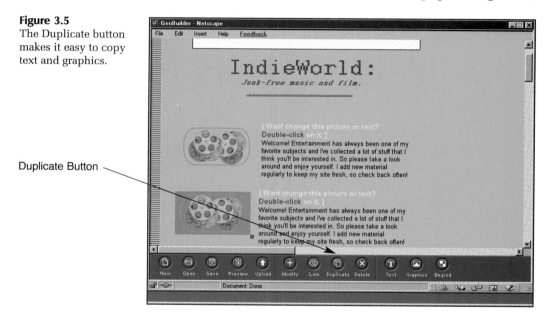

Finishing Touches

Now that you are familiar with adding text and duplicating images for your site, the second half of the chapter takes you through saving your page, changing colors and styles, and adding important contact information to your site.

Saving and Reopening Your Work

Hold on! She just realized she hadn't saved any of her work and had to take a break. Here's where the Save button comes in. Click **Save,** name the file (with the **.html** extension), and hit **OK**. You are told where the document was saved; press **Close**. Your page is saved and is still available to Web surfers, but you can continue working on it.

If you decide to close the page and work on it later, simply go to **File** in the top-left corner and select the **Exit** command. You are asked whether it is okay to discard changes to this page; that keeps you from accidentally closing the page without saving your changes. If you recently saved your page or don't want to keep the changes you made since your last save, click **OK** to close GeoBuilder.

Since she hadn't finished her page, our neophyte user needed to reopen GeoBuilder and the page to continue working on it after her break. Since she'd already worked with it, she opened GeoBuilder and clicked on the **Open** button, which gave her a scrolling index of her pages. If you highlight the desired page by clicking on it and hit **Open**, your page is presented and can be worked on.

Selecting and Adding Graphics

Back to work. She still had a lot of work to do—she had only a couple of sample graphics and text boxes (Figure 3.5). First she decided to replace the graphics, which can be done by either double-clicking on the graphic placeholder or by clicking the **Graphics** button. Doing either creates a New Image placeholder in the top-left corner and brings you to a directory of graphics, which includes dividers, buttons, clip art, or any graphics you have previously saved.

After selecting a graphic category from the left side of the directory (our user chose Clip Art), you can then choose a category of clip art from the middle segment (she chose People). This gives you a selection of specific graphics, any of which you can preview with a simple click (Figure 3.6).

Figure 3.6
Our user chose a clip-art hippie to complement her music text.

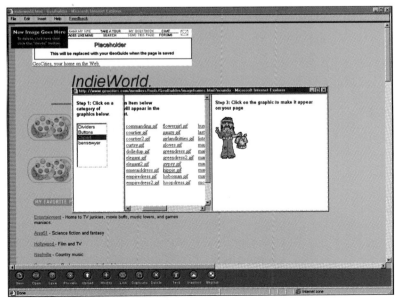

Clicking on the graphic places it on your page in the New Image placeholder. You can move the placeholder to its desired location before or after you click on the graphic. Our novice dropped the hippie into the placeholder at the top-left corner, deleted the top film roll graphic, and moved her hippie into place.

She snagged a cool-looking hobo and placed him under the hippie using the same process.

Customizing Your Web Page

Remember that the template is just a starting place. Let your creativity loose. Our user didn't want the text and the graphics stacked on top of each other, so she moved the GeoGuide placeholder, the header, and the divider to the middle of the page. She kept her hippie on the left, with the sample text to his right; the hobo and more sample text filled in the right side.

About that sample text—she got tired of reading it, so she replaced it with her own. You can click the **Text** button to do this, but she decided to double-click on the sample text. Up popped the Text Editor you saw in Figure 3.3, allowing her to change the text.

Changing Your Background

Once she finished the top part of her page, it was time to do something about the background color—the bright green was a little much and didn't go well with her red header text. Changing it was easy, especially since she knew all along that she wanted a white background.

To change the background color, click on the **Background** button. Much like the graphics selection, GeoBuilder presents a number of backgrounds from which to choose, including General, Margins, Natural, Templates, Tiles, and Solid Colors—all of which you can preview (Figure 3.7).

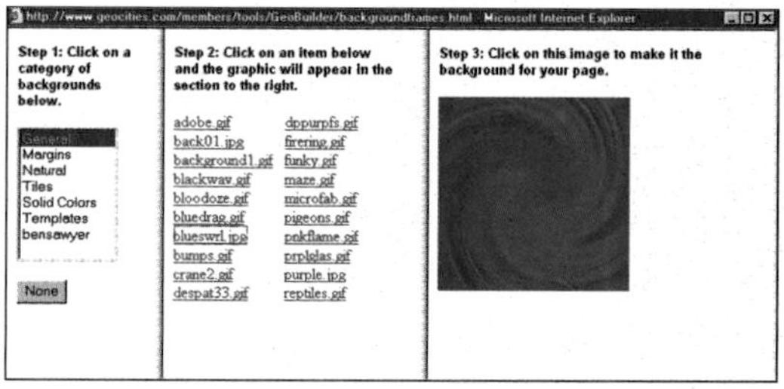

Figure 3.7
Although this swirling blue background looks pretty sharp…

After checking out a number of options, she decided to stick with her original plan (Figure 3.8). You can select the background from the list and, as the instructions tell you, click on the selected background to change it.

Figure 3.8
...our user preferred
keeping it simple with
white.

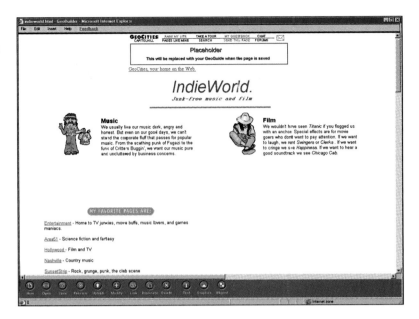

Links

Since she planned on eventually building more pages—some about
music, some about film—she decided to turn those corresponding words
in her slogan into links. The Text Editor allows you to do this by
highlighting the particular word and clicking on the **Link** button in the
Editor.

Since she had begun to lay out the page with music to the left and film to
the right, she continued the trend with the links. She did so by using
Duplicate and then clicking and dragging.

She then chose to fix the headers above the link section, to change the
text, and to create the links. She started by deleting the "My Favorite
Pages Are:" headers and clicking **Text** to change the headers to **Links**. She
also changed the main page header's color from black to red.

CAUTION

Overlapping Areas

One of GeoBuilder's unique attributes is that each element (text box, image,
and so on) on the screen has its own area on the screen. No two elements can
overlap without appearing as big red boxes on the screen.

At this point, our novice tried to save her changes, but was told she had
overlapping objects. You must fix this by either moving one of the objects or,
as was the case here, simply shrinking one object so that all its text was
displayed but didn't overlap with an adjacent object.

The Text Editor was used to change the supplied links to those the user wanted on her page. She also included a short description of each new link. You can use the Text Editor's **Link** button to transform a highlighted piece of text into a link (as described earlier in this chapter). IndieWorld is beginning to take shape (Figure 3.9).

Figure 3.9
IndieWorld: its slogan and a handful of links to music and film sites.

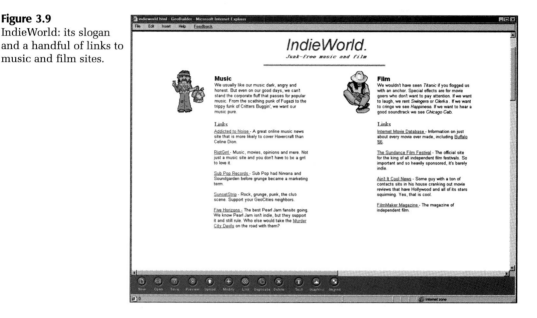

TIP
Use the Undo

Since the amateur site builder didn't feel like including her personal hobbies ("What business is it of yours?" she asked), she deleted those various template items. However, in her haste she accidentally deleted an item she needed. If this happens to you, go to **Edit** in the top toolbar and pull down to **Undo;** your item will reappear.

Adding E-mail Contact Information

You should always include an e-mail address (and other pertinent contact information) so that visitors can reach you. Our user wanted to finish her page by providing an e-mail link at the bottom. First, she used **Duplicate** to create a copy of the squished green film divider and then dragged it to the bottom of the page.

She dragged the provided e-mail link and centered it below the divider. A quick text edit, and her page was ready to go!

Figure 3.10
IndieWorld lives!

E-mail link

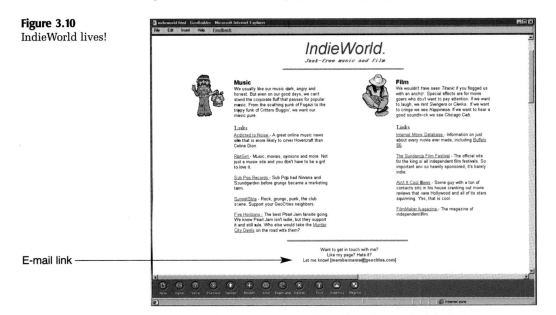

Save the page, open the browser, and there it is her first home page. Simple, just as she wanted it. GeoBuilder, however, will allow you to do much more.

Moving On

This page was just the beginning of what GeoCities can do. Of course, you can add your own music/bookstore, include audio/video clips of your favorites, build your own graphics from scratch, or include a survey. Once you are finished with your home page, you can register it with Internet search engines, hold online chats about your favorite topics, and build links between other great Indie sites. The rest of this book focuses on specific enhancements you can make to your Website using GeoCities' specific tools and techniques.

Part II
Tools & Templates

4

Building Your GeoCities Skills and Toolbox

In the last chapter you learned how to create a sample home page within minutes. You are now aware that GeoCities is much more than a place to store your Website; it is a vibrant community. In addition, GeoCities strives to make it easy for you to build your Website from scratch, upload pages you develop on your own, and integrate graphics and multimedia effects into your site.

This chapter introduces you to these specific GeoCities tools and explains how you can use other tools to create and manage your Website. Now that you're a member, all of your work begins in the GeoCities Members' Area (**http://www.geocities.com/members/**).

Web-Building Tools Provided by GeoCities

To create Web page files, you need to create HTML documents using an HTML editor. HTML editors are programs specifically designed to create Web pages; most of them are pretty easy to use.

GeoCities lends a hand by supplying a few preferred HTML editors you can use to create your GeoCities Web pages online—directly within your browser. Each HTML editor is geared to a different user level. If you aren't that familiar with HTML, you might want to stick with GeoBuilder (which is covered completely in Chapter 6, "GeoBuilder"), the Intel.com Web Page Wizard, or the Basic HTML Editor. If you know a bit more about building Web pages, you may want to try the EZ Editor. And if you know HTML well, try the Advanced HTML Editor—it's like an online notepad.

All of these editors are available from the Homesteading tool within the Members' Area.

TIP

GeoBuilder is Ready and Waiting!

If you are starting your site from scratch and don't want to worry about HTML at all, you probably want to investigate GeoBuilder, the new graphical tool that operates from a drag-and-drop philosophy within your browser. You can literally drag a headline or table from around the screen and place it exactly where it should appear within your Website. A truly unique tool, GeoBuilder comes with numerous templates and designs so you don't need to start each page blank.

GeoBuilder isn't exactly an HTML editor; it is a simple page-building tool that allows you to add images, edit text, and use your mouse to arrange your page. It's so useful, in fact, that Chapter 6 focuses specifically on GeoBuilder.

Each tool requires a different level of knowledge with HTML (Hypertext Markup Language)—the language that controls how text and pages appear on the World Wide Web (WWW). You should be able to build many great looking pages with the built-in GeoCities tools, without having to become an HTML expert.

From the GeoCities Members' Area, start your Web building by clicking on the link called **Homesteading** (Figure 4.1).

Figure 4.1
GeoCities provides the basic tools you need to start building your Web page.

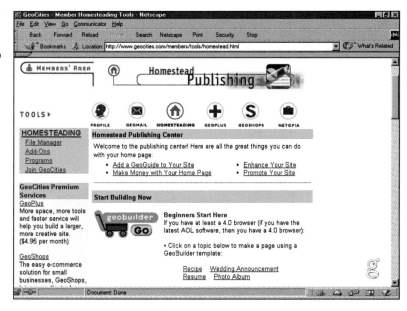

From here you can select from the various Homebuilding tools available and enter the GeoCities File Manager, which will help you manage your Website. Although Chapter 5, "Using the GeoCities File Manager," provides more detail about the File Manager, you should know a bit about this tool right now because the File Manager is your gateway to publishing Web pages. The File Manager allows you to transfer files between your computer and GeoCities' Web server. You can create, copy, rename, and delete files as well as edit or preview the files using the File Manager. You can also manage your Website by creating subdirectories and transferring files to them (that's how you get your Web pages onto the Internet), but let's back up. You still have to create your Web page files.

NOTE

What's a Web Server?

A Web server is a computer system that stores Web pages that you can visit. Each site on the Internet has a Web server behind it. Bigger sites like GeoCities have multiple servers that all work together to display pages. With GeoCities you'll interact with the GeoCities Web servers when you edit or send files that appear on your Website.

When you enter the Members' Area, you will be prompted to log on if you are using a new computer or if your computer has forgotten your username and password. From the Members' Homesteading Area, click on the link named **File Manager** to go to the online GeoCities File Manager.

TIP

Alternatively, if you click one of the **Start Building Now** links (except for the GeoBuilder icon), you will also be brought to the GeoCities File Manager (**http://www.geocities.com/members/tools/file_manager.html**). Then click on the button named **Enter File Manager**.

Part II Tools & Templates

Figure 4.2 shows the GeoCities File Manager.

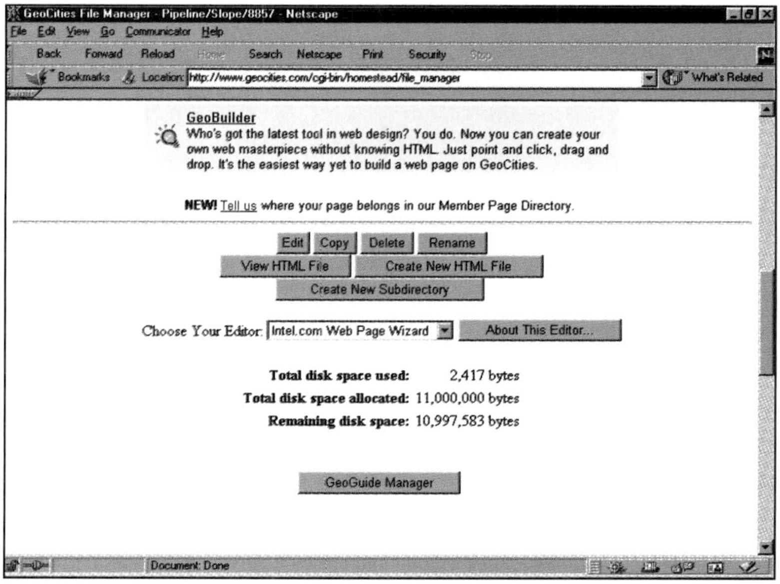

Figure 4.2
The File Manager is
where you can select
the online editor you
want to use.

CAUTION

Working Online Can Be Expensive!

The only disadvantage to many of the free and easy-to-use GeoCities tools is
that they require you to work on your site directly while you're online. This
isn't a problem if you are a user who pays a standard monthly access fee for
your Internet access, but it can be very expensive if your Internet Service
Provider charges you based on the time you're connected. That's one reason
GeoCities lets you use virtually any HTML editor you prefer. You can
download or purchase another editor (such as HomeSite or Microsoft
FrontPage), build your site on your computer, and then upload it once you've
finished—and save quite a bit of online time. Of course, you don't get the
benefits of some premiere GeoCities tools (such as GeoBuilder), but you do
get to use all other GeoCities member services.

Later in this section, we'll look at how to use other HTML editors effectively
if you can't (or don't) use the GeoCities editors to build your Website.

GeoBuilder

▶ Very easy to use

▶ Completely create a Website within your browser

▶ Graphical editor, no HTML knowledge needed

As mentioned earlier in this chapter, GeoBuilder is a graphical tool that simplifies creating your Website. We'll cover it in Chapter 6 in some depth because it is so exciting. The only drawback to this editor is that it requires a very current Web browser—Microsoft Internet Explorer 4.0 or Netscape 4.0 (or above)—and Windows 95, 98, or NT.

Intel.com Web Page Wizard

▶ Easy to use

▶ Provides four default looks

▶ Provides animation and video clips automatically

▶ Requires no HTML knowledge

▶ Limits direct HTML editing and customization

The Intel.com Web Page Wizard helps you build your page quickly even if you don't know any HTML. The tradeoff is that you must select from the default page styles provided by the Wizard. The interface is very intuitive and easy to use. You make choices in the left-hand frame, and the right-hand frame is automatically updated to show your changes. Follow these instructions to use the Web Page Wizard.

1. Choose **Intel.com Web Page Wizard** as your editor within the GeoCities File Manager.

2. Go up to the list of files in your site and either check the box to the left of the file you want to edit and then click on **Edit**, or don't click any of the boxes and click on **Create New HTML File**.

   The Intel.com Web Page Wizard is automatically launched.

Part II   Tools & Templates

3. The Wizard guides you through nine separate steps, once the editor has been launched. Begin at Step 1, in the top left corner or your screen, by choosing a graphic style from the drop-down box. Continue on through the next eight steps in the Wizard, adding a title, text, and links to your Web page. Each step lets you add a set of information to your page, including a title, links, paragraphs of text, animation, layout preferences, and even video clips. As you work on your page, your changes are reflected on the right-hand side of the screen (Figure 4.3).

Figure 4.3
The Intel.com Web Page Wizard builds your Web page for you.

4. When you reach Step 10, enter a filename. If you name your file "index.html," this file will appear as your main home page because all default home pages on GeoCities are named index.html. When you type in only your GeoCities address (for example, **http://www.geocities.com/TheTropics/8504/**), index.html is the page that will appear. If you name the Web page something other than "index.html," you will need to link to it from your existing index.html page so visitors will know it exists.

CAUTION

Overwriting Files Is Permanent!

The slightly tricky part to this step is that you receive a checkbox that asks whether you want to "Overwrite Existing File." If you check the **Overwrite Existing File** option and already have a file with the same name, your old file will be overwritten with the new file. Although this sounds straightforward, you really need to be careful. When you overwrite a file, the original file is *gone* from your GeoCities Website. Let's say you just created a Web page about your cat, Frenzy, and you want to name the page, frenzy.html. If you click the **Overwrite Existing File** checkbox, then any file you already have that's named frenzy.html will be replaced with the file for your new Frenzy page.

5. At Step 11, check **No** if you're finished creating Web pages for the day or **Yes** to build another page. Then repeat the steps for the Page Wizard until your entire set of color and design coordinated pages is complete. When you click on **Finish**, the Wizard assembles your page and saves it. Follow the link in the right-hand frame to return to the File Manager. You just built a complete page for your Website!

You can preview your page by going to the File Manager and clicking on the **View** link to the right of your file. For more information about using the Intel Wizard, visit **http://www.geocities.com/members/wizard/intel_wizard.html**.

Basic HTML Editor

▶ Works in 3.0 or later browser, on the Mac, and Web TV

▶ Very quick to create pages

▶ Less direct page coordination than the Page Wizard

▶ Requires slightly more HTML knowledge

▶ Useful for those new to HTML who want to test their knowledge

If you know a bit about HTML and want a Web page that allows a little more HTML customization than the Intel.com Web Page Wizard offers, try the Basic HTML Editor. Follow these instructions to use it.

1. Choose **Basic HTML Editor** as your editor within the GeoCities File Manager.

2. Go up to the list of files in your site and either check the box to the left of the file you want to edit, then click on **Edit**, or don't click any of the boxes and click on **Create New HTML File**.

Part II Tools & Templates

The Basic HTML Editor is automatically launched (Figure 4.4). If you're editing a file, the filename is automatically entered at the top of the page. If you're creating a new file, you have to type the filename in the box at the top of the page.

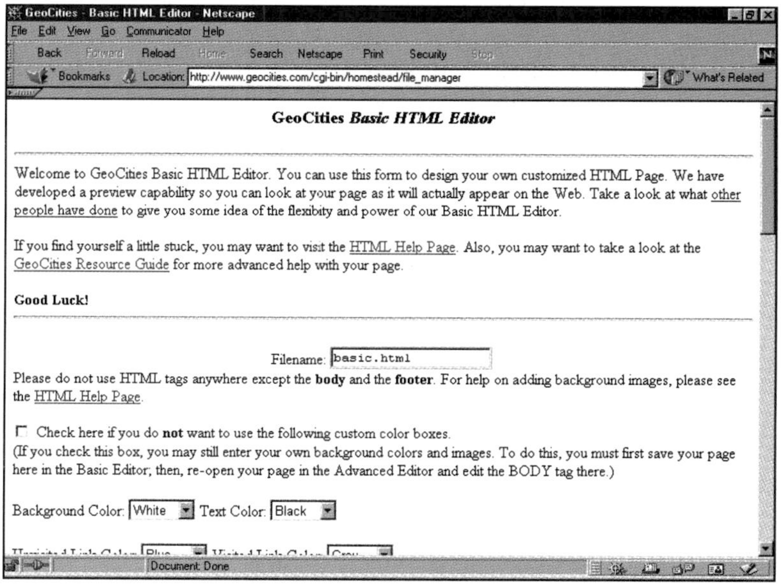

Figure 4.4
The Basic HTML Editor offers a different approach to building your page.

3. Using the Basic HTML Editor, you can choose from a variety of background colors, link colors, and line separators provided by GeoCities. You don't have to know HTML for most options; just use the pull-down menus to make your selections. In fact, the only places in which you can test your HTML knowledge are the fields for your body text and for your footer text.

TIP

Seeing Colors

Here's some cool news for more advanced users. If you don't like the color or image choices in the pull-down menu, you don't have to use them. You can click the box at the top of the page that says: "Check here if you do not want to use the following custom color boxes." Then, you can add your own colors. You'll then have to save the file in the Basic HTML Editor and edit it using the Advanced HTML Editor (that's where the "more advanced" part comes into play).

4. When you're done entering new text or changing existing text, you can use the buttons at the bottom of the page to save your work. Click on **Preview** to view your file as it will appear on your site. Keep in mind that Preview does not save your file. The preview appears at the top of the Basic HTML Editor page. To continue editing after you admire your work, simply scroll down until you see the Basic HTML Editor.

5. After you finish with your page, you must save your page so it can be added to your Website. Click the **Save** button to store your page and return to the File Manager. Click **Save and Continue Editing** to store your current edits and continue working on this page.

    If you prefer to pretend that your day's efforts never happened, you can cancel all your changes for this entire page and exit by clicking on the **Return to File Manager** button.

Advanced HTML Editor

▶ Requires adequate HTML knowledge

▶ Starts with a completely blank page

▶ Edit your HTML right on the GeoCities server

▶ Good for people who want to add scripts to their sites

▶ Good for HTML experts and those who are learning

Okay, so you've had some experience writing HTML pages. You'll probably be happy using the Advanced HTML Editor, which is just like Windows Notepad or SimpleText on the Macintosh. The Advanced HTML Editor is like a blank canvas on which you will start your painting. It has none of the benefits of standard templates and page designs, but does allow those of you who are more technically oriented to exploit the full functionality of HTML.

1. Choose **Advanced HTML Editor** as your editor within the GeoCities File Manager.

2. Go up to the list of files in your site and either check the box to the left of the file you want to edit and then click on **Edit**, or don't click any of the boxes and click on **Create New HTML File**.

Part II Tools & Templates

The Advanced HTML Editor is automatically launched (Figure 4.5). If you're editing a file, the filename is automatically entered at the top of the page. If you're creating a new file, you'll put the filename in the box at the top of the page.

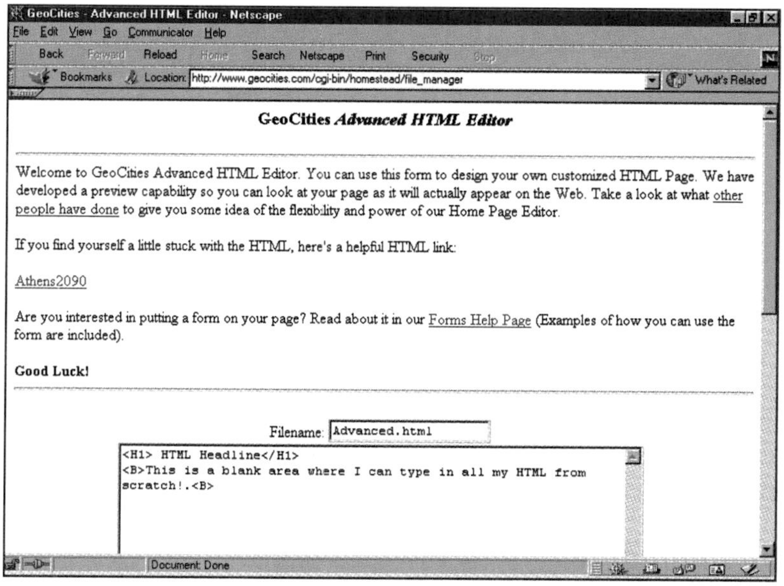

Figure 4.5
Despite its name, the Advanced HTML Editor is very easy to use.

3. If you choose to edit a file, then the file's contents will appear in a text box. If you're creating a new file, you'll see two text boxes on the screen, one for the filename and the other for the file contents. There are no built-in cool features or pre-designed choices even though this program is called the *Advanced* HTML Editor. It was the advanced editor until the GeoBuilder program came along. The Advanced HTML Editor still exists because some computers can't work with the Java technology that fuels the GeoBuilder program. This editor is also a great quick way to make code changes to pages on your site because it loads fast and gives you access to the entire, raw HTML code to your page.

    With this editor you're essentially editing the complete raw HTML-based code that produces a Web page. This means *you're* the one who has to be advanced to use this HTML editor. That means, you'll have to know HTML to use it.

4. If you're using this editor, then you know HTML, or you are in the process of learning it.

    You must type in every line of text and every HTML code, and debug all problems yourself. When you're done editing a file in the Advanced HTML Editor, you can preview, save, or reset your changes by using the buttons at the bottom of the screen.

> **TIP**
> **Do a Little Touch Up**
>
> One very common time to use the Advanced HTML Editor is to make small changes to pages that you created in another manner. If you want to simply fix a typo, or add a paragraph of text, many people use this editor because it is very easy to quickly edit and save your HTML file, instead of using another editor.

GeoCities has many sites that provide complete and useful information for building an HTML page from scratch. The most popular site is "The Home Page Home Page," which guides you through common HTML tags and how to use them on GeoCities. Visit this site at **http://www.geocities.com/Athens/2090/**.

GeoCities' EZ Editor

▶ More flexible than the Intel.com Web Page Wizard

▶ Lets you build your site with a different interface

The EZ Editor is an editor that helps you build complex pages without having to know a lot of HTML, yet it is much more flexible than the Intel.com Web Page Wizard. You cannot edit pages created by another application in the EZ Editor. You also can't use the EZ Editor with any browser that doesn't support frames such as Netscape Navigator 2. In fact, any browser that is 3.0 or higher will support dividing the page into different framed areas.

> **NOTE**
> **Before You Use the EZ Editor...**
>
> Keep these points in mind before you use this editor:
>
> - If you resize your browser window while editing, all unsaved changes will be erased.
> - The EZ Editor does not work on Windows 3.1x.
> - You can insert any HTML tag by clicking on Insert, choosing Text, and then entering HTML tags in the Input window.

To open GeoCities EZ Editor:

1. Choose **EZ Editor** as your editor within the GeoCities File Manager.
2. Go up to the list of files in your site and either check the box to the left of the file you want to edit, then click on **Edit,** or don't click any of the boxes and click on **Create New HTML File.**

The EZ HTML Editor is automatically launched. You now see four frames in your browser window. Figure 4.6 shows these four frames and how each is used.

Figure 4.6
The EZ Editor is easy, even though it looks different from the other GeoCities tools.

General Info Frame

Preview frame
Displays your changes to your page

Functions frame
Controls the EZ Editor with four pull-down menus

Input area
Where you type when the EZ Editor requires information

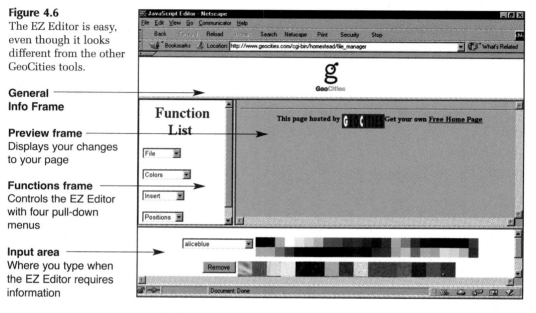

3.   Before you start, read the helpful instructions that are displayed in the Preview frame. Or, if you're editing a file and want a refresher, you can get back to the instructions by choosing **Help** from the File pull-down menu in the left frame.

4.   Choose **New** from the File pull-down menu in the Functions frame. The Preview frame now shows a file with the standard GeoCities footer.

5.   Change the background color by choosing **Background** from the Colors pull-down menu. In the Input area, you can now select the color you want to use in your page background or pick a graphical pattern instead. The Preview frame updates your page to display the background you selected. You can also remove a background completely from your page.

6.   Add a page title by choosing **Text** from the **Insert** menu in the Functions frame. Notice that the Input area has changed, asking you to type in a page title. Position your cursor in the text box and begin typing. You can also control your text color, font, and size using the appropriate drop-down boxes. When you're done adding and customizing your text, click **Submit**.

7.   To save your page, choose **Save As** from the **File** menu in the Functions frame. Enter a filename in the Input area, and click **Save**.

8. Use the commands in the **Insert** and **Colors** menus to add text paragraphs, lines, graphics, and other exciting customizations to your page. Don't forget to save all of your changes when you are finished.

> **NOTE**
>
> **Use Your HTML Knowledge in the EZ Editor**
>
> If you already know HTML, you can add your own tags using the EZ Editor. Choose **Text** from the **Insert** menu in the Functions frame. Begin typing your text and HTML tags using the text box in the Input area. When finished, click **Submit**. The Editor recognizes your HTML code and adds it to the file. The Preview frame is updated with the text and code you just typed.

BYO (Bring Your Own) HTML Editors

The previous section describes each of the editors that GeoCities provides for you to build your Website, and Chapter 6 focuses in depth on the best of the bunch—GeoBuilder. But you aren't limited to using one of these online HTML editors when building your GeoCities site; you can use any HTML editor that you download from the Web or purchase in a store.

HTML editors come in a variety of shapes, sizes, and degrees of complexity, but all offer similar functionality—they let you create individual and sets of HTML files on your own personal computer, whether you're using Windows, Macintosh, or another platform. HTML editors are software packages that you must install on your computer and use separately, not like the online GeoCities HTML editors that work within your Web browser.

Although GeoCities provides several HTML editors for your use, people often prefer using their own specific editors for reasons such as these:

▶ HTML editors installed on your personal computer allow you to work on your Website when you aren't connected to the Internet.

▶ HTML editors can have more features and flexibility than the editors provided by GeoCities. For example, you can map together a Website, add standard headers to every page in your site, and easily import large amounts of text from word processor documents and other files on your computer.

▶ HTML editors provide more detailed control over how images appear on your Website.

▶ HTML editors enable you to see results much more quickly rather than keep you waiting several moments after every click.

Part II Tools & Templates

On the other hand, most HTML editors usually cost money to purchase (generally between $30 and $100) and often require several days of experience for you to fully understand and use them. In addition, you're responsible for installing the software on your computer, keeping it up-to-date, and configuring it so that your files are sent to your GeoCities Website. Figure 4.7 shows HomeSite, a popular HTML editor from Allaire (**http://www.allaire.com**).

Figure 4.7
Allaire's HomeSite is a
popular commercial
editor.

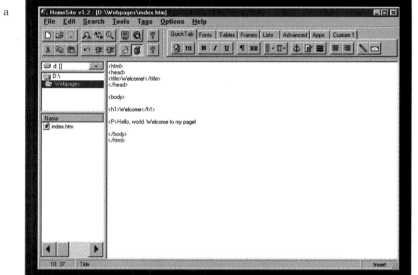

Given these tradeoffs, many people use GeoCities tools and many others use their own HTML editors, depending on their personal preferences and requirements.

There are literally hundreds of editors you can use. Most allow you to test drive, or evaluate, them before you purchase the software.

The following are some of our favorite recommendations for Windows users:

▶ Microsoft FrontPage or FrontPage Express (**http://www.microsoft.com**)

▶ HotDog Express (**http://www.sausage.com**)

▶ Allaire's HomeSite (**http://www.allaire.com**)

On the Macintosh platform, popular HTML editors include:

▶ BBEdit from BareBones Software (**http://www.barebones.com**)

▶ Adobe PageMill (**http://www.adobe.com**)

Many more editors are available in addition to these few. Try searching Yahoo! or shareware.com (**www.shareware.com**) to find the one that best suits your needs.

NOTE

Sending Your Files to GeoCities

Once you've created your Website with your favorite HTML editor, the next step is transferring those files from your computer onto your GeoCities address. Known as FTP (File Transfer Protocol) in the Internet world, transferring files is straightforward and easy to do. Most HTML editors have FTP functionality built in, which allows you to send files directly from within that program. "FTPing" requires an address, username, and password. You already know your username and password—they are your GeoCities account information. Your FTP address is **ftp.geocities.com**.

Don't worry if this is confusing now; we cover FTPing files in more depth at the end of next chapter, after discussing the File Manager.

Behind the Scenes, or "What Did I Just Create?"

Good question! You can look at a Web page in either a Web browser, like Netscape Communicator or Microsoft Internet Explorer, or in an HTML editor. When you look at a Web page with a browser, the browser interprets the HTML tags and makes your page look attractive and colorful. What you see are images and styled text in different locations of the browser's window. Figure 4.8 shows a standard Web page inside of Netscape.

Figure 4.8
This colorful Web page teaches you about the brain.

Part II   Tools & Templates

When you look at the plain HTML file that makes up that same page, you see a completely different picture. Figure 4.9 shows the HTML file that is behind the "brainy" Web page, telling it exactly how to look and what to do. (HTML is a lot like English instructions that tell the browser how things should appear on a Web page.)

Figure 4.9
Carefully compare this image to see how it translates into colors and good layout in a browser.

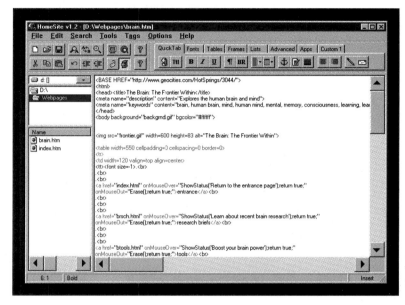

Most HTML editors don't give you much control over the HTML. They operate much more like Microsoft Word or Adobe PageMaker, where you create text, tables, images, and links and then drag them onto the proper spot in the page. The editor then translates your commands into quality HTML.

What about when you want to create a special effect that the editor doesn't do? It might not be a bad idea to get familiar with the basics of HTML so you are comfortable with the codes and tags that are the building blocks for the Web. Here are a few recommendations:

▶ As mentioned before, this site teaches you basic HTML that is commonly used by most GeoCities members: **http://www.geocities.com/Athens/2090**.

▶ *Blueprint* (**http://www.geocities.com/main/help/Blueprint**) is GeoCities' HTML Help 'Zine. Check it out for great design tips. It has everything from advanced HTML to tips on animating graphics.

▶ HTML is a worldwide standard that is maintained by the World Wide Web Consortium (**http://www.w3c.org**). Impress your friends by learning about the history of HTML and future developments.

Other GeoCities Goodies

GeoCities offers more than just HTML editors for your Web-page toolbox! It also provides useful add-ons that let you customize your site without any previous experience or programming knowledge. All add-ons are available through the GeoCities Homesteading site (Figure 4.10).

Figure 4.10
GeoCities not only helps you build a home page; it gives you furnishings as well!

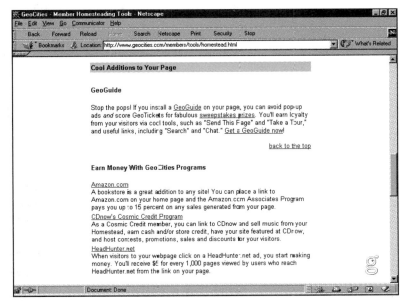

Available add-ons include:

▶ **Guestbook**—Allows your visitors to leave comments for you and future visitors to your page.

▶ **Counters**—Tracks the number of visitors who stop by for a look.

▶ **Forms**—Creates customized interactive forms that ask your visitors questions and let them submit that information to you.

▶ **Multimedia Things**—Specializes in helping you add multimedia *things* to your site, such as audio and video clips.

▶ **Virtual Reality**—Builds three-dimensional (3D) interfaces into your page for an out-of-this-world effect using a special Virtual Reality site-building tool.

Many add-ons such as these are covered in detail throughout this book. We show you all about images, multimedia, forms, guestbooks, counters, and much more—all available free to GeoCities members. And more add-ons are continually being developed. You can explore the Homesteading area now, or flip to Chapter 10, "Adding Special Effects to Your Pages," to learn more about using add-ons in your page.

Moving On

As you can see, GeoCities offers you a lot of useful and important tools when you become a member. Besides a handful of HTML editors, you get multimedia help, online advice and recommendations, and page wizards.

Getting familiar with these tools is just the beginning. Most of the exciting activities require that you set up a comfortable base using your favorite HTML editor, then customize and expand your site. The next chapter focuses on the File Manager, the tool that helps you keep track of all the files that make up your Website.

5

Using the GeoCities File Manager

The last chapter showed you some of the tools you'll need to create a killer GeoCities Website. At this point, we assume you've created at least the opening page to your brand new Website. It doesn't matter how great your Web page is, but if it just sits on your computer, all your work will be in vain. Of course, that's why you have an account at GeoCities—to make your site public. The place you'll usually go to put your site on stage, front and center, is GeoCities File Manager.

What Is File Manager?

File Manager is where you'll make your Web page a real living, breathing Website. From here, you can upload your files to GeoCities, rename them, and organize them. Once you've placed your files on GeoCities with File Manager, you can edit then preview them to make sure they look the way you intended.

You can get to File Manager (shown in Figure 5.1) in a couple of different ways. If you go to the Members' Area, you'll see a list of Quick Links down the left side of the screen. Click on the Quick Link that says File Manager. Of course, if you prefer (and don't mind more typing), you can go directly to **http://www.geocities.com/members/tools/file_manager.html**.

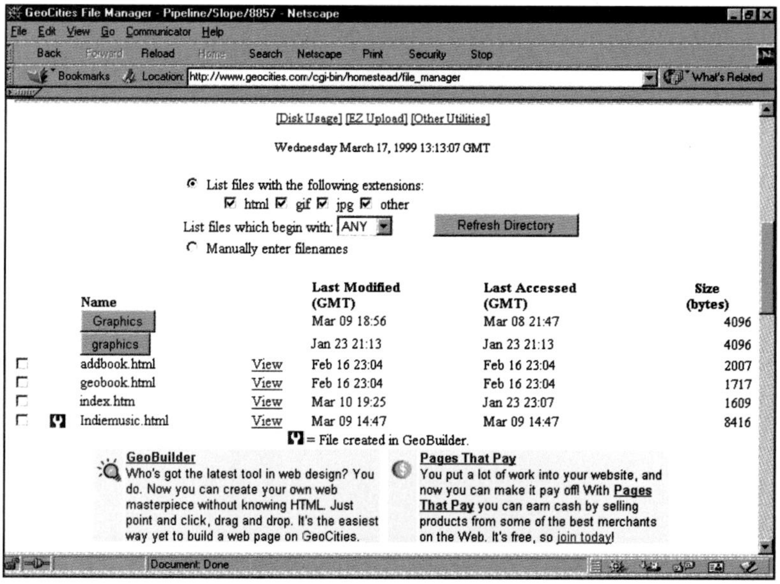

Figure 5.1
GeoCities File Manager
makes getting your Web
page online quick and
easy.

GeoCities gives you 11 megabytes of space to create your site, which is plenty of room to put whatever you want on your Web pages—within reason and within the rules GeoCities provides. (Make sure you read them before you start!)

CAUTION

Size *Does* Matter

If you plan a relatively intricate site with lots of graphics, check your files to see how much room they will take. If it looks like you have too much for your page, look ahead to Chapter 9, "Graphics," which tells you how to reduce the size of your graphics files so they'll load faster and take up less room.

Let's start with the most important function of File Manager: uploading your files.

Uploading Files

To upload files from your computer's hard drive to GeoCities, follow these simple steps:

1. Go to the File Manager sign-in page, located at **http://www.geocities.com/members/tools/file_manager.html.**

2. You'll notice you have a couple of choices, as shown in Figure 5.2. The top choice, **List files with the following extensions,** allows you to select the file types you want shown in File Manager: HTML, GIF, JPG, or other. If you have a lot of files in your Web page directory, you may be wise to uncheck **Other,** or you might have to scroll through dozens of irrelevant files. You can also reduce the list by having only files that begin with a certain letter appear in File Manager.

   The bottom choice, **Manually enter filenames,** requires that you manually type in the name of each file you want to upload. Although this saves you from having to scroll through lots of filenames, make your life easier by accepting the default choice (**List files with the following extensions),** which lets you see the files and choose the ones you want. Then click on the button labeled **Enter the File Manager.**

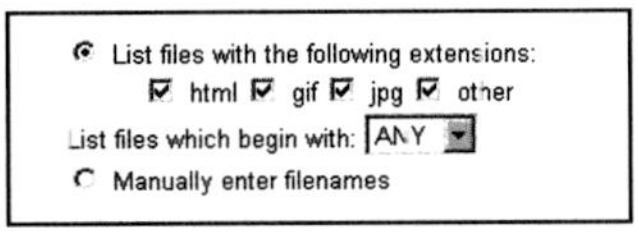

Figure 5.2
Choose which file types you want to see here.

> ⊙ List files with the following extensions:
>   ☑ html ☑ gif ☑ jpg ☑ other
> List files which begin with: `ANY ▾`
>   ○ Manually enter filenames

TIP

Fancy Fingerwork

Whenever possible, avoid typing in filenames or long URLs. Typing something as simple as "flower.gif" instead of "flowers.gif" prevents you from getting to the file you want. The best rule to follow in working with your Web pages is to keep the process *simple.*

3. You will be prompted to log in to your GeoCities account the first time each session you spend editing your site. GeoCities remembers your Username and password for several hours so you don't have to constantly type them in again, and again, and again. If prompted, enter your Username and password and click on **Submit**.

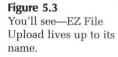

> **TIP**
>
> **Forget Your Password?**
>
> If you forget your password, you can find it in the original e-mail that GeoCities sent you when you signed up. If you lost or discarded that e-mail, you can click on the **Password Lookup** link at the bottom of the screen. GeoCities then e-mails you your password. Keep this e-mail in a safe place so you don't have to request your password again.

4. After you log in, the GeoCities File Manager appears with your Homestead address and your Username at the top of the page. A little ways down the page, you see three links: Disk Usage, EZ Upload, and Other Utilities. For now, click on link named **EZ File Upload**, or scroll down the page until you find that section. (We'll get to disk usage later.)

5. You should now be at the EZ File Upload part of the page, as shown in Figure 5.3. EZ File Upload is an FTP program, which you learn more about in a moment. Click on the **Browse** button to find the files on your hard drive.

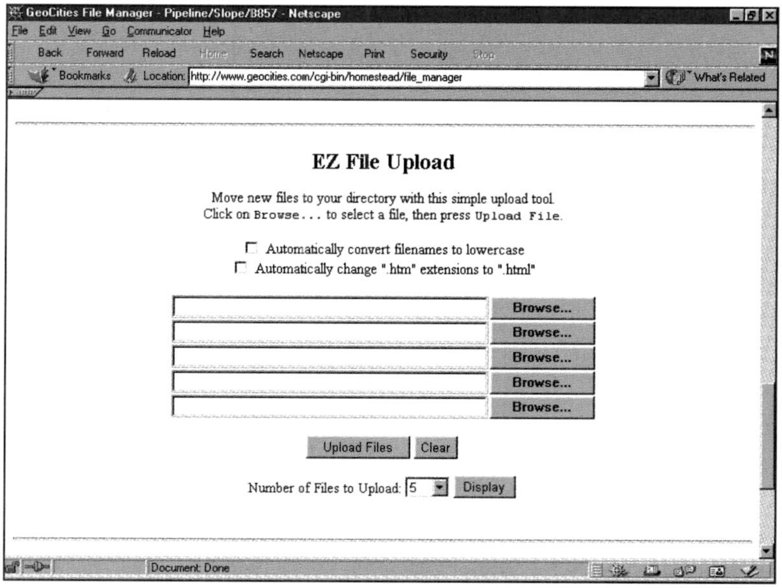

Figure 5.3
You'll see—EZ File Upload lives up to its name.

NOTE

What Is FTP?

FTP, which stands for File Transfer Protocol, is basically a way of transferring files between two computers. Many programs are available that let you upload and download files from a variety of sites, not just GeoCities. We discuss one of them—CuteFTP—later in this chapter.

6. A Choose File box should appear, as shown in Figure 5.4. This is where you choose the files you want to upload. Go to the folder in which you store your Web page files, choose a file, then click the **Open** button. The path to the file appears in the text box.

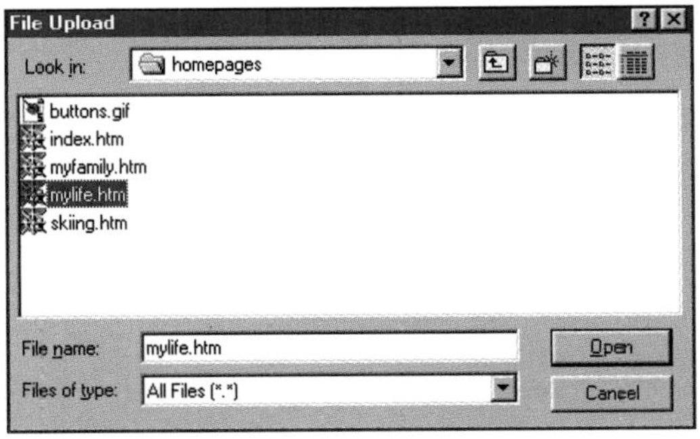

Figure 5.4
We've chosen to download a graphics file, **buttons.gif**.

7. Repeat this process for all the files you need to download. The pull-down box at the bottom of the screen lets you choose how many files you want to upload at one time. Choose a number other than five (the default) and click **Display.** Once you choose the files you want, click on the **Upload Files** button.

TIP

Once Again, Size Matters

Uploading is another area in which file size makes a difference. If you upload many files such as a large graphic or a video file all at once, you'll be sitting at your computer staring into space for a long time. You may want to limit your uploading to five files, which GeoCities sets as the default.

Part II Tools & Templates

Your screen appears to just refresh, but wait! Scroll down a bit, and you'll see a screen similar to that shown in Figure 5.5. A box at the top lists the names of the files you just uploaded, followed by a list of files that you already have on your Website.

Figure 5.5
The site is finally starting to show some life.

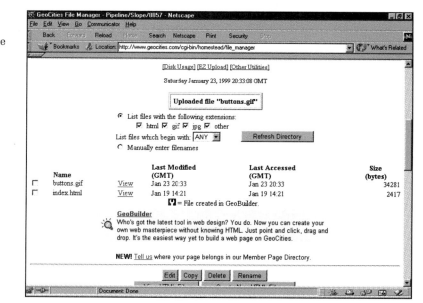

You notice our list shows two files, even though we uploaded only one. That's because **index.html** is the default name of the page GeoCities creates for you when you sign on.

Then, if you scroll down the page, you see three bolded lines. They tell you how much space you've already used, how much you were given at the beginning, and how many bytes you have left.

Viewing Your Pages

Now that your Web pages are up for the world to see, you probably wouldn't mind looking at them, too. Instead of typing your site's entire URL into the Address bar, you can preview your pages right from File Manager:

1.   Go to the File Manager sign-in page, located at
     http://www.geocities.com/members/tools/file_manager.html.

2.   Enter your Username and password, and click on **Submit,** if necessary.

3. Scroll down to the list of files that are on your Web page, and click on the **View** hyperlink next to a filename. That page then appears in your browser window, just as it would to anyone else surfing your site. If you click on a graphic, it will appear by itself in your browser window. Click on a sound and you'll hear it, and so on.

> **TIP**
>
> **Why Preview?**
>
> Looking at your files online is always a good idea, even if you saw them a million times while loading them from your hard drive. You might never know if you forgot to load an important graphics file, or if something just looks different than you intended. It's also a good idea to look at your page on someone else's computer. Various monitor sizes and screen resolutions can make a big difference in your Website's presentation.

4. Click your browser's Back button to return to the File Manager and view more files.

Editing Files

Okay, let's say there is a problem with your Web page. Perhaps you not only forgot a graphic, but spelled the heading wrong. (No matter how many times you double-check, something is *always* misspelled.) Do you have to go back to your hard drive, fix the file, and then re-upload it? Well, you certainly can, but GeoCities has a much easier way for you to edit files: the Edit button.

1. Go to the File Manager for your Website.

2. Click on the checkbox next to the file you want to edit, selecting that file. If you don't click on a checkbox, the File Manager screen will simply reload.

3. Scroll down past the mass of buttons located beneath your list of files to a pull-down menu that allows you to **Choose Your Editor**. At the time of this writing, you could choose from four editors:

    ▶ Intel.com Web Page Wizard

    ▶ Basic HTML Editor

    ▶ EZ Editor

    ▶ Advanced HTML Editor (the default)

To find out more about each editor, you can click a button (**About This Editor**) that you'll find next to the box.

> **NOTE**
>
> **A Bit About the Editors**
>
> You probably remember these editors from the last chapter, which covered them in more depth. Each of the four editors that GeoCities provides is geared toward people with a different level of HTML expertise. If you have never used HTML before, you may want to use the Intel.com Web Page Wizard (see Figure 5.6). It steps you through creating your first Web page, but you get little choice (four-color/graphics schemes) of what your page looks like. You just add text. If you are just fixing a small typo, the Advanced HTML Editor gives you the straight HTML in which to hunt and fix your mistake.

Figure 5.6
The Intel.com Web Page Wizard.

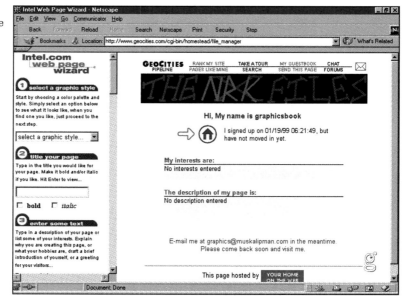

4. Let's assume you're going to use the default, Advanced HTML Editor. Click on the **Edit** button. A new screen, shown in Figure 5.7, appears with a giant text box containing your HTML file.

Figure 5.7
The Intel.com Web Page Wizard.

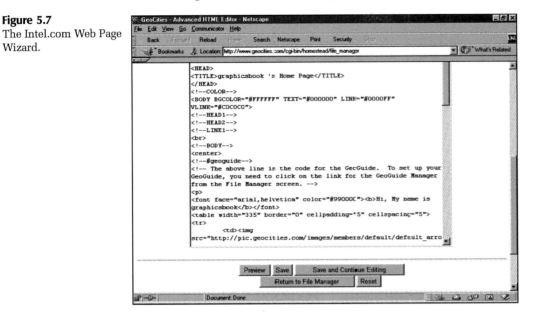

5. Make your changes. If you want to preview your page after you finish, click on the **Preview** button. Your page appears, but when you scroll down, the editing box is there for you to make more changes.

6. If you make a mistake, you can click on the **Reset** button, which will cancel everything you've done but haven't yet saved in this editing session.

7. At this point, you can either choose **Save and Continue Editing,** which saves your work and keeps you on the same screen, or choose **Save,** which takes you back to the File Manager page. You can also return to File Manager by clicking on the **Return to File Manager** button.

Deleting Files

As you work on your site, chances are that you will no longer need some files that you once put up on GeoCities, at some point. Rather than have them take up precious site space, you can easily delete them.

1. Go to the File Manager for your Website.

2. Click the checkbox next to the file or files that you want to delete.

3. Click the **Delete** button. GeoCities takes you to a page asking you whether you're sure you want to delete these files (see Figure 5.8).

Figure 5.8
Are you sure? Are you really sure?

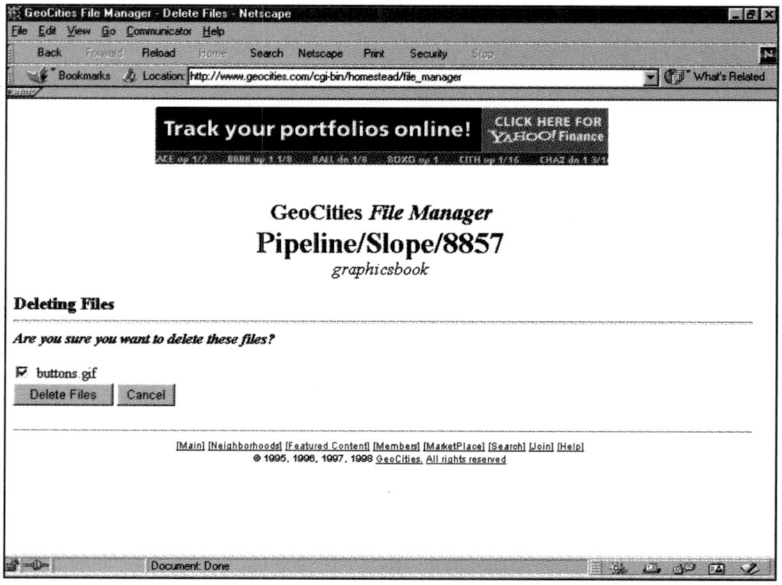

4. If you decide you don't want to delete some of the files after all, simply uncheck them. If you realize you don't want to delete any of them, click on **Cancel,** which will take you back to the File Manager.

5. When you've decided which files should be deleted, click the **Delete Files** button. You will be returned to the File Manager page; if you scroll down, you'll notice that those files have disappeared from your file list.

CAUTION

Make sure you really want to delete the files off the site. Once they're gone, you can't get them back unless, of course, you still have them on your hard drive. In that case, you can upload them to GeoCities once again.

Renaming Files

As we mentioned earlier, your GeoCities site already has a file named
index.html, which is the default page GeoCities created when you
opened your account. You know, the one that said "Hi!" and gave you
your e-mail address. Since you already loaded your own files to your site,
it would be nice if people could see them when they arrive at your
GeoCities address. Actually, you can do this in either of two ways. First,
you can edit GeoCities' index.html file directly in one of their editors,
adding HTML code to give your page the look you want. A simpler way
is to create a file in your favorite HTML and then upload it to your site.
Once you've done that, you can simply rename the files, as follows:

1. Go to the File Manager for your Website.

2. Click the checkbox next to the index.html file and then click on the
    Rename button. You'll be taken to the Rename Files page, shown in
    Figure 5.9.

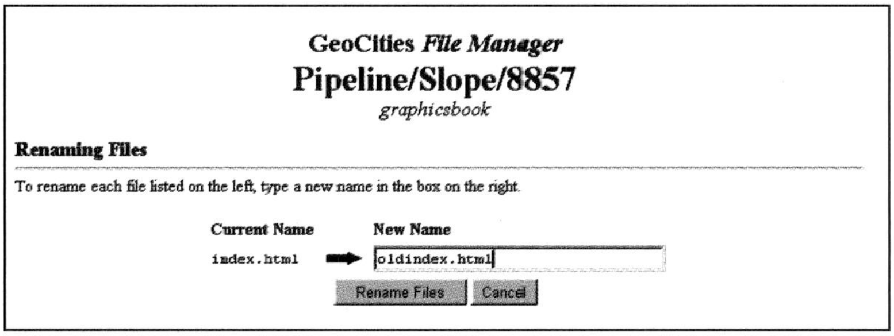

Figure 5.9
This simple screen
allows you to rename
your files.

3. Change the name of the original **index.html** file to something similar,
    like **oldindex.html**, and click on the **Rename Files** button, which
    returns you to File Manager.

g!

TIP

Deleting the Original File

You can delete the original index.html file, if you wish. But our motto when
working with Websites is "better safe than sorry." Whenever you're ready to
delete something, you would be wise to simply rename it first, and then see
what effect it has on your pages. After you make sure the file isn't needed,
you can delete it permanently. This may save you from disaster if, for
instance, you rename a graphics file, only to discover that it is still being used
on a page you forgot about.

4. Now click on the checkbox next to the HTML file that you want to be your home page—the first page people see when they come to your site. Click the **Rename** button.

5. Rename this file **index.html**, and click the **Rename Files** button. Again, you are returned to File Manager.

6. In the Address bar of your browser, type in your site's URL and press Enter. Your page is now out on the Internet for the world to see.

Getting File Manager Organized

As your site gets larger and more complicated, you will probably find it increasingly difficult to find files in your list. Scrolling through all those files is time-consuming and you can easily miss what you're looking for. It's time to get organized.

You can organize File Manager in much the same way you would organize files in an old-fashioned metal file cabinet. You create folders that contain files that somehow relate, keeping them separate from the generic files in the main part of the cabinet. Let's start by creating one file folder (called a *subdirectory*), and then we'll provide other tips on organizing your site.

Creating a Subdirectory

For this example, we'll create one folder in which you can put all your graphics files. We'll call it Graphics (pretty intuitive, huh?).

1. Go to the File Manager for your Website.

2. Scroll down and click on the **Create New Subdirectory** button. You are taken to the Create Subdirectory page shown in Figure 5.10.

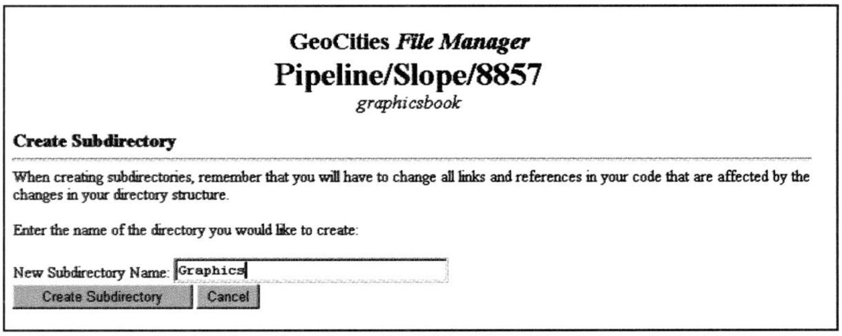

Figure 5.10
Creating subdirectories is the first step in getting organized.

> **GeoCities *File Manager***
> ## Pipeline/Slope/8857
> *graphicsbook*
>
> **Create Subdirectory**
> ___
> When creating subdirectories, remember that you will have to change all links and references in your code that are affected by the changes in your directory structure.
>
> Enter the name of the directory you would like to create:
>
> New Subdirectory Name: `Graphics`
>
> [Create Subdirectory] [Cancel]

3. Type the word "Graphics" in the text box, and click the **Create Subdirectory** button. You return to File Manager. Notice the new button, named **graphics** (Figure 5.11), located above all of your files. This is your new subdirectory.

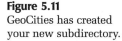

Figure 5.11
GeoCities has created your new subdirectory.

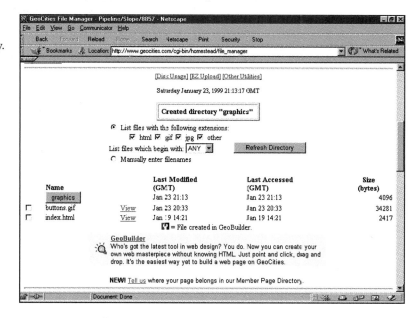

You may also notice four new buttons at the bottom of the button grouping:

▶ Move Files to Subdirectory

▶ Copy Files to Subdirectory

▶ Rename Subdirectory

▶ Delete Subdirectory

Rename Subdirectory and **Delete Subdirectory** work in much the same way for subdirectories as do the Rename and Delete buttons for files. **Copy Files to Subdirectory** does just what it says: It makes a copy of the selected file(s) and places it in the subdirectory, leaving the original where it is. If, for some reason, you want more than one copy of a file on your hard drive, you can choose this option. We'll talk about the other button, **Move Files to Subdirectory**, in a moment.

Part II Tools & Templates

NOTE

Cleanup Detail

Remember this when you move your graphics files (or any files): You'll need to redirect all your pointers. For instance, if your image file is called **button.gif**, your source code would look like this:

```
<IMG SRC=button.gif>
```

However, if you move the file to a new folder, remember to include the name of the folder in the HTML code:

```
<IMG SRC=graphics/button.gif>
```

If you don't, the HTML page won't be able to find the graphic, and you'll end up with a missing picture icon on your screen:

4.   Click on the **Graphics** button. You notice that you're still in File Manager, but now only one button appears in your file listing; it's labeled **Up One Level**. This means that no files are currently in your subdirectory.

5.   Click on the **Up One Level** button to go back to the main file listing.

6.   Click on the checkbox to the left of the files you want to move to the subdirectory, and click on the **Move Files to Subdirectory** button. You are taken to the Move Files to a Subdirectory screen, shown in Figure 5.12.

Figure 5.12
Getting your Website a little more organized.

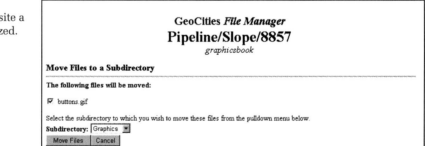

7. All the files you checked should be listed on this screen. Directly below them is a pull-down menu that lists all the subdirectories in your site so you can choose to which one you want to move your files. Because **Graphics** is the only choice right now, you can safely click on the **Move Files** button. Of course, if you change your mind, you can prevent any of the files from moving by unchecking them, or just click on the **Cancel** button. For now, click on **Move Files**.

8. You are returned to the File Manager. Notice how much less cluttered it looks with some files moved. To see what files your new subdirectory contains, simply click on the **Graphics** button. The new screen now shows all the graphics files that you moved (see Figure 5.13).

Figure 5.13
The newly populated
Graphics subdirectory.

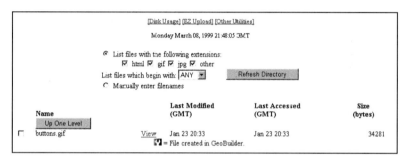

Part II Tools & Templates

Organizing Your Site

Of course, one subdirectory won't magically streamline your site. If your site consists of more than a page or two, you should probably create a system to keep it under control and organized. Organizing not only makes your File Manager page look neater, but it helps you easily update pages and graphics when you know exactly where to go.

Let's say your main page has three links on it: one to a page about you, a second to a page with photos of your dogs, and a third to a page with pictures and links for your favorite band. One way to organize your site is to create subdirectories for each page. You can store all the components— the HTML file, graphics, sounds, and such—on each page. Figure 5.14 shows the site's organization.

Then in your root (read main) directory, you keep your site's index.html home page file and all the graphics and other files from that page.

If you eventually decide to add a link from the page about you to one about your kids, you can easily add a sub-subdirectory. This sort of structure, or any well-designed subdirectory structure, can help you better manage the files that make up the pages on your site. Imagine having a site with 80 pages and hundreds of graphics listed in the same directory—a mess to say the least!

Figure 5.14
Only files that belong on the opening page of this sample Website (with three subdirectories) show up on its main directory.

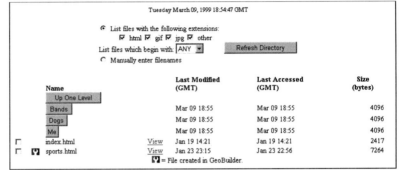

Of course, if you plan a site of only one or two pages, then the system we discussed under Creating Subdirectories (placing all graphics into a Graphics subdirectory, for example) may be all the organization your site needs. Don't feel you must choose one of the organizing methods presented here. The key is that you feel comfortable with your site's organization and can easily manipulate your site when necessary.

Once your system of organization is in place, you can easily find and replace graphics files whenever you want. Perhaps you'll want to substitute a photo of your dog sitting charmingly in the bathtub for an outdated one of him as a puppy.

Using Another Program to Upload Your Files

EZ File Upload, the FTP program provided in GeoCities File Manager, is a quick and easy way to upload files. But what if you want to use your own FTP program? It's easy enough to do. We'll step you through downloading the popular PC FTP program, CuteFTP, and show you how to use it.

Actually, you can do a lot more than upload and download files using CuteFTP. You can delete files, create subdirectories, reorganize your site—perform many of the functions you can with File Manager. You can choose the method depending on which way you find easier (and whether you prefer using the free File Manager or paying for an outside tool like CuteFTP).

Downloading and Installing CuteFTP

CuteFTP (see Figure 5.15) is a shareware program that you can download and try for free. If you decide to keep it, you must pay the program's creators. That's the premise of shareware—try before you buy. So, let's try out CuteFTP and see whether we like it.

1. Go to **http://www.cuteftp.com**.

Figure 5.15
Here is where CuteFTP can be found. CuteFTP lets you delete files, create subdirectories, and reorganize your site.

2. Click on the link that says **Download**. You'll be taken to a page asking you for some information:

    ▶   E-mail address

    ▶   Your computer's operating system

    ▶   Site from which to download the program

Part II Tools & Templates

TIP

Mac Users Included

Macintosh users should download Fetch, the most popular FTP program available for the Macintosh. Fetch doesn't work exactly as CuteFTP, although they are very similar. Fetch is located at **http://www.dartmouth.edu/pages/ softdev/fetch.html.**

3. Enter the appropriate information for you and your computer. It doesn't really matter from which site you choose to download the files. When you're done, click on the **Download Now** button. CuteFTP then downloads to your hard drive.

4. Go to the folder to which you downloaded and run CuteFTP's install program. It should install quite quickly.

Using CuteFTP to Upload Files to GeoCities

The first time you open the CuteFTP program, you'll notice that a lot of site addresses are already included in the program. This is a great way to explore sites you might not have heard of, from which you can download a variety of programs.

However, that's not what we're going to use CuteFTP for right now. Let's add GeoCities to the list of sites, then upload a file from your hard drive to your GeoCities site, so we can take CuteFTP out for a test drive.

1. Open the CuteFTP program. The opening screen is shown in Figure 5.16.

Figure 5.16
The opening site screen of CuteFTP.

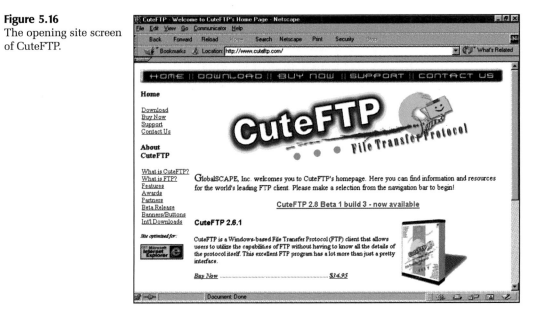

2. When the program starts, the FTP Managers window appears. Click the **Add Site** button.

3. The Add Host dialog box appears, as shown in Figure 5.17.

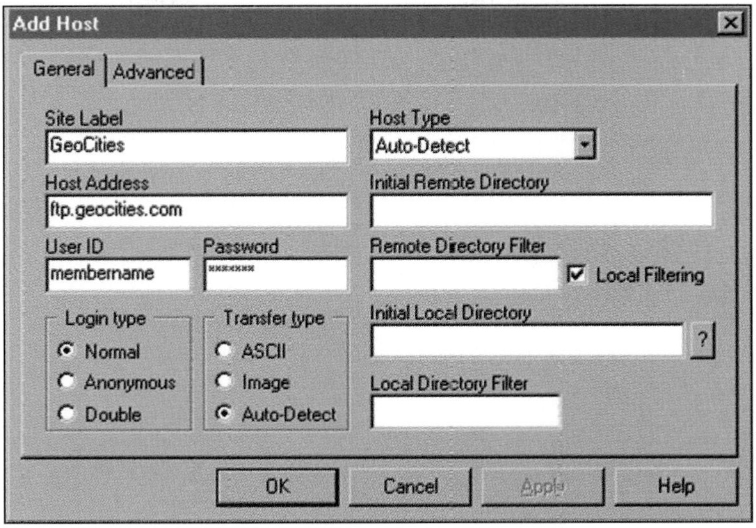

Figure 5.17
The Add Host dialog box.

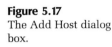

Add Host

General | Advanced

Site Label
GeoCities

Host Type
Auto-Detect

Host Address
ftp.geocities.com

Initial Remote Directory

User ID
membername

Password
****

Remote Directory Filter

☑ Local Filtering

Login type
⦿ Normal
○ Anonymous
○ Double

Transfer type
○ ASCII
○ Image
⦿ Auto-Detect

Initial Local Directory

?

Local Directory Filter

[OK]   [Cancel]   [Apply]   [Help]

4. In the Site Label box, enter the word "GeoCities." In the Host Address field, enter "ftp.geocities.com." For Username and Password, use your GeoCities Username and password.

5. Click on the button with the ellipsis (. . .) next to the Initial Local Directory box, and go the directory in which you keep your GeoCities files. Select the directory and click on OK. This will be the default directory that CuteFTP goes to when you decide to connect to the GeoCities site. Leave all the other buttons at their default settings. When you're finished entering information, click on OK.

6. You'll be returned to the main screen, where you'll see GeoCities added to the Personal FTP Sites folder. Now, click on the **Connect** button.

7. A pop-up screen appears welcoming you to GeoCities. Click on the **OK** button. You see a three-paned window (similar to the one shown in Figure 5.18). The left pane contains the contents of the directory on your hard drive that you specified earlier. The right pane contains whatever files are present on your GeoCities site. The top or bottom pane displays the "queue" of files waiting to transfer.

Part II Tools & Templates

Figure 5.18
CuteFTP's main screen.

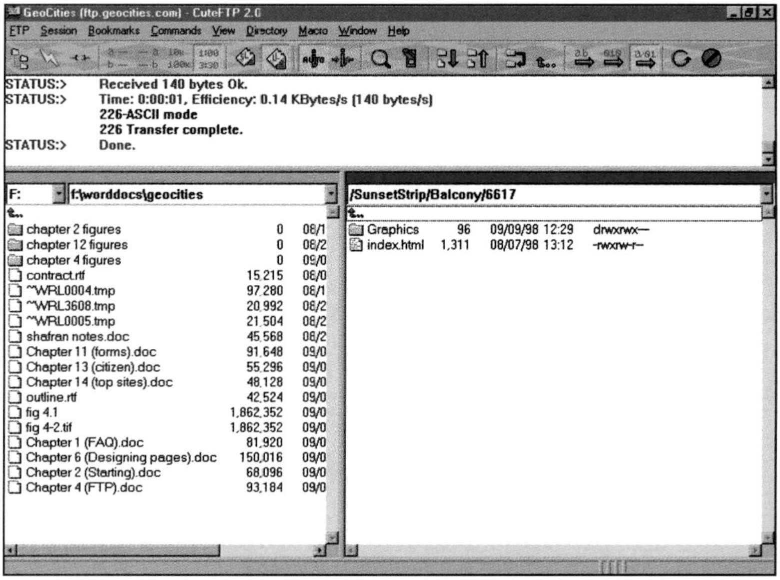

8. Drag the file or files that you want to upload from the left pane to the right pane, and release the mouse button. (Do the reverse if you want to download files from GeoCities to your hard drive—drag right to left.) Click **Yes** when CuteFTP asks you whether you want to upload the selected files. After a period of time (how long depends on the size of the files you're uploading), CuteFTP will let you know the files have uploaded successfully. You then see them displayed in the right pane.

9. When you're done uploading files, click on the third button from the left, which looks like a disconnecting plug. That will disconnect you from GeoCities, and then you can go to another site or close CuteFTP.

Moving On

Hopefully, this chapter has covered everything you need to know to start putting your site online at GeoCities. If you need to know more about something that was mentioned here, go to the Members page and click on Help. You'll find a ton of information to help you through almost any problem. And if you don't find the information you need there, go to one of the Help Forums, where someone will answer your questions.

The next section of this book helps you with developing the actual pages of your site. Now that you know how to upload pages and get organized, turn your attention to the fun part—creating actual pages. Let's get started!

6

GeoBuilder

In the fall of 1998, GeoCities launched GeoBuilder, an intuitive Web-page builder for members with little technical expertise, especially with HTML. This WYSIWYG (What You See Is What You Get) editor provides you with authoring, site management, and image-editing tools without the need for HTML knowledge.

With GeoBuilder, you can

▶ move items by drag-and-drop;

▶ resize your graphics and photos;

▶ establish links to other Websites;

▶ position multiple items simultaneously.

Also included are an expanded clip-art library, numerous templates, and animated images. GeoCities members can even import existing pages into GeoBuilder.

GeoBuilder offers you design shortcuts to simplify your Web page-building process. You can choose from an array of templates, including one for each of the fourteen GeoCities Avenues. Minimum requirements for using GeoBuilder include a Pentium processor-based PC and a version 4.0 or better Web browser.

Getting Started with GeoBuilder

To use GeoBuilder, you must be a GeoCities member. Click on a GeoBuilder link on the home page or go straight to **http://www.geocities.com/ members/tools/editor/inter.html.** Here you can visit the GeoBuilder FAQ (**http://www.geocities.com/members/tools/editor/faq.html**). The FAQ is another good reference as you move forward with GeoBuilder. You can also click on a link to launch GeoBuilder. We advise those of you who are new to page-building to begin by clicking on the Home Page Template. There are at least twenty different templates you can select from. We will show you how to create pages from each of them in this chapter.

Each template is designed to get you jump-started on creating a page for a specific topic-area—such as Computers and Technology, or Entertainment. Templates come with custom-orientated graphics (such as graphical sports banners for the Sports Template) and page designs that are clever.

For the purpose of this chapter, we selected the Home Page Template.

After clicking on the Home Page Template link, you will be asked for your username and password to access GeoBuilder, if you haven't logged on to GeoCities already. The GeoBuilder appears (Figure 6.1) with a blank page created from the Home Page Template. This template contains several pre-built sections that you can customize, and a default section, containing the standard GeoCities information that appears on all pages (the GeoGuide, an ad, and a banner), which is marked Reserved. The template gives you suggestions for a layout; however, you can make as many changes as you want.

Figure 6.1
You have arrived at the GeoBuilder Home Page Template.

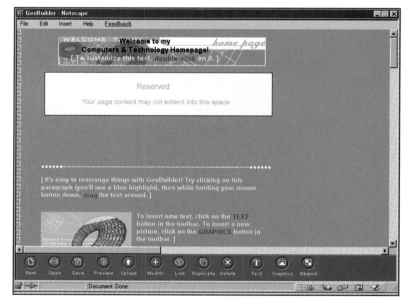

To change the size of a picture or text block, click on it, then click on the resulting small red square. Hold down the mouse button and move the mouse to change the size to fit your needs.

To edit text, double-click on it.

To move something such as a block of text, click on it, hold the mouse button down, and drag it wherever you want to place it.

To create a link to another Web page, click on a picture or text, then click on the Link button in the toolbar.

The GeoBuilder Toolbar

Resist the urge to start tearing through the template and plastering pictures, links, and words every which way. Instead, check the options you're offered on the toolbar and leave the main area of the template alone for now.

The toolbar that runs across the bottom of the page includes the New, Open, Save, Preview, Upload, Modify, Link, Duplicate, Delete, Text, Graphics, and Background buttons. So what does button do? We're going to click on each one to find out.

New

Do you think that clicking the New button will create a new page? Whoa. If you click this button on the toolbar, you'll get a prompt asking whether it's okay to discard changes to the current page. Since we haven't made any changes, discarding them is fine. However, to save the current page, click Cancel and then use the Save button in your toolbar. This gives you the chance to save your current work before building a new page.

Clicking on OK presents you with the opportunity to select a template (Figure 6.2). You can select from a number of choices such as Campus Life, Arts and Literature, Society, or Wedding Announcement. One of the options from this list (at the top) is Blank Page. Choose Blank Page to start from scratch or select one of the templates and click Create.

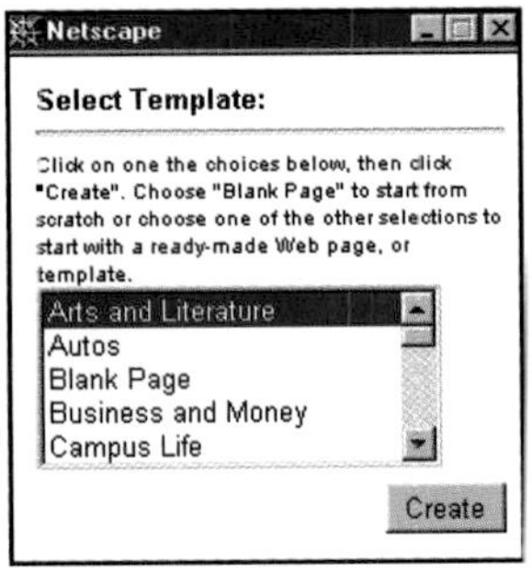

Figure 6.2
Well, go ahead! Select a template.

Part II Tools & Templates

If you select Sports and Recreation, you are greeted by a template that includes a little photo of football helmets, along with a suggested layout. (This is similar to the initial GeoBuilder template you received when you signed in.)

From here, you can start building your page—but we're getting ahead of ourselves. You can also perform the following functions and a handful of others using the File, Edit, and Insert menus at the top of the page. If you need more assistance, select the Help menu. If you love GeoBuilder (or have problems or suggestions), click on **Feedback** at the top of the page.

Open

To get a scrolling list of files that are already on your Website, click Open.

You can open any file in your Website to work on within GeoBuilder (see Figure 6.3):

1.   Find the file you want to edit by browsing through your main directory or subdirectories. Select the file.

2.   Click on the **Open** button in the dialog box. GeoBuilder is ready to let you start editing.

3.   If the file was not created with GeoBuilder, you'll be asked whether you want to import it. If you do, click **OK**. If you don't, click **Cancel**.

Figure 6.3
Pick a file you want to edit within GeoBuilder.

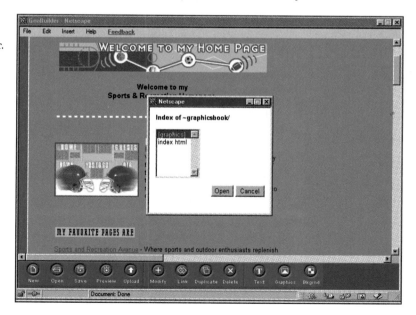

Part II Tools & Templates

TIP

You Can Always Use Another Editor

If you don't want to convert your files for GeoBuilder use, remember that you can use one of the other four editors (Intel.com Web Page Wizard, Basic HTML Editor, Advanced HTML Editor, and EZ Editor) that were covered in Chapter 4, "Building Your GeoCities Skills and Toolbox." As you recall, these editors are provided for free by GeoCities.

Save

As you may suspect, this is where you give your page a name and save it. Pick a name for your file (remember to end with either the .HTM or HTML extension to mark it as an HTML file) and click the OK button (Figure 6.4). Once your file has been saved, GeoBuilder shows you a confirmation box with a complete URL to that new file (Figure 6.5).

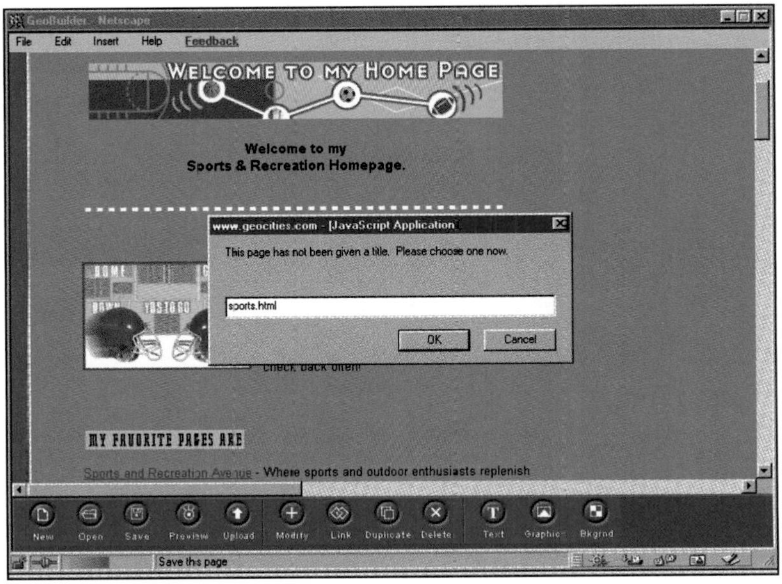

Figure 6.4
Give your file a relevant and useful name for future re-use.

Figure 6.5
Here's the complete
URL to the new
SPORTS.HTML file.

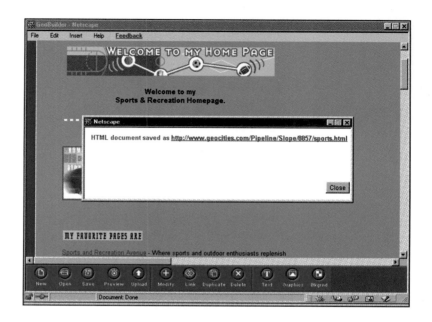

Preview

If you want to look at your page before saving it, click on the Preview button and GeoBuilder will let you preview it.

Previewing is helpful because sometimes there are subtle differences in the way a page appears within GeoBuilder and how it appears within your browser, not in Edit mode. Preview lets you check out the whole page to make sure everything is placed right and looks fine.

Upload

Should you want to upload a file from your computer, here is the place to do it. Click on the Upload button and you can enter a filename or browse the files on your computer.

If you want to edit the page you just uploaded, you then have to click on the Open button.

Modify

To use the Modify tool, you must first select an object on which to work, such as a block of text or a photo. Selecting a block of text and choosing Modify opens a text editor that allows you to change the existing text. Selecting a graphic or photo provides you with a number of image options.

You can also activate the Modify tool, by just double-clicking on an item and the same Modify boxes/options appear.

Link

Choosing Link asks you to select a Web address, a file in your directory, or an e-mail address that you would like to link to. First, you must select an object that you want to be the link (what visitors will click upon) and then click on the Link button. Figure 6.6 shows the Link to dialog box.

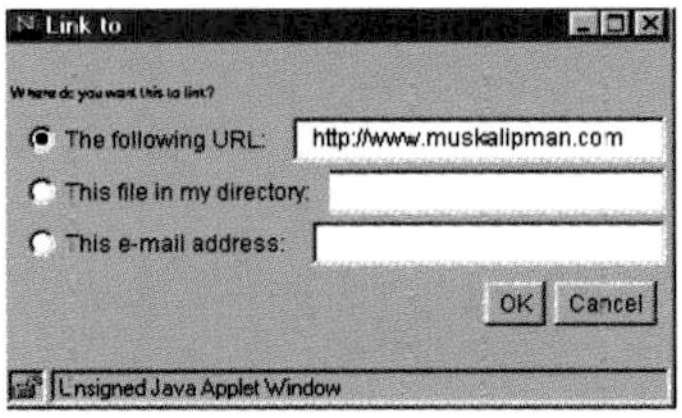

Figure 6.6
Here's how you can link text or a graphic to another site on GeoCities or the Internet.

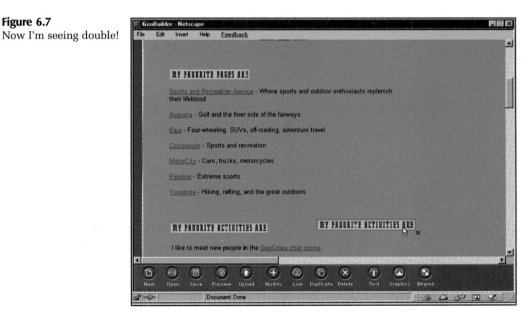

Duplicate

To use the Duplicate button, select text or a graphic, click on the button, and guess what—you have another copy of it. This is great for adding more icons and buttons to your same page. So if one picture of your dog isn't enough, just start cloning!

Once the new copy of an object is created, you can then drag it to the right spot on your page! Figure 6.7 illustrates a duplicate image being dragged next to its original.

Figure 6.7
Now I'm seeing double!

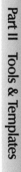

Delete

No need to insult your intelligence here. Click on an object, click on Delete, and the object goes away, forever.

If you accidentally delete something, you can close your page and re-open it, *without* saving your changes. Deletions aren't written in stone until your page is saved.

Text

Click on the Text button and get a text editor. The editor allows you a number of options to change how text appears, including a handful of fonts, sizes, faces, colors, and more (Figure 6.8).

Figure 6.8
All your Website's text goes through this text editor.

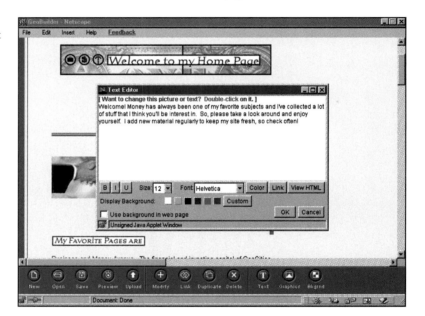

Graphics

Want to add some graphics? Here's the place. GeoCities has hundreds of sample buttons, navigation bars, and clip-art images you can immediately use on your Web page. Figure 6.9 shows a golf image being picked for our Sports & Recreation page.

Figure 6.9
The free images GeoCities provides cover a lot of different topics.

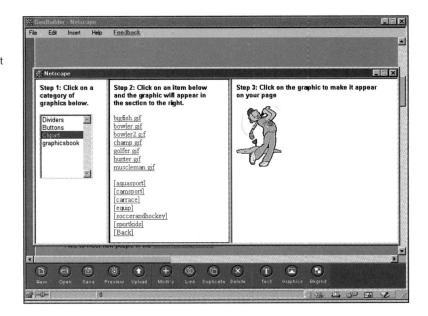

You can also select images that you've uploaded onto your GeoCities account, such as a photograph, or graphic that you built yourself. We talk more about graphics and images in Chapter 9, "Graphics."

Background

If you don't like the background of the template or page you're working with, change it by selecting the Background tool. The background is the layer behind your page's text and graphics. You can use colors or images for your page background, but make sure you can still read the text when you're through making any changes!

Figure 6.9 shows the GeoBuilder drop-down box that lets you select a background. Basically, you can select either solid colors or images to appear in your page's background. Like the Graphics button previously, GeoBuilder has a stock set of graphics you can use for your page's background, or you can use an image that you uploaded yourself.

Figure 6.10
GeoBuilder has many different background types to pick from.

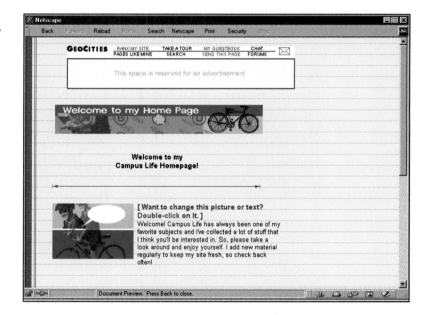

Figure 6.11a shows a plain background of just one color, while 6.11b shows a page with a tiled image set in the background.

Figure 6.11a
Pick a single color for easier color coordination between your text and page.

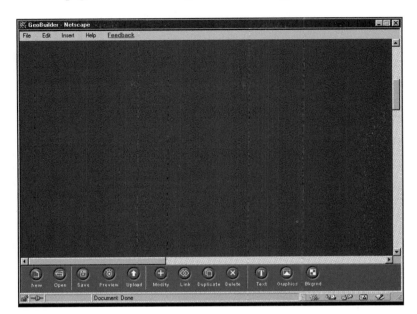

Figure 6.11b
This background makes the page colorful and fun!

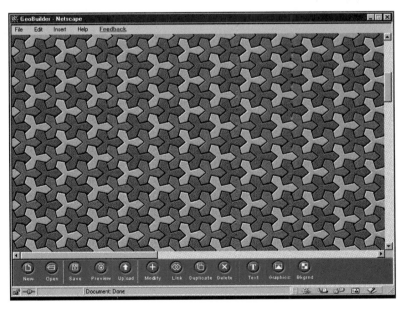

Part II   Tools & Templates

Understanding the Templates

Now that you have the GeoBuilder basics down, this section lets you
get comfortable with all of the default templates that GeoCities provides
for you.

We show you each template (before we make any modifications or add
any of our own custom graphics or text). Remember that, like all pages on
the Web, you can completely customize and change the way any of the
pages appear from any of these templates.

**Computers and
Technology**

Health and Fitness

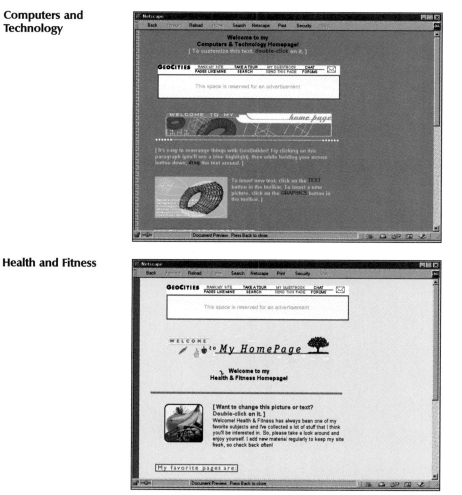

Business and Money

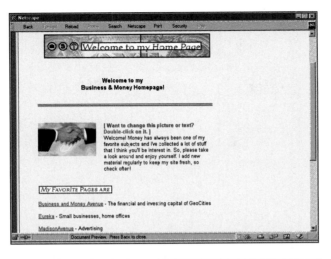

Shopping

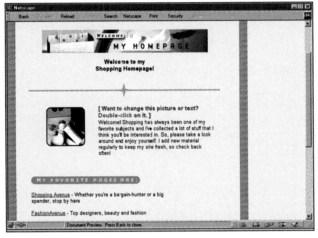

Personal Ad

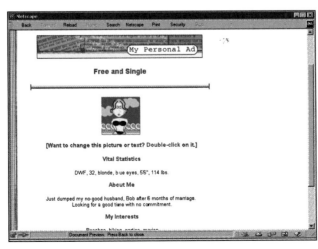

Photo Album

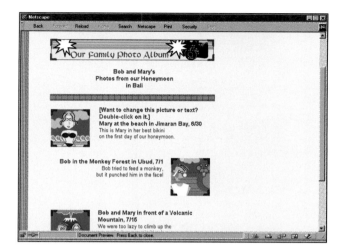

Entertainment

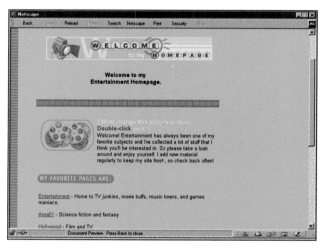

Family and Kids

Home and Living

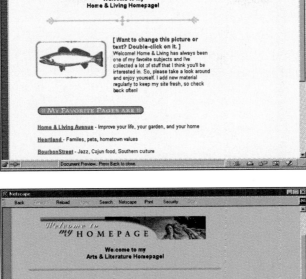

Arts and Literature

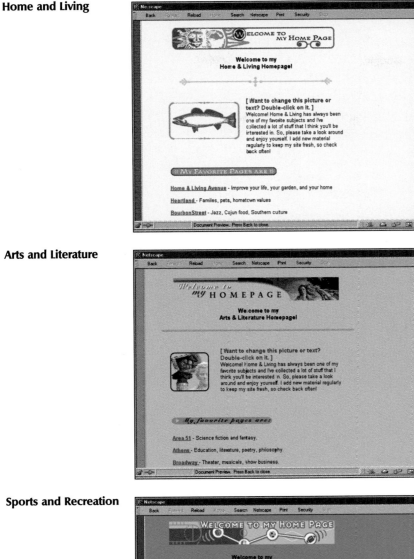

Sports and Recreation

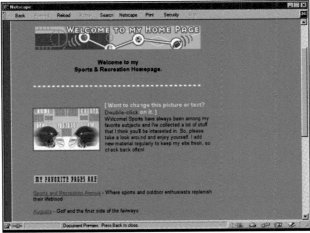

Travel

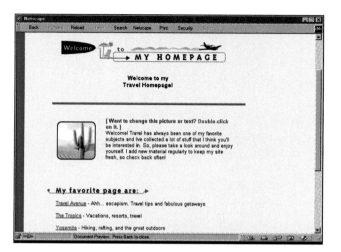

Women

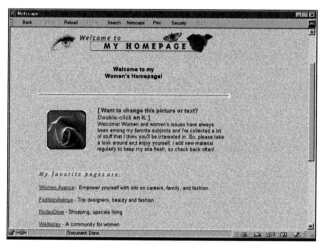

Society

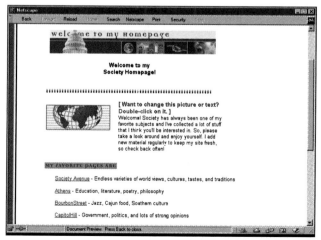

People and Chat

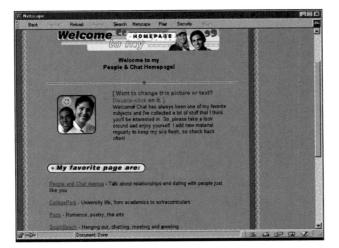

Autos

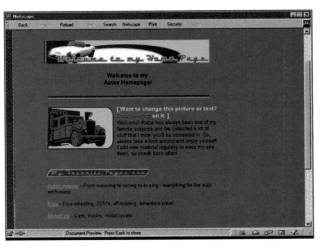

Resume

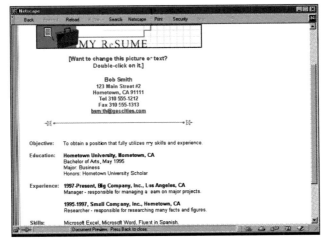

Recipe

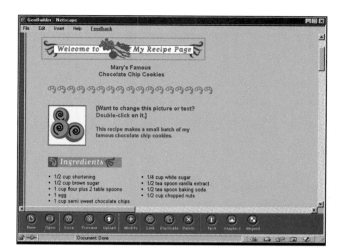

Wedding Announcement

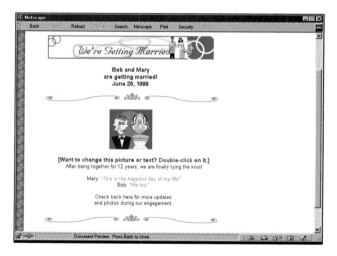

Other Useful Tasks

Now that we've covered most of the basics in GeoBuilder, you are probably ready to start building your site and reading through the rest of this book. This last section describes some of the other useful things you can do within GeoBuilder to enhance your Website.

Manipulating Files

Under the File menu, you can execute many of the tasks (New, Open, Save, Save As, Preview, and Upload) that are included in the toolbar. Two other functions are File Manager and Import (which allows you to import a Web page). In other words, you can pull an existing page into GeoBuilder and work on it.

The File Manager option takes you to the GeoCities File Manager that we discussed in Chapter 5.

Changing Object Properties

Each item you add to your page has certain properties that GeoBuilder assumes as a default. For example, all images are sized to their maximum size on your page, and text is left-aligned.

You can modify these default properties by selecting Edit, Properties from the GeoBuilder menu bar. Each object has its own set of properties that can be controlled, all of which are covered in-depth during this book as we come to a related topic.

Part II Tools & Templates

Update the Page Title

Another particularly useful command allows you to control your Web page's title (the text that appears at the very top of your browser's screen when you visit a site). Choose Edit, Page Title to make this change (see Figure 6.12).

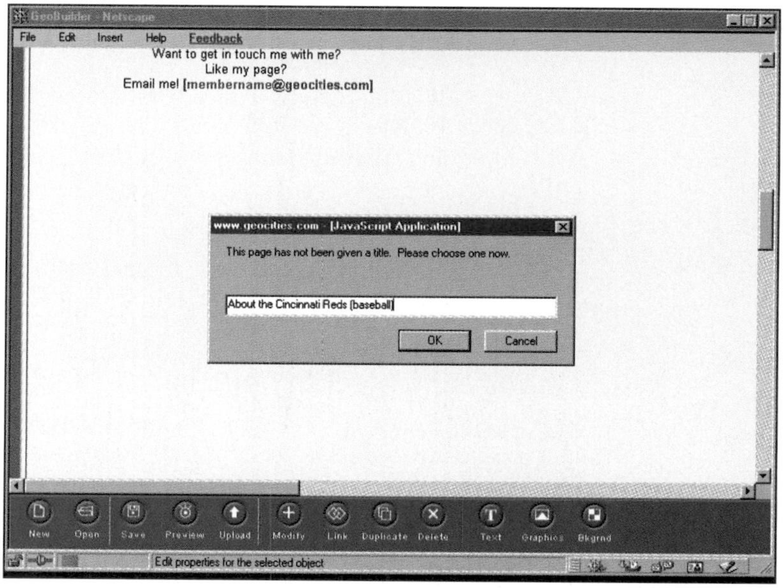

Figure 6.12
The page title is what often shows up in search engines, so pick one that describes your site accurately!

Inserting Items

The Insert menu (seen on your screen's menu bar) allows you to insert items such as text and graphics. It also helps should you want to add a numbered list, a bulleted list, a rectangle, a horizontal line, or other page elements. Figure 6.13 shows a simple numbered list we added by using the Insert menu.

Figure 6.13
This numbered list isn't
in any particular order.

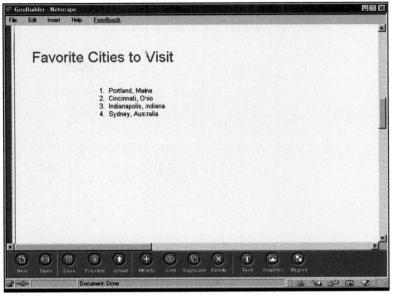

Within the Insert menu, select Input element and you can add a drop-
down list, a check box, an entry field and all other items you'll need for a
Web form (see Chapter 12, "Developing Forms on GeoCities"). You can
also add a button that provides stock quotes for you or your visitors, and
other neat activities under the **Insert, Addons** menu item.

Moving On

You'll find building a Web page easy when you use GeoBuilder.
Obviously, the more HTML you learn, the more options you have. But for
those of you who want to start a site but have yet to master HTML skills,
GeoBuilder is an excellent tool.

Now that you know how to start a basic GeoCities page, you're ready to
learn much more.

7

Page Templates and Popular Designs

So you've decided to create your own Web page. Good for you! After all, that's why you signed up for GeoCities, right? Now comes the hard work: What will your page be about? Even if you've already decided, how do you put it all together and make it look good? That, my friend, is the subject of this chapter.

Of course, everybody wants his or her site to be different. The Web would be a much smaller place if every page displayed the same information and layout. However, many of the popular home pages can be boiled down to about a dozen different types. We'll cover each common type in this chapter so that you'll get a good idea how to start.

Page Building 101

As talked about in Chapter 1, you don't need to learn HTML in order to build a page on GeoCities. Neither the GeoBuilder program (see Chapter 6) nor an offline editor, like Microsoft FrontPage or Adobe PageMill, requires that you learn HTML.

> **TIP**
> **Learn from Other Sites**
>
> What we present in this chapter isn't written in stone. While Web design does involve many do's and don'ts as well as some common layouts that we'll cover, don't feel beholden to our ideas. Learn from them (or copy them exactly if you *really* like them!), but if you have your own cool ideas, go ahead and experiment. We can't possibly cover every great layout idea or design tip in a single chapter.

However, by gaining some understanding of HTML, learning the basics of building Web pages, and checking out some design templates, you'll be a better page builder. Table 7.1 includes some good links to useful HTML and Web design sites. Table 7.2 lists some excellent books, including some that are available at a deep discount in the GeoCities Store. While we think this book is your best one-stop shop for creating sites on GeoCities, many of these sites and books help focus on HTML specifics, high-end design concepts, or are simply useful reading when you get involved in building Websites. Between the available Web tutorials, the listed books, and this book, you should find plenty of help in designing good pages.

Table 7.1
Some Good Links to
Design Sites

GOOD GEOCITIES HOSTED SITES ON HTML

<HTML> For the rest of Us
http://www.geocities.com/SiliconValley/Lakes/3933/index.html

The HTML Resource Center
http://www.geocities.com/Baja/8767/index.html

The "Home Page" Home page
http://www.geocities.com/Athens/2090/

Annabella's HTML Help
http://www.geocities.com/Heartland/Plains/6446/basics.html

The How Do I Web Design Reference
http://www.geocities.com/SiliconValley/6763/howdoi.html

GOOD SITES ON HTML ELSEWHERE ON THE WWW

Yale C/AIM Web Style Guide
http://info.med.yale.edu/caim/manual/

Web Design Tips
http://www.colin.mackenzie.org/webdesign/

Web Page Design for Designers
http://www.wpdfd.com/

Webmaster Resources Design Guidelines
http://www.webmaster-resources.com/guidelines.shtml

Table 7.2 Some Good Books on Web Page Design	*HTML 4 for the World Wide Web: Visual QuickStart Guide* by Elizabeth Castro. Published by Peachpit Press, ISBN: 0201696967.
	HTML: The Definitive Guide* by Chuck Musciano, Bill Kennedy, Mike Loukides. Published by O'Reilly & Associates, ISBN: 1565924924.
	Home Sweet Home Page and the Kitchen Sink by Robin Williams, Dave Mark, John Tollet. Published by Peachpit Press, ISBN: 0201886804.
	The Non-Designer's Web Book by Robin Williams, John Tollet. Published by Peachpit Press, ISBN: 020168859X.
	Web Pages That Suck by Vincent Flanders, Michael Willis. Published by Sybex, ISBN: 078212187X.
	The Web Design Wow! Book by Jack Davis, Susan Merritt. Published by Peachpit Press, ISBN: 0201886782.
	Web Concept & Design* by Crystal Waters, Andrew Mundy. Published by New Riders Publishing, ISBN: 1562056484.
	Creating Web Pages for Dummies* by Bud E. Smith, Arthur Bebak. Published by IDG Books, ISBN: 0764501143.

* You can get these books at a special discount at the GeoCities Store by trading in some of your GeoPoints (see Chapter 14 for more info).

It is important that you learn the types of pages and some basic page-layout schemes used on the Web, with personal home pages in particular. You can start by understanding how a Website is broken down into distinct, separate pages and how you can organize those pages by dividing them into distinct sections through some simple layout schemes.

Part II Tools & Templates

Building a Site Page by Page

As you probably know from your own Web surfing, a complete Website is divided into separate pages, each of which holds different information usually devoted to a distinct part of a site's content. For example, a Website about your kid's soccer team might include pages for box scores, the team's roster and biographies, the team schedule, the team record, and pictures of the team in action. If each area is included on its own specific page, your site would comprise six pages (unless you had multiple pages of photos or a roster of more than one page). Add a seventh page for the introductory home page and—voilà—you've got a site!

As you can see, the way to start constructing your site isn't to meticulously design each page, but rather to decide on the sections your site will include, and then to divide the sections into separate pages. Some pages will link to further sub-pages, creating a simple hierarchy similar to a family tree. Finally, decide the specific titles for your pages and how you will link them together. You can easily sketch this out by hand, as you'll see in Figure 7.1.

Figure 7.1
This simple sketch illustrates the planning behind a Website about a kid's soccer team.

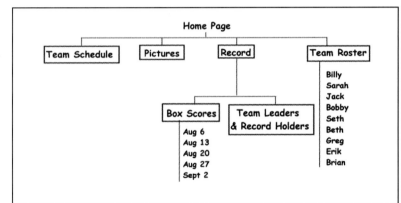

TIP

Link Your Pages Together

Once you've gotten your overall site layout together, we recommend you build very simple pages, each one including links that take you to the other pages. Eventually, you'll have a file saved for each page you intend to design, and you'll be able to see how visitors will navigate through your site.

Now that you have a site map, it's time to focus on some page-design basics. Then we'll dive into personal home pages and give you some pointers specific to each common type, sections they commonly contain, and sample layouts.

The Basics of Web Page Layout

Good Web pages have a clear, clean layout and are set up using distinct sections that will become familiar to users. For example, many pages use a simple menu of links on the left side of the page, the main content in a wide area of the middle, and additional links or small side content on the right. This simple, three-column layout is used in another way—links on the right and content on the left—by the realRankings college football page (see Figure 7.2).

Figure 7.2
Understandable page design makes your site easier to navigate.

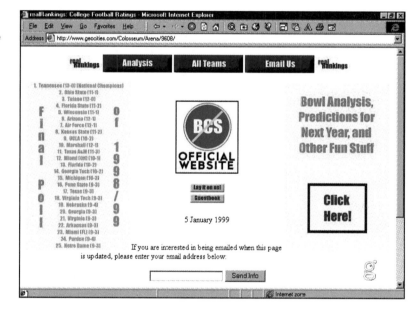

The realRankings college football page uses a three-column layout that includes (from left to right) poll results, graphics, and links to other areas of the site. You can use either of two ways to create a site with clearly sectioned pages: Divide a single page into sections using tables, or divide your site into various pages assembled into a single view using frames. For example, Mike Cahill's fan page for actress Neve Campbell (**http://www.geocities.com/Hollywood/Set/2070/neve1.htm**) uses frames to place a long menu on the left side of the site. This menu acts independently from the main window and leaves a simple navigational frame alone at the bottom.

Figure 7.3
Mike Cahill's Neve
Campbell page makes
good use of frames.

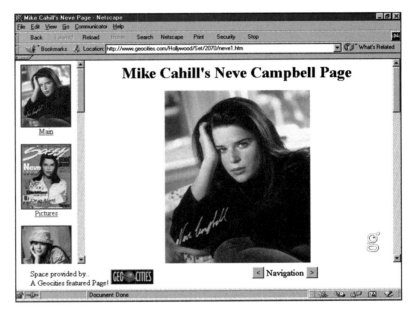

When building a nice sectional layout, the big difference between using frames and using tables is that frames take a bit more expertise and you'll have to design more pages. However, frames offer some fundamentally different options. For more on frames, check out the frame tutorials found in Table 7.3.

Table 7.3
Frame Tutorials
Found on the Web

Gilpo's Frame Tutorial
http://www.geocities.com/SiliconValley/6763/frame.html

The Frames Tutorial Page
http://www.geocities.com/Area51/4525/frametut.html

To keep this lesson simple, you can build most design ideas we present hereafter using simple tables. Table 7.4 lists some HTML table tutorials for those of you who want to build tables using HTML. Even if you plan to use a visual editor, these tutorials are worth a read.

Table 7.4 Table Tutorials Found on the Web	**Anabella's Table Tutorial** http://www.geocities.com/Heartland/Plains/6446/tables.html
	Roxy's Table Tutorial http://www.geocities.com/~roxys-place/WebPageHelp/4Tables.html

Looking at the Basic Elements of a Web Page

The basic elements of most good Websites usually include at least four key areas or sections of content. However, not all sites will include all four areas.

▶ Title area

▶ Area displaying links to other parts of the site

▶ Main body of the page containing the bulk of content

▶ Footer area displaying copyrights, buttons, and other information about the page

Figure 7.4 shows a Denver Broncos fan page (**http://www.geocities.com/ Colosseum/Stadium/3877/awayindex.html**), a great GeoCities Website that uses all four main elements in an excellent fashion.

Figure 7.4
This Denver Broncos fan site uses all four major page elements in an intelligent manner.

Title

Site links

Main body

Page footer

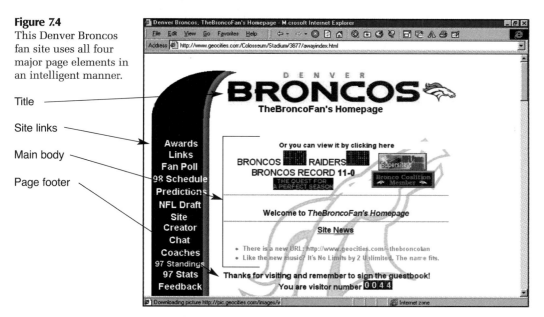

Let's look at each element as it relates to GeoCities pages in the following sections.

Part II Tools & Templates

Title Area

Most GeoCities pages have a title. The title usually rests in the center area at the top of the page and takes up perhaps one-quarter to one-third of the browser window. Many GeoCities members also insert their GeoGuide here (see Chapter 13, "Promoting Your GeoCities Home Page," for more on GeoGuide). Web page designers often treat their title as a graphic to give it a nice colorful look. An example of a title area utilizing a graphical banner can be found at **http://www.geocities.com/TimesSquare/Arena/ 2708/index.html,** a site devoted to the game Battletech (see Figure 7.5).

Figure 7.5
This site includes a title banner that incorporates the "Battletech" logo into the title area.

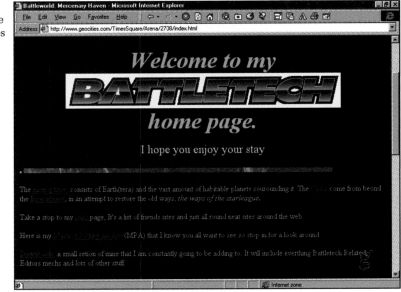

Navigational Area

Once you determine your site's main sections, you'll want to build simple sections for each page. These should include a list of links (perhaps with explanations) that will let people quickly jump to those sections. Some page designers put the links section in a frame on the bottom of their page; others place it on the side of the main home page. Other designers replicate the links section on every page on the site. Whether you decide to put it on top, bottom, left, or right, you should place the section in the same place on every page.

Magun's Compass (**http://www.geocities.com/TheTropics/8106/**) is a travel site on GeoCities. The site is divided into major destinations as well as some additional pages. On the left side of the home page (Figure 7.6), you'll see links to each page that deals with a destination or additional topic.

Figure 7.6
Users can click on any link in this simple section to get to the page they want.

Navigational Links

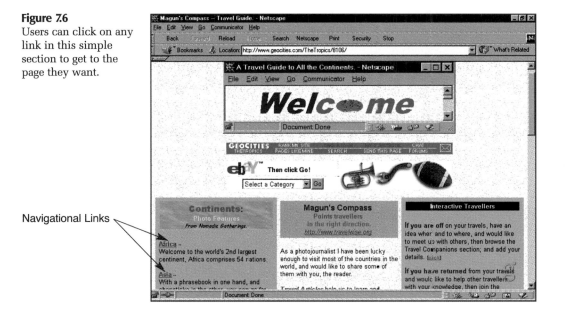

TIP

Always Include Navigation

We suggest you put your links section on every page or use frames. You never know which page users will enter first or where they'll end up. If the body of your pages is quite long, you might consider placing a group of links at the top or side of your page and a similar group in the footer area at the bottom of your page.

Main Body

The core of any page is its main content—whether a story, a tutorial, an image or an image gallery, or just a long list of useful links to core content.

The body of most pages consumes the bulk of your layout (think 60 percent or more of your total area). You should break the content into manageable chunks (see Figure 7.7 for an example). If you have text, use plenty of headings and short paragraphs, and keep the text concise. Images should be presented in thumbnail form, allowing people to click through to larger images. Links should be clearly marked, and a list of links should provide some details of the destination.

Figure 7.7

This text-heavy page describing IRA types uses short paragraphs, a table, and accented text to make it very readable.

Main Body ──────▶

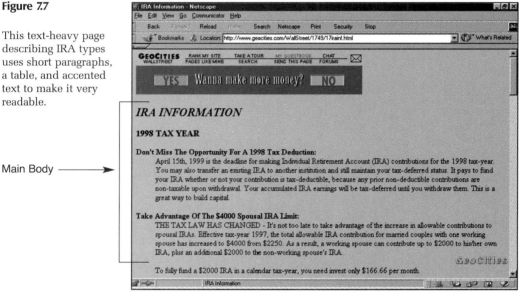

Footer Area

At the bottom of many GeoCities pages, you find simple information concerning the page. This usually includes the copyright ©, the author's name, e-mail links to the author, any special acknowledgments, and a "Hosted by GeoCities" logo. The footer on Jim Clatfelter's Garden California page **(http://www.geocities.com/RainForest/1079/),** shown in Figure 7.8, is a good example.

Figure 7.8
Jim Clatfelter's Garden
California page features
an informative footer
area, author contact
information, and a plug
for free graphics used
on the site.

Footer Section ────────▶

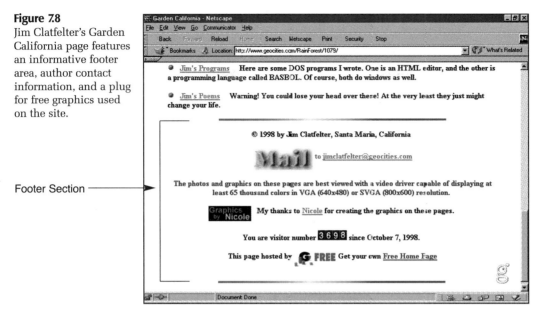

Other Page Elements You'll Commonly Find

Besides the four main sections of a home page, there are several other
things you'll commonly find on a home page. These include:

▶ Update information stating
    when the page was last revised

▶ Buttons denoting the tools
    used to build the page

▶ Web forms for visitors to fill out

▶ Hit counter

From General Issues to Specific Site Styles

Now that you have a flavor for the basic components of a Website, and the basic areas of a typical Web page, let's use that knowledge to identify some specific styles of sites and pages you can build. We broke out thirteen different types of sites (and several more sub-styles) you can build and then listed some specific pages each type of site will have. In addition, we included links to example sites for each and provided other tips for people building these page types.

The Expertise or "All About…" Page

Most of us have some expertise in what interests us. For example, if you've built models since you were a kid, you must be something of an expert in model building. If you are a piano teacher, you might choose to build a site about various pianos or how to play one. Whatever your level of expertise—professional or hobbyist—you can build a great page that shares your knowledge with others.

A standard way to begin building this type of site is to figure out how to divide your content. Start with a simple home page that contains a title area, some introductory information about your site and perhaps, since you are the expert, a brief bio that explains how you gained your expertise. Try to place an interesting graphic on the page that will instantly define what your site is all about. If you're an expert on sailing, a sailboat image makes more sense than a picture of the ocean.

From the home page you can build out to your different pages, usually including:

▶ Articles written by the site author on his or her area of expertise

▶ A news area or site newsletter

▶ A list of events

▶ Links to other sites with similar subject matter

▶ An associate bookstore with recommendations of books that pertain to the subject matter

▶ Other places to purchase items relevant to the subject matter

Your own writing and information are the keys to establishing your expertise. While linking to other areas of the Web and providing news, events, and book/product ideas are good, the periodic updates of information you personally construct and present are what will distinguish your site from similar ones. Most people make their mark in the form of simple articles or tutorials.

This is best done on a consistent basis (once a month is good, unless you feel like doing more), and you would be wise to keep updates fairly short (1,000 words or less). Round out your site with links and the other items listed.

The Review or Opinion Site

This is a variation of the expertise site, but one tinged with more personal opinions and criticism. Everybody has an opinion about something; some consider themselves experts on certain subjects. If you count yourself in that group, you can create a review site that offers your opinion on anything from movies to books to video games. However, you'll probably want to stick to one topic.

Let's say you want to review the latest movies. You can start by including listings for your favorite recent releases. Then, you might create a separate page for videos—the best and the worst. From there, you can simply add new reviews for the latest movies you've seen in the theater and on video. You might even specialize: For instance, review just foreign films or action movies. In fact, the more specific you are, the better your chance that fellow fans of that genre will come to your site.

TIP

Stay Focused

Hundreds, if not thousands, of general-interest sites flood the Web with reviews of whatever the page owner feels like writing about. You're more likely to be considered an expert outside your own home and get more traffic to your Website if you concentrate on one aspect, and stick to it.

Part II Tools & Templates

The site shown in Figure 7.9 provides a good example of a specialized review. Loretta and Dave's Movie Review (**http://www.geocities.com/ Hollywood/Set/9280/**) is dedicated to what they affectionately call "cheesy movies." That's right, those movies that are so bad, they're good (or at least hilarious to watch). The opening page of their site contains a recent review of a cheesy movie. Visitors can then go to another page to see previous reviews, alphabetized and linked to a separate page for each one. It's a simple site, but apparently works: According to their site counter, over 600,000 people have visited in the past year and a half. Pretty good for a non-commercial site!

Figure 7.9
All the cheese that's fit to watch.

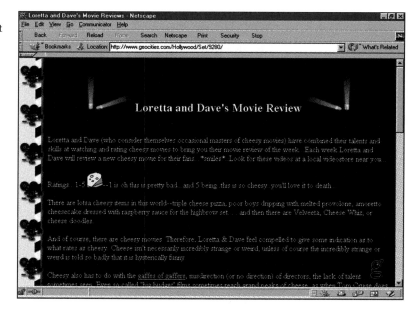

TIP

Do It Yourself

It's not hard to create simple art if you have a graphics program, such as Paint Shop Pro (a popular shareware program that can be found at **http://www.jasc.com**).

Good Review or Opinion Ideas

Here are some ideas for pages/sections to place on a review/opinion site:

▶ Put current reviews on the home page and add a section devoted to all your past reviews.

▶ Have a links page to other top review sites on your subject, other pundits, news sites, etc.

▶ Include a form that lets people submit their own reviews or opinions.

▶ Maintain a news area or site newsletter.

The Link or Portal Site

As Yahoo!, Lycos, and other sites have shown, an important site type can simply be a well-done set of links and pointers to information about a subject that resides elsewhere on the Web. We used to call these sites "link sites" or indexes. Now people call them "portals" since they act as doorways to the rest of the Web.

In truth, the best portals are not always huge sites like Yahoo!, but are extremely focused sites run by people who truly live for the interest and material. No search engine can replace a dedicated human who scours the Web and lists only the crème-de-la-crème of the Web.

Building your own portal or link site on GeoCities is fairly easy. Choose a subject area that interests you and search the Web for sites, downloads, movie files, sounds, news items, and more that pertain to your subject matter. Organize them into common groups and provide a summary for each. You can even review them or add rankings.

Most link or portal sites try to fit every link onto one page or, if there are too many, break the links into sub-pages organized by subcategories. Start with a simple home page that contains a title area. Subdivide the home page into several areas of links that pertain to each of the sub-areas of content that you've collected. For example, if your site is a portal to programming resources, you can divide the page into links for source code, development tools, tutorial sites, news, and job listings.

A good portal site includes the following:

▶ **Last update:** Since links can grow stale, dating each page lets users know whether this site is fresh or not.

▶ **News page:** Contains links to press releases or news articles about the subject matter.

▶ **Search engine:** An area on the home page that lets you submit directly to popular search engines. (See Chapter 10, "Adding Special Effects to Your Pages," for more information on embedding a search engine on your page.)

▶ **Forms page:** Lets people submit links and information to be placed on your site.

▶ **"Top Ten" page or area:** Lists the most popular links on your site.

My Favorite...

One of the most popular home page topics on the Web is "My Favorite..." —whether it's an actor, band, sports figure, movie (you get the picture!). These are fun pages to create, because they're about one of your favorite topics, and you always learn something new while you're putting together the site.

A standard way to start with this type of site is to have a picture or logo of your subject at the top of the screen, with a large heading proclaiming exactly what your page is about. Then comes the fun part: Include anything and everything about your favorite subject. For instance, Figure 7.10 shows a fan's *Pulp Fiction* home page (**http://www.geocities.com/ SouthBeach/Marina/3095/pulp.html**). It's actually quite simple. At the top of the screen is a picture of a main character, followed by a famous quote from the movie. Then you'll see a number of links to other pages on the site that deal with the movie. Different topics include *Pulp Fiction* trivia, photos, and some ongoing discussions about different aspects of the film.

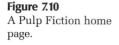
Figure 7.10
A Pulp Fiction home page.

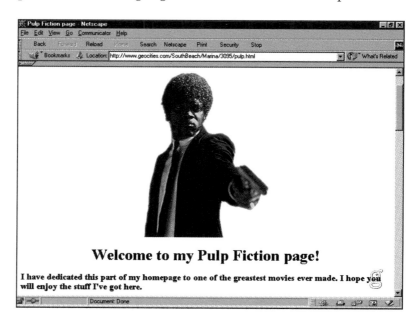

So where do you get information for a page like this? Obviously, you already know something about the topic yourself, and you'll find plenty of sites on the Web where you can do some research.

Information about Movies, TV Shows, and Stars

▶ Internet Movie Database (**http://www.imdb.com**): Everything you want to know about practically every movie every made.

▶ Hollywood Online (**http://www.hollywood.com**): Lots of information on current movies, including sound bites and an enormous amount of photos and gossip.

▶ Cinemania (**http://cinemania.msn.com**): Movie news and gossip, filmographies, and more, with lots of links to take you to related subjects.

Information about Music, Musicians, and Bands

▶ The All-Music Guide (**http://www.allmusic.com**): An incredible variety of information on everything from pop to reggae to classical. You can search by artist's name, album, or even record label.

▶ The International Lyrics Server (**http://www.lyrics.ch**): More than 100,000 archived song lyrics, searchable by artist, album, and song.

▶ Addicted to Noise (**http://www.addict.com**): Updated daily with rock music news, reviews, artist biographies, and discographies.

▶ The Ultimate Band List (**http://www.ubl.com**): Music news and reviews and extensive links to official band sites and fan sites for every rock artist you've ever heard of and a lot who you haven't.

Information about Sports, Teams, and Athletes

▶ ESPN SportZone (**http://www.espn.com**): The place to go online for current sports information on the major professional and college sports. It's cooler than the other side of the pillow.

▶ CNN/SI (**http://www.cnnsi.com**): A partnership between two leaders in the information industry, CNN and *Sports Illustrated*.

Once you've collected enough information, break it out among the typical pages you'll see for most "My Favorite" sites, as shown in Table 7.6.

Table 7.6
Tracking your site's content

Interest	Accomplishments	Bio/History Information	Articles/News	Links	Multimedia Goodies
Movie	Awards	Cast and crew bios	Reviews	Links to the official site Links to fan pages about cast	Images from the show Favorite sounds AVI clips
TV show	History of show Awards	Cast and crew bios	Episode guides News about the show Reviews of episodes Favorite Lines page	Links to the official site Links to fan pages about cast	Images from the show Favorite sounds AVI clips
Entertainer	Filmography page Individual awards	Biography page	Latest news Gossip page Interviews Articles	Other fan pages	Images, sound clips, movie clips
Sport	Past champions Past great games Places to watch it	History of sport and its stars	News about latest games Reviews of teams Fantasy rosters Rules book	Links to teams Links to athletes Links to fantasy leagues	Images, sound clips, movie clips
Team	Year-by-year record Year-by-year box scores Year-by-year rosters	History of team Bios of current players	Latest news Interviews with team players Latest score and standings	Team home page Links to articles on top sports sites about team Other fan pages Links to local papers covering team	Downloadable desktop themes, images of the team, team logos, team fight song, movie and sound clips
Athlete	Career statistics Awards he or she has won	Biography page	Latest news Gossip page Interviews Articles	Links to his or her team page Links to other fan pages Links to news about the athlete	Image gallery Autographs Sounds
Music	Popular bands in this category	History of the music style, award winners through the years	Latest news Award nominees Latest touring information Reviews of latest albums	Links to bands	MIDI files Authorized or non-copyrighted musical performances
Band/Musician	Discography Band members through the years Videos released Awards won by band or musician	Bios of the band members Background on each album	Latest news Gossip page Interviews Articles Tour announcements Concert dates and past tours with set lists	Link to official band home page Link to other fan sites Link to band's or musician's albums through associate store	Approved concert audio files MIDI files versions of songs

Family Website

One of the most positive aspects of the Web is its ability to bring together people who live across the country or around the world. In this day and age, Mom and Dad might live in New York, a brother in Florida, a sister in Mexico, and you in Arizona. Chances are that it's hard for the family to get together. With the Web, as long as everyone is connected, you can put up the latest pictures of the twins, photos from the family album that you just dug up, and shots of your new house and yard.

Figure 7.11 shows an excellent example of a family album (**http://www.geocities.com/SiliconValley/Lakes/5705/album.html**). The creator of this page made a giant table, and in each table section he put a small picture of some member of his family. This is a great way to put a lot of pictures on one page without forcing the page visitor to wait for all those large files to load. The small pictures load quickly, so the user can get an overview of what's there. Then, when Mom decides she wants to get a closer look at her grandson's birthday party picture, she can click on the picture and go to another page that features the picture, a caption, and maybe even some music.

Another site worth visiting as you build your family site is FamilyBeat (**http://www.familybeat.com**).

Figure 7.11
Bringing the family together through pictures.

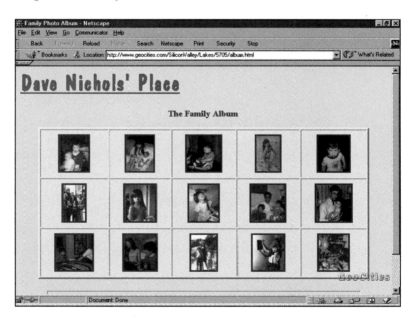

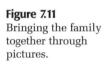
Part II Tools & Templates

Another way of putting together a family album is to put one picture on each page, as shown in Figure 7.12. To move on to another page, you click on the Next button; to return to an earlier page, you click on the Back button. This type of presentation is known as a *slide show*, as presented at **http://www.geocities.com/Athens/Forum/5454/pa1.html**.

Figure 7.12
A slide show of the kids.

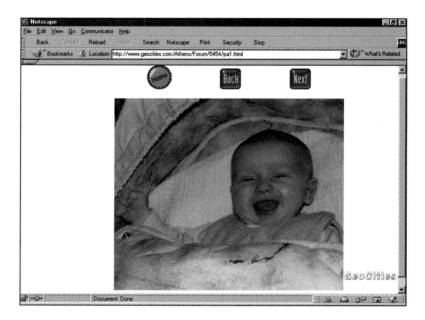

You can go about putting a family album together in a couple different ways. If you already have some pictures, you can scan them into your computer using a flatbed or handheld scanner.

Or, if you plan on updating your family album more often, you can invest in a digital camera. The price of digital cameras is beginning to come way down. Plus, you don't have to invest in film—just hook the camera up to your computer, download your pictures, and then start again.

NOTE

Get the Kids Involved

Kids love playing with computers and going online. What better way to get them away from the computer (temporarily) and reading books than having them create a book review site with their friends? You can give them a page on your site, or, since GeoCities Websites are free, you can even give them a whole site in the Enchanted Forest or a similar kids' area. See "Kids on the Web" later in this chapter for more information.

Good Family Site Info

A Good Family Info site might include the following pages or sections:

▶ Family photo album with pictures of the family through the years

▶ Artwork by kids

▶ E-mail links to each family member

▶ Links to the schools, companies, and other associations related to the family

▶ Links to the hometown papers or sites about the family hometown

▶ Pictures from family vacations

▶ Updates on accomplishments of family members

▶ Genealogy of family

▶ Online holiday greetings card/pictures

TIP

Include Personal Information, With Caution

When it comes to including e-mail or personal information, you'll certainly want to be careful. Don't allow e-mail access to a child without an adult being able to first screen those incoming messages.

Don't place day-to-day schedules on your site, and certainly don't put information you might be using as "code word" information with your children in case of emergencies. In essence, share the type of information you would share with anyone about your family and keep the stuff you wouldn't off your site.

All About Me

Another fairly common Website deals with everyone's favorite subject: yourself. This type of page can contain elements from the two previous pages, as well as other information that is specifically about yourself, your family, your dog—whatever makes you who you are. And alongside the personal stuff, you can include favorite links to other sites, tips on how you created your page, information on your hobbies or hometown, or other subjects in which you are interested.

An example of a "Me" page is shown in Figure 7.13. "Walt's Place" (**http://www.geocities.com/Heartland/Meadows/2001/**) is a relatively simple page to create, with some attractive graphics at the top and bottom of the screen, and some information about Walt. Then, at the bottom of the page, he included some of his favorite links.

TIP

Add Links AND Descriptions

If you're going to add links to your page, be sure to give the name of the page to which you're linking, and maybe a brief description. That way, people will know whether they want to go there or not.

Figure 7.13
All about Walt.

Another, more elaborate, personal Web page is Jessica's home page (**http://www.geocities.com/SouthBeach/Pointe/2501/**), shown in Figure 7.14. Jessica has a clever site that includes a lot of links to various school-related photos and activities, as well as other interests of hers, such as quotations and life lessons. As we suggested earlier, she has made each link very descriptive, so you know whether or not you want to visit. Also, she's placed a different icon next to each link—many of them animated—that somehow relate to the link. She even included some background music.

Figure 7.14
This fun site tells us a
lot about Jessica.

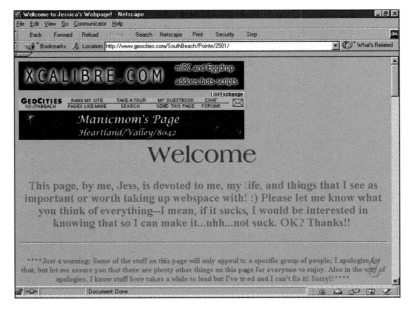

A number of sites offer free icons, bullets, art, sounds, and the like. These
include:

▶ GeoCities Clip Art page (**http://www.geocities.com/Avenues/
Computers_and_Technology/Internet/Clip_Art/**): Links to lots of
different clip art pages, both inside and outside of GeoCities.

▶ The Web Developer's Virtual Library (**http://www.stars.com/Vlib/
Providers/Images_and_Icons.html**): Another, even more exhaustive
list of sites that provide free Web images and animations.

Between these two sites, you should be able to find most of what you
need to add spice to your personal home page.

About Me Ideas

An About Me site can include the following pages/sections:

▶ Personal biography and picture

▶ Articles you've written about various subjects or areas of
interest/expertise

▶ Accomplishments and awards

▶ Links to organizations you belong to, schools you attended, and places you lived in or worked in

▶ Links to other family member sites or sites created by friends

▶ A photo gallery of pets, significant others, family, trips, etc.

▶ Personal links page to your favorite Websites, books, music, people, etc.

▶ Online resume

Online Resumes

Another logical step in creating a personal Web page is to create an online resume. An online resume is especially useful if you are involved in any aspect of the computer or graphics industries. You can display samples of your work, along with a list of your qualifications.

TIP

Keep Them Separated

Keeping your professional resume separate from your personal home pages is often a good idea. Do you really want a potential employer to know all about your Beanie Babies collection, or see your baby pictures?

An impressive resume can be found at **http://www.geocities.com/ Pentagon/2607/ratznestresume/ratzt.htm** (see Figure 7.15). This is similar to what you would find on a paper resume. A white background, normal-sized black text, and well-separated sections make it easy to see what kind of experience this person has.

Figure 7.15
Resumes work well on GeoCities.

![Screenshot of a Netscape browser window showing a resume at http://www.geocities.com/Pentagon/2607/ratznestresume/ratzt.htm]

OBJECTIVE

Full time position focusing on communications and computer networks design, engineering, implementation, fault isolation, management, consulting, quality control, and trend analysis.

SUMMARY OF QUALIFICATIONS

AutoCAD, Novell and Windows network operations, trained on GTE transmission media and equipment, Digital Patch and Access System, Integrated Digital Network Exchange, Transmission Control Network, Web Page Authoring/Mastering, and extensive background and experience with computer architectures, peripherals, operating systems, configurations, troubleshooting, and numerous software applications.

WORK EXPERIENCE

1998 -   Systems Engineer, Fort Campbell, Kentucky

1994-1997 Communications Systems Supervisor and Controller, Okinawa, Japan

• **Automation Manager**: Supported computer and network configuration, troubleshooting, and requisition needs for over 100 users. October 1995 – August 1997
• **Circuit Activation Manager**: Provided circuit actions coordination, work orders, and test and acceptance testing for multinational and joint service agencies worldwide. June 1995 – August 1997
• **Configuration Manager**: Provided configuration management functions centering on AutoCAD drafting of network layouts, topologies, circuit/trunk/link routings, facility layouts, and alarm circuitry which resulted in company savings of over $50,000.00. July 1997 – August 1997
• **Communications Security Manager**: Accounted for and controlled over 50 cryptographic materials essential for secure communications for the United States Military. July 1996 – August 1997

g!

Part II Tools & Templates

> **TIP**
>
> **It's the Electronic Age**
>
> When you're including your contact information, don't forget to include your e-mail address as a link on the resume. That way, people can get in contact with you instantly.

If you're in a "creative" field—such as dancing, game programming, or the arts—showing your creativity with an interesting background or different size or color fonts is perfectly appropriate. Just remember that you want people to actually read your resume. If you have a wild background or yellow on white type, the reader might decide it's not worth the effort.

An example of a more elaborate resume site is located at **http://www.geocities.com/Vienna/4099/resume.html**. The owner is a dancer, and the opening page of this person's site lists not one, but two resumes—one dance-related and one teaching-related—as well as a list of performances he's been in and a short biography. You'll notice that the background of this site is white with silhouettes of ballet dancers. Because it's not overwhelming, the design is suitable to use in a resume for a creative field like dance. The Web has a lot of different sites dedicated to helping you with your resume, electronic or otherwise.

These sites include:

▶ Catapult Resume Writing Tips (**http://www.jobweb.org/CATAPULT/ jsguides.htm**) and Guide to Resume Writing (**http://www.jobweb.org/ CATAPULT/guenov/restips.html**): Two pages from the JobWebSite dedicated to resume building.

▶ Michigan Technological University Department of Education (**http://www.ed.mtu.edu/jobs/resume.html**): Information here includes resume-writing tips, a guide to effective resume writing, some resume templates, and more.

A personal resume site can include the following pages/sections:

▶ Links to articles/papers about you or items you've written or produced

▶ If you're a visual artist or artisan, a photo portfolio of your work

Creating a "How-To" Site

Another variation on showing your expertise in a given area is to have a site or page showing users how to do something that you are good at. A particularly popular way to do this is with recipes and cooking tips. Everybody loves to eat, and people are always looking for new dishes to whip up. It's especially convenient, if you're working at a computer all day, to do a quick search for recipes on the Web to spice up that evening's meal. (Don't worry, no one's looking!)

Figure 7.16 shows one woman's GeoCities site that's dedicated to "Just Plain Ole Cookin" (**http://www.geocities.com/Heartland/8462/**). At the top of the page, she includes a table with links to different food categories (cookies, cakes, and pies—how can you go wrong?). Below the table is a list of different recipe links that people can visit.

Figure 7.16

Yum, a recipe site on GeoCities.

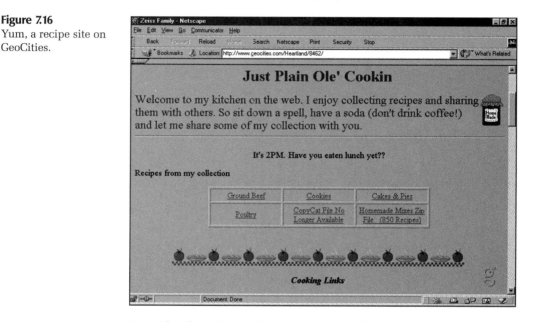

As with other sites we have seen in this chapter, this site is very simple, but attractive. It has a pink background, befitting the recipes theme, as well as simple food-related clip art placed sparingly throughout the page.

TIP

Giving Credit Where Credit Is Due

You may have noticed a graphic at the bottom of the recipe page that says "Some of my graphics by VikiMouse, The Mouse Pad." Often, when you want to use graphics on your site, the creator will allow you to use them for free, simply asking you to add a link to his or her site so other people know where you got your graphics. The Mouse Pad (**http://www.vikimouse.com/page3.htm**) is actually a good site for free art, including, appropriately enough, the kitchen and cooking collection (**http://www.vikimouse.com/kitchen/kitchen.htm**), part of which is shown in Figure 7.17

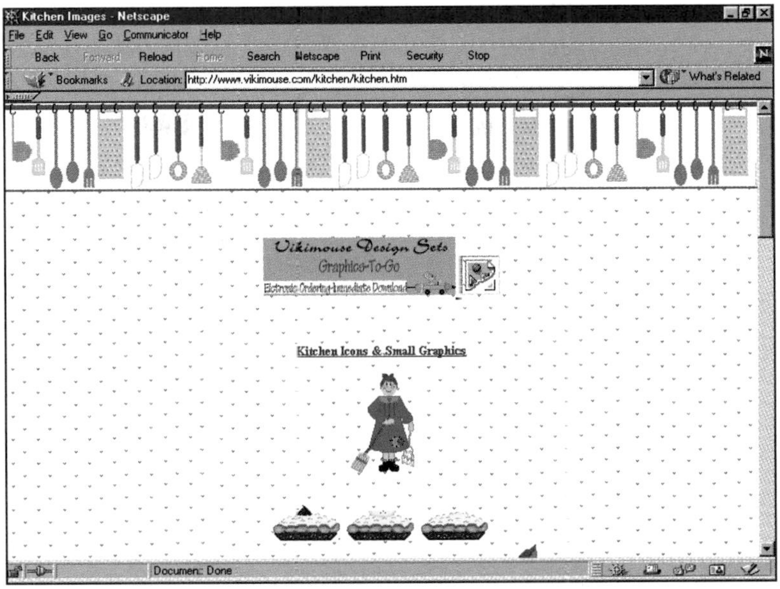

Figure 7.17
The VikiMouse kitchen and cooking collection offers an impressive array of cooking-related icons.

A more, well, masculine version of the how-to site can be found at **http://www.geocities.com/Heartland/8108/contents.html**—the Woodshop Notebook. As you can probably guess by the name, the site is dedicated to all things related to woodworking. The site includes woodworking plans and special features on everything from building a rocking horse to maintaining a table saw. Plus, you'll find links to other woodworking-related sites. This site is so good because it goes out of its way to include as much information as possible about its topic, and then sends you to other pages to find out even more.

g!

> **TIP**
> **Keep 'Em Coming Back for More**
> One way to ensure that people will return to your site is to make sure you update it frequently—at least every few weeks. That way, you'll have a regular set of visitors coming to your site to find out what you're going to talk about next.

Good How-To Information

A personal how-to home page can include the following:

▶ Weekly, monthly or routine how-to articles periodically placed on the site

▶ An archive of past how-to articles

▶ Links to places to buy materials or associate bookstores to help people get things they might need

▶ Video clips or audio narration of how-to projects

▶ An image gallery of how-to illustrations (such as blueprints)

▶ Links to other tutorial pages

▶ An overall tips and tricks page

Genealogy

If you've ever tried to research your family's history, you know that every piece of information that you find can be potentially valuable. So why not add information about your family's history to the Web for other researchers to find? An excellent genealogy can be found at **http://www.geocities.com/Heartland/Acres/8310/mcgrew.htm**.

Genealogy is a very popular topic on the Web. There are literally thousands of sites relating to particular families, as well as areas devoted to genealogy resources. A small sampling of resource sites includes:

▶ Treasure Maps, The How-To Genealogy Site (**http://www.firstct.com/fv/tmaps.html**): This site lives up to its name, with detailed information on how to get started on your family history, a discussion on using the U.S. Federal Census, and even a tutorial on how to decipher old handwriting, complete with photos. This site received four stars from Yahoo! Internet Life and good reviews from a number of other Internet rating sites.

▶ Government Sources (**http://www.geocities.com/Heartland/Plains/6106/govment.html**): This site contains a number of government-related genealogy resources, including land records, social security number lookups, and vital records.

▶ The A to Z of Irish Genealogy Websites (**http://www.irish-insight.com/a2z-genealogy/index.html**): Just one of many country-specific genealogy Websites available on the Web. Includes emigrant ship lists, Catholic parish lists, and information on various clans.

Travel

Although you can make a simple travel site in a similar manner to either a photo gallery or a personal Website, such as the ones described earlier in this chapter, that isn't what we have in mind here. We're talking about pages with information that will be useful to other travelers: little-known, out-of the-way places; that great, inexpensive hotel you stayed at in Stockholm; the wonderful *trattoria* you found on a side street in Venice; or even the most unusual places to visit if you're traveling across the good old USA. It's information like this that will set your page apart.

One example of a very specialized travel page is the Ukraine Travel Guide, located at **http://www.geocities.com/TheTropics/Shores/9405/** (see Figure 7.18). The site's creator says the Ukraine is the "best place for those who like trying new things." Near the top of the page is a color image map of the Ukraine with the five largest cities highlighted. Users can click on one of the cities to find more information, or they can scroll down to the table beneath it and find information on everything from hotels and resorts to places to visit to the weather.

Figure 7.18
The Ukraine—a new tourist destination.

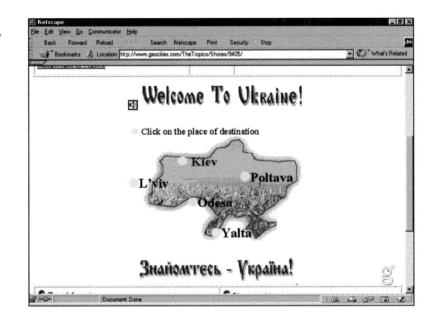

NOTE

Understanding Image Maps

An image map is a graphic that has been divided into sections—each section will take you to a different place, depending on which area you click on. You can use any graphic for an image map, but it's best to use one that has obvious divisions or markings so the user will know where to click. Image maps will be discussed in more detail in Chapter 9.

If you would like to check out some professional travel sites to see what they offer, here are a few:

► Microsoft Expedia (**http://www.expedia.com**): From this one site you can comparison-shop air fares, find hotel rooms around the world, and rent cars. But you can also find information about the area or country you're visiting and get tips on everything from when the best time is to visit Michelangelo's *David* in Florence to how to tip on-board a cruise ship.

▶ Travelocity (**http://www.travelocity.com**): This site is a great place to find out the latest information on the air fare wars. You can also sign up to receive a free e-mail newsletter, as well as a service that will e-mail you when low fares to your chosen destination become available.

▶ The Well-Informed Traveler (**http://www.armchair.com**): "A compendium of travel information and advice." This site has a lot of good information for Americans traveling abroad, including tips on driving in foreign countries and dealing with health care abroad.

Good Travel Information

A travel-related home page can include the following:

▶ Local guides and travel tips for places you have visited

▶ Archive of travel diaries

▶ Travel photo gallery

▶ Links to sites about places you've visited

▶ Links to popular travel sites

Kids on the Web

As we mentioned before, kids love the Web. It's easy to get around and has lots of fun activities in which they can participate. GeoCities has entire neighborhoods devoted to kids. These areas are considered safe places where "our youngest GeoCitizens can shine." Want to get your kids involved with more reading and creative writing? Get them started creating their own Web page.

g!

TIP

The Reviews Are In

Guestbooks are a great way to find out who has been visiting your site and what they think of it. They're also a good way of interacting with your audience. For an example of a guestbook program, go to **http://www.Guestworld.com**.

Even very young kids can get into the act, as demonstrated by Alex's Web Port, shown in Figure 7.19 (**http://www.geocities.com/EnchantedForest/ 1646/entrance.html**). Enchanted Forest is specifically for children. We're thinking that Alex had a little help with the artistic and HTML side of his page, but the content is pure seven-year old, with a big paragraph talking about himself and his family and links to sites like Disney, Crayola, and Reading Rainbow. This is a good page to show your younger kids to give them some ideas.

Figure 7.19
You're never too young to have your own Web page.

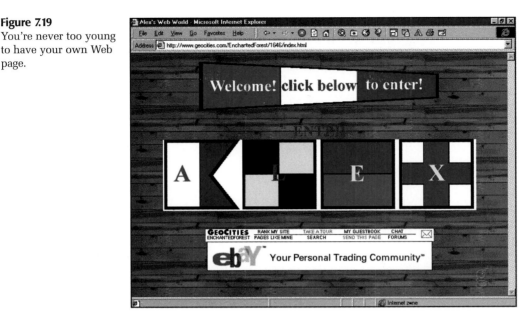

Small Business Sites

Our final site example is a little different from our other discussions on personal pages. But, if you own your own business or work out of your home, oftentimes your business *is* your personal life. Having a Web page on the Internet is a good way to get your business some free publicity.

> **TIP**
>
> **Always Include Contact Information!**
>
> Along with information about your company, don't forget to let people know how to get in touch with you. And make sure your contact information is easily found on your site. It doesn't do you any good to have potential customers come to your page if they don't know how to reach you to do business.

Good Business Information

A personal business site can include the following:

▶ Links to people you've worked for or do business with

▶ Write-ups and pictures of company projects

▶ Links to articles or news about your company

▶ Links to personal home pages for company employees

▶ Information or expertise articles about your field

TIP

Going beyond the ideas presented here and offering prices, contact information or advertising will probably cross the line into a commercial site, which is against GeoCities' policies (unless you are a GeoShop operator). All the details on GeoShops can be found in Chapter 17, "GeoShops: E-Commerce Made Easy."

The Best Layout: Mix It Up

Many ideas for building sites and laying out individual pages are almost interchangeable. Although similar sites clearly use similar page and layout types, some of the best personal home pages will combine all the best ideas and page types. This will create an exceptionally well-done, unique mix of content, links, articles, image galleries, and more. As you lay out your site's structure and gather content that will comprise its individual sections, look beyond the basic ideas for each site type. Imagine how you might integrate the ideas and layouts you see elsewhere.

Moving On

As you've seen by looking at the sample Web pages in this chapter, anybody can create a site on the Web—young or old—for personal or business use. You have no excuse for waiting to start your own. Of course, as we said, the page ideas provided in this chapter are just ideas—you can create one of hundreds of other types.

The following chapters will give you the mechanics of how to put together an attractive site using HTML, graphics, and some cool extras that GeoCities created just for its members. The next chapter deals specifically with gathering your site's individual components.

Good luck, and don't be afraid to use your imagination!

Part III
Making an Exciting Site

8

Pulling Your Page's Contents Together

Chapter 7, "Page Templates and Popular Designs," gave you some good ideas as to the different types of personal sites you can create on GeoCities. In this chapter, you see the various ways you can put your home page together, different items that make a site complete, and what you should think about when placing them on your page. We will also discuss how you can find fun items to put on your site.

Keep in mind that the point of this chapter is not to tell you *how* to create images or record background music—items like these are covered in detail in later chapters. What we offer here is insight into what you can and should (as well as shouldn't) include on your page. Then, we'll point you in the right direction to create or find what you want.

Planning Your Web Page

Some of the most important work on your Website should happen before you write even one line of HTML code. If you want a truly attractive and well-constructed site, you must *plan* what you want to accomplish with your page.

Let's say you want to create a "My Favorite" page for your favorite actor. What do you want it to include? Photos of the star in question, of course, but what photos? And where will you get them? Information about the star is another natural choice. But how should you organize it? How about one page for a filmography and another for the latest gossip? Perhaps you have the information on his films, but where do you find the gossip? Do you want to include various graphics, like film reels, or just a dividing bar across the page to separate elements? What should your dividers look like?

I think you see the point. Sure, making a page with the help of visual editors can be easy (even writing HTML code is not too difficult for those who wish to learn it!). The hard part is collecting and developing the content for your page and figuring out how to organize it. Remember that the content your site delivers is just as important as a lovely design.

Five Steps Toward Collecting Your Content

When getting your pages together, use these five simple steps to move from concept to reality. To further illustrate this, imagine that you are building a home page about your local little league team.

Step 1—Write Your Plan Down

Put exactly what you want to include on your site in writing. This includes any text on the page, as well as graphics and multimedia effects. Turn this into a checklist so you can mark off each piece of crucial imagery, text, or other content as you find it. For your little league team, you can create a plan that includes getting the names and stats of all the players, the team schedule, pictures of each member, season highlights, and so on.

Step 2—Create a Flowchart

Unless you plan to have just one page on your site, the next step is to create a flowchart showing how you are going to organize the elements of your home page. For instance, the main home page could have links to a filmography page, a page of photos, a gossip page, and a page of links to other fan sites. Using the templates included with GeoBuilder and some of the ideas from the previous chapter should allow you to do this easily.

For your little league site, you might divide the site into four key pages all descending off the main home page. Have one for the schedule, one for the highlights, one for team pictures, and one for stats.

Step 3—Determine Your Contents

The next step is to decide exactly what you want on each page and, more importantly, where you're going to get each item.

You may already have information from clippings and the like, but where are you going to find more up-to-date information? Are you going to include a list of links or put them in a table? If you're creating a list, do you need graphical bullets to put next to each link? You can see the detail this gets down to! You don't need to decide exactly what your graphics are going to look like yet, but you *do* need to decide whether you need them.

With the little league site as an example you would want pictures of all the team members, the coach, some shots of them playing other teams, and maybe even some video collected from other parents to turn into highlight clips. You might also want to scan the team logo.

Step 4—Collect Your Material

At this point, start gathering the pieces one page at a time. There is plenty of public domain art, music, information, and multimedia on the Web. Plus, you can utilize what you already have. We'll explain how you'll do this later in the chapter.

Step 5—Sketch Your Pages

In this step, it may be helpful to do a quick drawing of each page and make sure you have all the pieces (remember the checklist from Step 1?). We realize that most people don't really want to sketch out pages. What is important, however, is that you decide the format of each page and get a picture in your head of what you want.

The rest of this chapter focuses on Steps 3 and 4—deciding what items you need and figuring out where to get them.

For the little league site, you might choose to create a simple layout and tables for stats and the schedule. Then for the team pictures you might create a simple baseball field and place each player's picture in the position they play. By sketching out your home page on paper, you can more creatively conceive what you want to do when you sit down with your editor.

The Information Superhighway

Okay, we know it's a cliche. But the term is basically accurate—the Internet is filled with information. The problem is in sorting it all out.

Let's say you want to create a travel page dedicated to places you've visited. You choose the Bahamas, one of your favorite vacation destinations. You've been there before, but want to learn about other aspects of the Bahamas that you haven't yet experienced, such as exploring the smaller islands. The easiest way to find that information is by using a search engine on the Web.

> **TIP**
>
> **Make It Personal**
>
> Your personal experiences are what make your Website unique. Don't forget to include information you've learned or already have on hand. Not everything has to come from the Web.

As we're sure you already know, a *search engine* is a program on the Web that finds information based on *keywords* you type in. In this instance, appropriate keywords might be "Bahamas and islands" or "Bahamas and scuba."

Let's try an example. One of our favorite search engines is Lycos (**http://www.lycos.com**). Perhaps your friend mentioned hearing something about swimming with dolphins, and you thought that sounded like something good to mention on your page. So you'd enter "Bahamas and dolphins," click on the Search button, and see what happens. The results are shown in Figure 8.1.

Figure 8.1
Our Lycos search yields some promising sites.

This type of search worked perfectly for something as specific as Bahamian dolphins. But what if you want more general information? For instance, if you're dedicating your page to reviews of British movies, a search for "British movies" won't turn up much. In this case, you need to narrow down your search parameters. For instance, if you want to find out about specific stars, like Kenneth Branagh or Emma Thompson, you can search for their names. Or you can search for the names of specific movies or directors.

TIP

More Than One Way to Skin a Search Engine

You can always find more than one way to search for something. And you're guaranteed to get different results each time, even by just changing one word. For instance, searching "British films" instead of "British movies" turned up lots of sites. Film is just a more proper word, isn't it?

An amazing number of search engines roam the Web, and each one will give you different results. Your best bet is to try them out and see which ones work best for you. A list of the most popular search engines includes:

- ▶ Excite— **http://www.excite.com**
- ▶ Lycos— **http://www.lycos.com**
- ▶ HotBot— **http://www.hotbot.com**
- ▶ Infoseek— **http://www.infoseek.com**
- ▶ AltaVista—**http://www.altavista.com**
- ▶ Yahoo!— **http://www.yahoo.com**

NOTE

For More Information

Obviously, we can't cover everything about search engines in just a few pages. If you want more information on searching, an excellent guide is *Search Engines for the World Wide Web: Visual QuickStart Guide* from Peachpit Press by Alfred and Emily Glossbrenner (ISBN 0-201-69642-8).

Making Your Page Attractive with Graphics

If you just include text on your Web page, don't expect too many visitors. One reason the World Wide Web became so much more popular than the previously text-driven Internet was because users could make their pages attractive, with graphics and other effects. These days graphics don't just include big pictures. Almost everything you see on a Web page that isn't a word is a graphic—and some words, like page titles, are often graphics as well.

Let's start by looking at the big picture—actually, the big pictures, or main graphics you want people to notice on your page. These pictures could be the main reason you're creating your page if, for example, you're doing a family album.

First you need to figure out where you'll get the pictures. As mentioned in the last chapter, if you're doing a family album, you'll want to use some pictures you already have, which you can scan into your computer. Or you can use a digital camera to take new pictures and download those to your computer as well.

NOTE

Don't Forget the Unusual

If you have access to a scanner or digital camera, you can put much more on your site than just pictures of people. You might include an old cross-stitch sampler that's been in your family for generations. Or, if you have a genealogy site, a great idea is to scan the family tree you have hanging on your wall. An artist might include scanned photos of her work. A small business can scan employees' business cards or create an online catalog by taking photos of its products. Your list is limited only by your creativity.

But what do you do if you don't have the graphics you want? Well, it's time to turn to the Web. Let's say you decide to do a page about cats. Obviously, you'll want to include a picture of your prized specimen, but you decide it might be nice to have a cartoony image of a cat at the top of the page. A quick search on Yahoo! helped us find CatStuff (**http://www.xmission.com/~emailbox/catstuff.htm**), which has about 3,000 cat-related graphics. You can also look at the pages we mentioned in the last chapter for links to lots of graphics pages:

▶ The GeoCities Clip Art Page
   **http://www.geocities.com/Avenues/Computers_and_Technology/
   Internet/Clip_Art**

▶ The Web Developer's Personal Library
   http://www.stars.com/Vlib/Providers/Images_and_Icons.html

TIP

Don't forget there are also tons of clip art CDs found in many stores that sell software. Some are as cheap as $9.99. In addition to these and the free clip art found on GeoCities and elsewhere on the Web, you may have lots of free art sitting on your computer right now. If you have Microsoft Word, Publisher, or FrontPage, chances are that you can find clip art included with those programs. If the clip art isn't on the hard drive, check the program CD-ROMs as you might not have installed the artwork during original loading of the programs.

CAUTION

Read the Fine Print

Whenever you take a photo or graphic from anywhere make sure you have permission. Many sites, like the CatStuff site, tell you the terms and conditions for using the graphics. (In the case of CatStuff, the graphics are **not** "public domain." *Public domain* means you're free to use graphics as you see fit.) CatStuff allows the use of its graphics on non-commercial sites. However, some sites use original graphics that the site's Web designer created. If you use such graphics on your site without permission, the designer might consider this stealing. If he or she finds out, you may have to remove the graphic from your site.

You need to be especially careful with photographs, particularly of celebrities. Unless you're using a picture you've taken yourself, you may run into problems. Some celebrities, such as Alyssa Milano, have employees search the Web looking for illegal images of their clients. And if you don't desist (remove the pictures), you could be sued. If you find a photo on the Web that you would like to use, e-mail the owner of the site and ask him or her where they got the picture and whether you can use it on your site. This is also a great way to establish contact with people who have interests similar to yours. It's just another way of networking.

Now that you have the main graphic of your page set, it's time to think of other graphics you want on your site. For instance, you may want a bar separating the top of your page from the main part of the page, and another bar separating it from the links at the bottom of the page. If you have a list, you'll probably want to put a small icon or bullet next to each item so they all stand out. You may want to include some images as links to related areas.

To continue on the cat theme, if you have one part of your site dedicated to feline health, you may want a little icon of a doctor to serve as part of your link to that page. Then, of course, that page will need its own set of graphics. As you can see, figuring out what graphics you're going to need on each page is going to take some time. Figures 8.2 and 8.3 show some GeoCities pages that make good use of graphics.

Part III Making an Exciting Site

Figure 8.2 (which you can find at **http://www.geocities.com/Hollywood/ 2549/**) is an eclectic collection of information that uses most of the types of graphics we mentioned earlier. At the top of the page is a title, separated from the rest of the page by a bar. The creator of this site (Julie) uses bars to separate different sections of her home page. Then she has a number of links with small graphics that represent where the link will take you. She also places bullets that relate to the topic of the link they're next to. And she uses a couple of animated GIFs to give her page some movement.

NOTE
What Are Animated GIFs?

Animated GIFs, as their name suggests, are GIF graphics that use some type of animation. They can be simple, such as a blinking bullet, or complicated, like a fish swimming back and forth on your page. The great thing about using animated GIFs is that they're not any more difficult to use than regular GIFs. You'll find more about animated graphics in Chapter 9, "Graphics."

Figure 8.2
This eclectic page uses different graphics types to break up and make the page interesting.

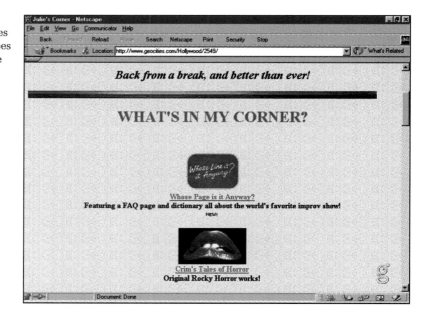

Figure 8.3 shows a Hogan's Heroes Homepage, that uses fewer graphics than Julie's page; however, the ones that are included really stand out. For instance, at the top of the page you'll see small pictures of the stars of the show. Further down the page is a graphical link to another site, and at

the bottom of the page is a small graphic you can click on to e-mail the page's author. The lines that divide the page into separate sections are in fact not graphics, but are created directly in HTML.

Figure 8.3
This fan page keeps the graphics simple.

One important aspect we haven't yet discussed is your page background. If you decide you want a simple black, white, or colored background, you can simply type that right into the HTML code. However, Figure 8.3 shows an example of a good graphical background. The German helmet, a simple gray sketch on a white background, is a perfect theme for the Hogan's Heroes Homepage. Because it's a large image and is very light, it's not hard to read the words on the page.

NOTE
Eyeball Benders

Do you remember eyeball benders? They were those optical illusion games in which you tried to figure out what a distorted picture was really supposed to be. Don't let your page be an eyeball bender! Very colorful or "busy" backgrounds make it *extremely* hard to read your page's text. And although repeated rainbow tie-dye swirls might be a great idea for the background of a Grateful Dead site, think for a minute about how hard it would be to read black text against all those different colors. Go ahead and experiment with your page's background, but be sure you test it before you put it up on the Web. Remember, if you have even a slightly hard time reading your page, someone else may decide it's not worth the trouble.

Part III Making an Exciting Site

You can also use scanned images as a background. If you're creating a page devoted to your dog, you could consider putting a picture of him in the background. Or the cross-stitch sampler mentioned earlier could make a very nice background. Just make sure your image is not overwhelming.

You always have the option of creating your own custom graphics. This isn't always as hard as it sounds, though it's certainly not as easy as borrowing public domain clip art. To create your own graphics, you'll need some type of graphics software. One relatively inexpensive product to consider is Paint Shop Pro, which is available on the Internet as shareware and costs under $100. On the more expensive side, there's Adobe Illustrator. For more information on creating your graphics, see Chapter 9. An excellent book on the subject is *Designing Web Graphics.2* by Lynda Weinman, available from New Riders Publishing (ISBN 1-56205-715-4).

And of course, if you're really serious about your Web page, another option for getting graphics is buying them. Literally hundreds of companies and individuals out there would love to design custom graphics for your pages—for a price. Now, if you're just creating a home page, you may be better off seeing whether one of your artistic friends would be willing to take a stab at it. But if you have your own small business site, professional graphics are the way to go. You want people to see your site and think of it as polished and professional, not just something that appears amateurish. At the very least, you should have your company logo on your site, like Art Connections **http://www.art-connections.com** does in Figure 8.4.

Figure 8.4
A small business site should always include the company's logo.

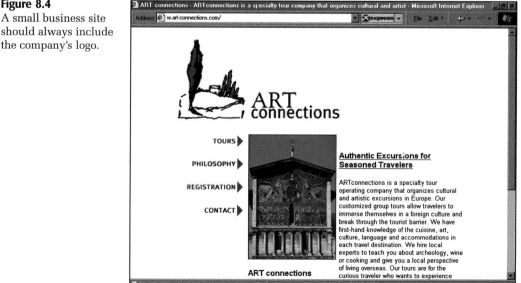

Graphics Checklist

Once you're ready to start working on your site, you can make sure you've considered all your options by going through this checklist.

Background:

___ Scanned
___ Single color
___ Web graphic

Questions to ask:
Is it too dark?
Will it be hard to read text on it?
Does it go with my page's theme?

Bullets:

___ Animated
___ Themed (animal-related, letters, and so on)

Questions to ask:
Will the bullets' color show up against my background?
Are they too big, or are there too many of them?
    (This will make the page slow to load.)
If you include animated bullets, is the blinking/movement annoying?
Do the bullets look good in relation to the size of the text?

Bars:

___ Plain HTML
___ Simple bars
___ Graphical bars (such as chains, a line of animals, a train)
___ Animated bars

Questions to ask:
How many bars do I need to break up the page?
Do different types of bars clash with each other?
Can this bar be seen easily against my background?

Other graphics:

___ Photographs (scanned or taken with a digital camera)
___ Scanned objects (such as postcards or stamps)
___ Images you draw (scanned from paper or drawn directly)
___ Images rendered from 3D programs
___ Related clip art
___ Animated graphics
___ Other

Questions to ask:
Does this art enhance my page, or is it just another graphic?
Do I have too many animated graphics on my page?
Do I have too many graphics in general on my page?
Should this graphic be made into a link?
Should I use thumbnails of graphics, which lead viewers to a larger
    version of the image?
Is this image too big? (Will it take a long time to load?)
Do I have permission to use this image?

Part III Making an Exciting Site

Listen Up–Implementing Audio in Your Website

Certain types of sites just beg for audio—and others just shouldn't make any sound at all. Of course, a Website devoted to your favorite band just screams for some type of sound. And imagine how nice it would be to have a family home page to include a spoken message from your two-year old.

Of course, on the other side of the coin, nowhere is it more inappropriate to have sound on a page than on an online resume (unless you're a musician). And most small business sites probably shouldn't have music (though you could offer a spoken message from the president, or something similar).

As with graphics, you have two basic ways to go about getting music, sound effects, and other audio for your site: create them yourself or find them on the Web. (And, as with other aspects, there's the third way: If you're willing to spend some money, you could buy it.)

CAUTION

Talk about Spending a Lot of Money

Just as when you're working with graphics, you have to be careful about the source of your sounds. As nice as it would be, it's illegal to copy music from your CD and place it on your Website. If the record company or musician finds out, it could cost you a lot more than just removal of the song from your page.

MIDI Format

First, let's talk about what you can find on the Web. One very popular sound format is MIDI. MIDI music is solely instrumental (it's created with a synthesizer), but can be quite well done. In fact, some MIDI music is downright good these days. You can often find popular songs that are in the public domain done in MIDI format. MIDI files are relatively easy to place on your site, and because they're small, they don't take a lot of time to download. (See Chapter 11, "Adding Multimedia to Your GeoCities Site," for more information.)

One excellent site for finding MIDI downloads for everything from rock to pop, classical, and movie and TV themes is the Super MIDI site (**http://www.geocities.com/SunsetStrip/Palladium/7728/midlink.htm**), shown in Figure 8.5. This site also has a ton of links to other MIDI sites with even more selections from which to choose. If you want a piece of popular music, chances are you'll find it by starting at this page.

Figure 8.5
A great collection of
MIDI music and links.

WAV Format

Another type of audio file that you're probably already familiar with is WAV (pronounced "wave"). These are the sounds you hear on your computer when you open or close Windows, receive e-mail, and the like. They're usually relatively short and generally small in size, which makes them fairly usable for Web pages. (Some can be rather large, though, so keep an eye on the file's size.) They're perfect for adding a small accent to your Web page. For instance, you could use a WAV file to have a bird sing when a visitor opens your hiking-and-great-outdoors page. Or, you could have the "Ta-da" noise play when you're displaying a picture of your stained glass masterpiece.

CAUTION

Use Sounds Sparingly

Although sounds can add a bit of panache to a Website, they can also be *extremely* annoying. For example, we visited one site, which shall remain nameless, that played a sound each time you clicked on a link. It was cute the first couple times, but you had to click on a lot of links to get around the site and had to hear that same noise over and over and . . . You get the picture: We left the site.

TIP

Recordings more than 75 years old and out of print should be okay to copy. However, be careful as recent re-recordings of classic songs are not okay.

Part III Making an Exciting Site

Now, WAV and MIDI (love those acronyms) are fine if you want to have some music or simple sounds on your site. But what if you want music with vocals or even somebody talking?

AU Format

That's where formats like AU come in. (*AU* is the UNIX equivalent to a WAV file and is widely supported on the Web.) You can have AU format files of everything from cats meowing to music you're promoting for your favorite local band. (Again, make sure you have permission before you put any music online.)

RealAudio

Programs like RealAudio are also available. You can use RealAudio to create everything from messages from the president of your company to creating a narrated tour of your site. All a visitor has to do is click on the link and the RealAudio RealPlayer pops up. The mechanics of RealAudio are discussed more in Chapter 11.

Here are some great resources for public domain files and information on all the different audio file types:

▶ Audio Searcher (**http://www.webplaces.com/audio/**) is a site containing three search engines (Lycos, Filez, and 1-Click) that have been set up to search for audio files. For instance, Filez searches for specific audio clips in the MIDI, RealAudio, and WAV formats, as well as in a general Sounds category.

▶ The MIDI Home Page (**http://www.eeb.ele.tue.nl/midi/**), as the name implies, contains a wealth of information about the MIDI format, links to pages with even more information, as well as links to downloads.

▶ Audio Browser (**http://www.webplaces.com/html/sounds.htm**) is a page that is associated with the Audio Searcher site. It contains lists of links to either categorized or assorted sounds, ranging from animals to greetings (a good idea to use when a page first opens) to, uh, bathroom sounds.

▶ The World Wide Web Virtual Library: Audio
(**http://www.comlab.ox.ac.uk/archive/audio.html**) is an in-depth site
about all aspects of audio. Along with a list of many sites containing
audio files, it also has links to information about the different file
types, and a list of online radio sites as well.

▶ RealAudio's RealGuide (**http://www.real.com/realguide/index.html**)
highlights the best RealAudio clips you can listen to. It's not
necessarily a place to get audio files, but it can give you some idea of
how much you can do with RealAudio.

Audio Checklist

Once you're ready to start working on your site, you can go through this
checklist to make sure you've thought about all your audio options. This
checklist has considerably fewer items because audio should be used
much more sparingly on your site than graphics.

Type of Audio:

___ Sound effect
___ Instrumental music
___ Music with vocals
___ Narration

Questions to ask:
How will adding this audio improve my site?
Is the file size too big and will it take too long to load?
Do I have permission to use this music/narration?

Trigger:

___ Loading a page
___ Clicking a link (unknown to user)
___ Clicking a link (labeled as audio file)

Questions to ask:
Will this sound be annoying if heard repeatedly by frequent visitors?
Will a user be happily (or unhappily) surprised if she hears a sound
   by clicking on a link?
Will the sound playing when the page is loaded slow down the
   loading of the page?

Video and Multimedia in Websites

Video is certainly one of the more engaging pieces of content you can add to a site, but with file size and production requirements being what they are, you will have to use it sparingly and with creativity to get the most out of it. Even a short video can take up a lot of space; however, if you have at least 11 megabytes of free space you should have room to add video to your site.

There are two major types of video found on the Web, each with their own flavors.

▶ The first type is *standard video files*. These are files such as MPEG, AVI (Windows), and QuickTime (Apple), which contains entire movie clips. While good with quality, these files take much longer to download and to view.

▶ The sometimes lengthy download time of standard video files helped to create *streaming video*, a derivative file format that lets the user see the video nearly as fast as the next frames can be downloaded. In the streaming video category, you find several flavors with RealVideo and Vivo being the most popular.

Video Checklist

You can go through this checklist to make sure you've thought about all your video options.

Audio:

Type of Audio:

___ MPEG/AVI/QuickTime Clip
___ Streaming Vivo or RealVideo

Questions to ask:
Is the file size too big and will it take too long to load?
Is this a clip I could link to on another site?
Will this clip autoload and be embedded in the page?
Do I have permission to use it?

TIP

Look for original music by undiscovered musicians who are all over the Internet. Music clips to link to can be found on major online record stores like CDNow.

Will it have accompanying audio?

Video:

Trigger:

___ Loading a page
___ Clicking a link

Questions to ask:
Will the video take too long to load?
Are the dimensions of the video too small?
Do people have the proper plug-in or player for this video?

> **TIP**
>
> Royalty-free video is rare to find; however, some movie sites let you use their trailers, and there are archives on the Web of video trailers you can link to.

Multimedia and Special Effects Checklist

If you've surfed the Web a bit, you've certainly come across various multimedia elements such as ThingMaker, or a snazzy Shockwave application. You've probably also come across a variety of Java applets or ActiveX controls that provide special effects like an LED Scrolling Ticker or a Lava Lamp title effect.

In many cases, you may not have known what these elements were specifically (after all who can tell a Java applet from a Shockwave applet from a Thing! these days anyway?) but you certainly saw them do neat things. This is the power a self-contained multimedia program that is displayed on a page can bring to your site.

The Web today is filled with all sorts of interesting special effects and multimedia programs that you can embed into your page. From chat rooms and message boards to cool games and multimedia programs, there are literally dozens of items to add. However, adding too many can make for a slow-loading and overwhelming site.

In addition, certain programs—like pictures, sounds, and music—are also protected by copyright. In Chapter 10, "Adding Special Effects to Your Pages," we cover all the GeoCities sponsored effects—as well as other effects, applets, and tricks—that you can add to a page.

Here's a checklist concerning the use of special effects on your GeoCities site.

Type of Effect:

___ Multimedia effect (examples: lava lamp, LED text display, PhotoCube)

___ Communication effect (examples: Web board, Guestbook, Messaging)

___ User application (examples: calculator, drawing tool)

___ Interactive game (examples: arcade game, educational game)

___ 3D effect (examples: 3D text, 3D Object Viewer, VRML Scene)

___ Interface addition (examples: drop-down menus, animated Things)

Form of Effect:

___ Java Applet

___ JavaScript Effect

___ Macromedia Shockwave or Flash Program

___ ActiveX Control

___ ThingMaker Things

___ VRML File

___ Dynamic HTML Effect

Questions to ask:

Will effect run on most of my visitors' machines? (Not all browsers support Java.)

Is this effect allowed on my GeoCities page? (User rules may prevent various effects.)

Will the effect take too long to load or prove to hard to understand?

Do I have permission to use this effect on my page from the developer?

Will this effect improve my page? (Never add things for the sake of using them.)

Gathering various special effects to use on your page isn't difficult.

As you'll see in Chapter 10, GeoCities already hosts a number of special effects you can cut and paste right into your page. In addition, indexes like Gamelan.com, JARs, and ShockWave host various special effects programs you can add to your site provided you agree to whatever terms are laid out both by GeoCities and the creator of the effect. Once you've decided what to add, visit these sites, pull down the appropriate programs or special Web code, assemble them into your page, and upload the associated files to your site.

Copyright Law, Web Content, and Your GeoCities Page

Many of you will want to use appropriate pictures of stars, athletes, or various other celebrities who are the subject(s) of your page. It is also tempting to take other imagery, sound files, video clips, and the like. We've all come across sites that are electronic scrapbooks to our favorite sports teams, TV shows, movie stars, models, and more. However, is it legal to take all this work and just use it to build your page?

First, let us state that we are not lawyers and are not dispensing direct legal advice. If you are really interested in copyright law, we advise you to consult with a lawyer.

About now you must be asking yourself why so many people violate numerous counts of copyright law to place photos and other scraps of material on their sites. First and foremost, many of these people probably don't expect to get called on it. However if they do, they will most likely lose their site and possibly even find themselves facing a lawsuit. Many people also probably think it's permissible—after all, they're not profiting from this work and the sites in question are usually fan shrines to the subject matter in question. As nice as that may be, it doesn't give you permission to steal the work of someone else. All the copyright holder has to do is prove that you are hindering his or her potential to earn money from that image.

In most cases, people building fan sites and the like have tended to use material that in the most enforced circumstances would be illegal. People who use content they shouldn't usually receive a letter or e-mail first. This letter will notify you that you are in violation of someone's specific copyright to the work you are posting.

That being said, the object of the game is not to put stuff out there and wait for letters to arrive. In fact, many stars, TV shows, and movies are getting hip to the fact that people are building fan pages. In these cases, they are making legitimate content available to their page-building fans to use that will protect both the fan and celebrity as it pertains to copyright issues.

As GeoCities' policy states, you are responsible for your site's content. Therefore, you are at risk when you put photos, music, and other copyrighted content on your page. The majority of problems usually result in nothing more than a terse e-mail demanding you pull the content down or (as in GeoCities) removing the page in question.

TIP

Copyrights © are automatic

Just because an image, text, sound, or other content item doesn't have a copyright symbol (©) next to it, don't assume it's free to use. Instead, you should always assume this: Unless you see verifiable proof the item isn't copyrighted, it is. In fact U.S. copyright law protects text and images automatically unless it is explicitly stated that something is free to use.

So what is allowable? You can freely use a number of item types:

▶ **Works deemed to be in the public domain.** If a piece of art or other material was created prior to January 1, 1922, in the U.S. it is considered to be in the public domain. However, you should always check.

▶ **Facts are not copyrighted.** For example, if you get the statistics on your favorite basketball player from *USA Today,* feel free to post them. However, the formatting, presentation and expression of a fact may be copyrighted. So if you get those statistics from *USA Today,* don't lift the exact formatting or presentation.

▶ **Some pieces of existing images.** You may be able to use small pieces of existing images. Again, be careful. You can legally take a small piece of a picture and use it in a collage or as the basis for a piece of another picture. But, if it is a major part of a picture or a clearly identifiable piece of work, you may have taken too much.

▶ **Federal government works.** You would be amazed at the amount of art and other information contained in books, publications, and other works by the federal government—all created at the expense of taxpayers and thus available in the public domain.

▶ **Work explicitly stating it may be reused without permission (or through a displayed disclaimer).** However, be sure that those offering the disclaimer have the right to do so. In general, if you feel good about the source, go ahead. For example, GeoCities offers access to a large library of clip art free for your use.

▶ **Work the copyright holder says you can use.** Nothing stops you from writing a copyright holder, explaining why you want to put their image, photo, or other work on your site and asking for permission to do so. You may find the creator willing to let you use their work when nicely asked.

Plenty of items out on the Internet are not copyrighted. If you decide to knowingly violate copyright laws, you do so at great risk and a risk that is yours alone.

Moving On

A site is always going to be the product of what you originally bring to the table in terms of content. No amount of great design and cool effects will make a good site if you haven't collected the appropriate graphics, text, multimedia, and other content elements. Now that you've had time to fully understand the scope of what a effective site can contain, it's time to understand better how to produce those special elements you want on your site.

9
Graphics

When the Internet first emerged, it was a text-based medium. All Internet information was text, followed by text, and then some more text. Text on the Net was cool at the time, but the information was usually targeted to specific audiences, namely researchers (mostly of the government type) and academicians. For a while, they were the ones having all the fun on the Internet.

Then, one day, along came the World Wide Web, and with it came graphics! Suddenly, a visual way for users around the globe to communicate with each other became widely available. The advent of a graphical means to communicate on the Internet sparked universal interest. And faster than you could say World Wide Web Consortium, the Web opened the Internet to an international crowd, many of whom had never even seen an ivory tower or a Pentagon wall.

Now, as you create your own Web pages, the power-of-graphics torch is passed to you. Carrying that torch might seem like a lot of responsibility at first, but, as you'll see, adding graphics to your Web page is easy. Furthermore, adding graphics is the quickest way to communicate your ideas and add pizzazz to any page. So, put down that torch, and see how you can use graphics on your GeoCities Web page.

NOTE

A Word From the Sponsors

Information on graphics abounds. Take a quick look in any bookstore, or run an Internet search on the term *graphics*. You'll be faced with an overwhelming array of resources. Keep in mind, as you sift through the world's resources about graphics, that you're working with graphics on a *Web page*—not a hardcopy page. Web page graphics come with their own set of rules. (Now you can eliminate a couple million resources on hardcopy page design!) This chapter aims to point you in the right direction by addressing some rules and special considerations for Web pages and providing a number of resources. However, this book can only get you started in the right direction. Ultimately, great graphics are up to you.

Part III Making an Exciting Site

A Concise Look at Web Graphics

Web page graphics serve two purposes: They can be illustrative items or interface elements. Illustrative graphics include photos, charts, drawings, and artwork. Interface graphics include buttons, rule lines, banners, backgrounds, and image maps. Of course, you can use both types of graphics for the same purpose because illustrative graphics can serve interface purposes (such as a photograph that is also a hyperlink), and vice versa. Figure 9.1 shows both illustrative and interface graphics. If you want to view this page, visit **http://www.geocities.com/Eureka/7475/**.

Figure 9.1
Web graphics come in three genders—illustrative, interface, and both.

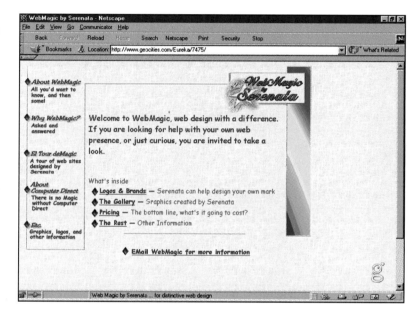

The key to any Web page graphics is *appeal* and *size*. Your graphics should be appealing, but they should also be small (no larger than 20KB, if you can avoid it). From a designer's point of view, that might seem contradictory, but from a Web surfer's point of view this makes sense. Large complex graphics (the ones that take minutes to download) are clearly unappealing, no matter how awesome they look once (*if!*) they make it to your computer. Fortunately, the Web helps out somewhat on this issue by accepting only certain graphic file formats.

Web-Friendly File Formats

Graphic files that have the GIF, JPEG, and PNG extensions (such as picture.gif, picture.jpg, or picture.png) can be used on the Internet. These file formats are all compressed (saved as efficiently as possible) to help speed up transmission time. Of course, all images stored in these formats won't download fast automatically—they'll just download faster than they would if stored in another graphic file format (if that format was supported on the Web).

> **TIP**
>
> You commonly see people refer to JPEG files as either JPEG or JPG files. Both refer to the same file. While JPEG is the official name of the file, JPG is used as the three letter filename extension to denote a JPEG file.

The following sections give a brief explanation of each file format.

GIF

GIF stands for *Graphics Interchange Format*. GIFs load fast and take up small amounts of space. The GIF format can only support 8-bit graphics, which means that it supports values up to 2^8 colors, thus the number of colors in a GIF graphic is limited to 256. You should use GIFs for graphics that don't require many colors (for example, GIFs are great for icons). A widely used feature supported by GIFs is *transparency*. This means that GIFs enable you to assign one color in the image as a transparent color. Then, when a browser encounters the transparent color, the browser doesn't show any graphic information, which enables the Web page background to show through. That's how Web pages create the illusion of non-rectangular figures. Finally, GIFs can be layered on top of one another to create *animated* GIFs. Moving icons are prime examples of animated GIFs. They are simple images that repeat a specific movement.

Perform a quick search of GIF in GeoCities, and you'll find all kinds of links to GIF pages (animated, transparent, and plain GIFs). For example, visit the RagLand Free Resources page at **http://www.geocities.com/ ~rmikulec/graphics.html** (shown in Figure 9.2). This page lists links to a number of GIF pages (and other Web page resources). You can also search Yahoo! by searching for *GIF* and *Collection*. Yahoo! will reward you with a long list of GIF collections on the Web.

Figure 9.2
Your neighbor at RagLand uses typical GIFs for the top banner and the two wheels, while the two "moving" awards on the right are animated GIFs.

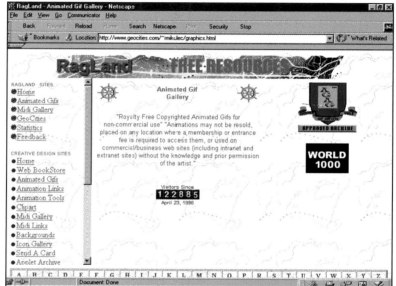

JPEG

JPEG stands for *Joint Photographic Experts Group* (they're the ones that created this file format). Because JPEG files support millions of colors and compress well, photographs on the Web are usually JPEGs. JPEGs can be encoded as standard or progressive:

▶ *Standard* encoding means that the JPEG image loads line by line from the top of the screen down.

▶ *Progressive* encoding means that the image first appears blurry but slowly becomes more focused as the image data is downloaded.

Loading an image progressively enables viewers to see what's going on before the entire image is downloaded. You should keep this differentiation in mind when you create graphics for your Web page (more about creating graphics later in this chapter). Figure 9.3 shows a JPEG image of military helicopters used as a background, courtesy of Alexander Ivanchev's Web page at **http://www.geocities.com/ Pentagon/7486/Aircraft.html** in the Military Aviation Neighborhood.

Figure 9.3
A JPEG photograph of military helicopters is used as a background image.

TIP
Check Your Compression Level
Most programs let you set the amount of compression used to create a JPEG. The more you compress the image, the smaller it becomes. However, the resulting image will not be as sharp as a less compressed image. Be sure to save your images at various levels of compression to see what level works best.

Part III Making an Exciting Site

PNG

PNG stands for *Portable Network Graphics*. PNG was created because the makers of GIF's compression algorithm decided to start enforcing the algorithm's patent. You really don't need to know the details; just know that PNG is a newer alternative to GIF. PNGs support the same types of graphics as do GIFs and have an even more powerful compression scheme. The drawback is that PNGs, because they are fairly new to the Web scene, are only supported by later browser versions. Figure 9.4 shows the PNG Group's home page (**http://www.group42.com**)—they helped develop the PNG format. You'll find helpful information and tools, and even some free "Psycho Clip Art" on their products page.

Figure 9.4
Visit the PNG Group's Website for the latest PNG information and tools.

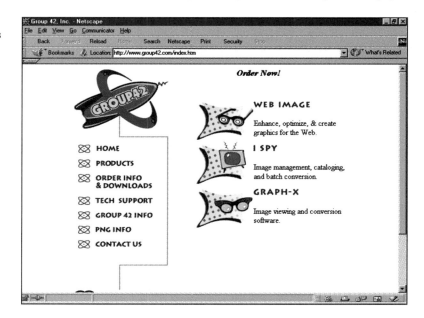

That completes the quick background check on Web graphic formats. You now know that as long as you stick with these file formats for your Web page graphics and keep the "appeal and size" requirements in mind, you'll do fine. But you're still sitting there—ready to create a Web page, with not a graphic at hand. Or so you might think. In reality, you have a generous supply of graphics within easy grasp.

Acquiring Graphics

Web graphics are plentiful—you just need to know where to find them. You can obtain graphics in a number of ways, including:

▶ Buy clip art CD-ROMs, available at your nearest computer store retailer.

▶ Use clip art that comes with applications you already have on your computer.

▶ Download images from Web collections.

The last option—downloading images from Web collections—presents a wealth of opportunities. You can either download freeware or purchase clip art from major vendors. (See some good clip art vendors on the Web mentioned throughout this chapter.) To download an image from a free Web collection, follow these steps:

1. Display the image you want to use on your Web page.

2. Right-click your mouse over the image, and save the image to your computer.

The image is now readily available for you to use on your Web page (as long as you remember where on your computer you saved it). You can modify images you download (as we'll touch on later in this chapter), or you can use the graphics exactly as they appear.

As mentioned, a number of sites sell graphics to you online. Here are some recommended vendors:

Vendor	Web Address
Artville	http://www.artville.com
Corbis	http://www.corbis.com
Cyberphoto	http://www.cyberphoto.com
Definitive Stock	http://www.definitivestock.com/
Goodshoot	http://www.goodshoot.com
EyeWire	http://www.eyewire.com/eyewire.html
John Foxx Images	http://www.johnfoxx.com
Photodisc	http://www.photodisc.com
PhotoEssentials	http://www.photoessentials.com
Rubberball	http://www.rubberball.com

And here are some sites you can go to which offer free imagery:

Site	Web Address
Free Images.com	**http://www.freeimages.com/**
GIF Art	**http://www.gifart.com/**
The Graphics Zone	**http://www.website-designs.com/graphic.html**
Andy's Art Attack	**http://www.andyart.com/index.html**
A+B+C Graphics	**http://www.abcgiant.com/**

In addition to finding and purchasing graphics, you can create your own. If you own photographs or can take a snapshot, you're well on your way to creating Web graphics.

Creating Graphics

If you'll be creating your own images, you might want to pick up some Web graphic handbooks that explain how to keep your file sizes small (such as by limiting the number of colors in your images by using color palettes). Also, check out graphics sites on the Internet for more Web graphic tips. For example, visit the Creating Killer Web Sites page (**http://www.killersites.com**) for graphics tips and other Web-page creation information. The Killer Sites home page is shown in Figure 9.5.

Figure 9.5
Click the image, then visit the Design Tips page for some quality information on Web page design.

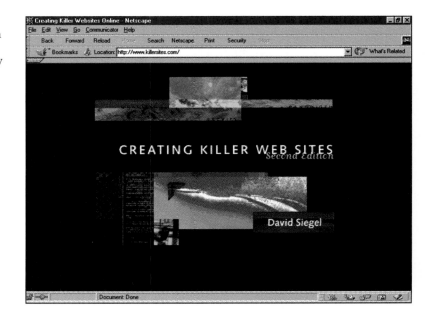

Now, let's get down to the business of creating your own graphics.

Scanning for Quick Results

If you have photographs, you're halfway to having Web page graphics. You can scan your photos using a traditional flatbed scanner, such as Hewlett-Packard's ScanJet. Basically, a scanner takes a picture of your photograph and saves it as a file on your computer. After you have scanned a picture, you can manipulate the file just as you manipulate other graphic files. One note about scanned photographs: You may have to clean them up if the original isn't in the best shape. You can use graphics programs, such as Paint Shop Pro (**http://www.jasc.com**), to clean up your pictures.

There are a number of popular scanners around, including Agfa (a favorite among graphic artists), Microtek (popular among production types), HP, and Umax. If you don't have a scanner, you can purchase one for a few hundred dollars. For the most part, you can probably get by with using a low-to-medium level scanner (priced around the $100 to $200 range). Check out major computer magazines to read up on the latest scanner deals.

In addition to traditional scanners, there are a couple newer types of scanners—Slide/film and Photoscanners. Slide/film scanners scan filmstrips or high-quality slides directly. Because they cost from $800 to $2,000, this type of scanner represents a major investment. Photoscanners, which are used to scan 3.5" x 5" and 4" x 6" photographs, represent the opposite end of the spectrum. They're inexpensive (usually costing less than traditional flatbed scanners) and are even built into some computers. This is a good choice for casual users.

Finally, you can also pay other people to scan your photographs using a new film development process known as PhotoNet. PhotoNet is a process in which you drop off your film, the developer scans the film into a high-resolution format, and then uploads photographs to the Web for you. Scanned photos are usually available within 24 to 48 hours from drop-off. Not a bad turnaround, and all the work is done for you. Friends and family can even view the photos on the Web and order their own prints. Visit Kodak's PhotoNet site (**http://www.photonet.kodak.com**) for more information (see Figure 9.6). Kodak isn't the only site that offers PhotoNet services. AOL and other companies also provide PhotoNet services.

Figure 9.6
Consider using
PhotoNet services to
develop your film as
scanned images instead
of prints.

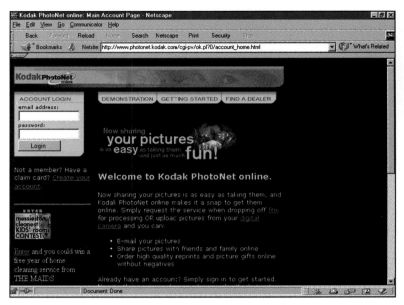

Furthermore, other companies provide scanning services aside
from the PhotoNet service. For example, Seattle Filmworks
(**http://www.filmworks.com**), one of the older Web-based photo
developers, will scan your film and e-mail the files to you. All you
do is send them your film and indicate that you want a scanned
picture. Within a few days, they'll e-mail scanned versions of your
pictures, ready for you to use on your Web page.

TIP

Other Film Development Options

Seattle Filmworks, along with most other film developers, can develop your
film on disk or CD-ROM as well as scan the photos for you.

Along the same lines as scanning, you can also take pictures with special
cameras for the express purpose of creating digital files.

Say Cheese—It's a Digital Camera

Digital cameras are one of the fastest selling consumer products around. A digital camera enables you to snap a photo and then instantly send the picture into your computer. It's a great device for people who want or need a quick and easy way to get images into a computer. The main drawback is that most affordable digital cameras do not operate with fancy lenses and other features included with most 35mm cameras. The few digital cameras that offer 35mm capabilities cost well into the thousands of dollars, which makes them impractical for most people creating Web pages.

Purchasing a Digital Camera

Quite a few models of digital cameras are on the market, and because the product is relatively new, people know very little about digital camera basics. Here are some hints and tips you can use when looking to purchase a digital camera:

▶ **Decide what type of camera you want to purchase.** For low-resolution (640 x 480 pixel) images, cameras run below $400. Higher resolution (1024 x 768 and greater) cameras will cost you from $600 to $1,000.

▶ **Do some online comparison shopping.** Visit CNet's Computers.com Website (**http://www.computers.com**) and Ziff-Davis's Computer Shopper site (**http://www.zdnet.com/computershopper/**) to find reviews, prices, and other information about the latest digital cameras.

Figure 9.7
Browse CNet's Computers.com Shopper Website for information on the latest digital cameras.

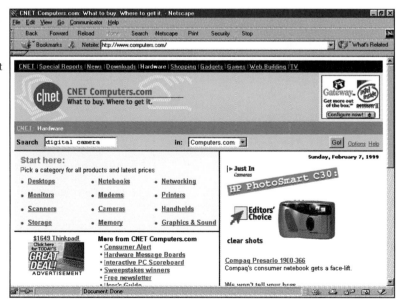

Part III Making an Exciting Site

► **Wander through local camera shops**.

► **Read reviews in major computing magazines**. Don't miss *Digital Camera* magazine (**http://www.digicamera.com**).

► **Remember, instead of using film, you'll be going through a lot of batteries.** Many cameras also include or offer power packs that you can plug in when using the camera near an electrical source. You might also look into buying a battery charger and rechargeable batteries.

► **Consider the number of photos the camera can take in one setting.** Consider whether the camera offers removable memory cards, and whether the camera offers a preview screen.

Using Graphics Programs

Finally, if you're game, you can create your own graphics for your Web pages. You can use any paint program, such as Paint Shop Pro, Adobe ImageReady, and Photoshop to name a few. Often, people create their own background images, buttons, rule bars, and other small Web page graphics by using paint programs. Many Web design books are packed with information describing how to create these smaller Web page elements.

TIP

Smoothing Backgrounds

If you're thinking of creating custom backgrounds for your page, make sure you find a resource that explains how to create a "seamless" background. When you use an image for a Web page background, the image tiles, or repeats, to fill the browser window. You want to make sure that the edges of the repeated images blend cleanly.

You can also visit product Websites for downloadable programs, tips, hints, and links to valuable resources:

Vendor	Web Address
Paint Shop Pro 5	**http://www.jasc.com**
Adobe ImageReady	**http://www.adobe.com**
Adobe Photoshop	**http://www.adobe.com**
Lemke Software's Graphic Converter 3.3.1(for the Mac)	**http://www.lemkesoft.de/us_gcdownload.html**

When you use a graphics program, you can modify existing images. You can recolor, resize, and crop pictures to suit your particular needs. A quick trip to a graphics program to customize an image is usually well worth your while. Remember to save your efforts as GIF, JPEG (a.k.a JPG), or PNG before you attempt to include the image on your Web page.

NOTE
Drawing Tablets

If you're pretty good with freehand drawing, consider getting a drawing tablet. Drawing tablets enable you to draw on a special pressure-sensitive tablet to create pictures on your computer. Many graphics packages support drawing tablets (including Paint Shop Pro). There are also several tablets on the market. Wacom (**http://www.wacom.com**) offers two of the most popular models—the ArtPadd II series (around the $150 to $200 range) measures 4" x 5" and is great for casual users. For higher-end graphic work, the ArtZ series offers 6" x 8" up to 12" x 18" tablets (from $350 to $700).

Creating Basic Web Graphics

Every person creates graphics differently, using different programs. That makes it tough to provide you with specific information on how to create graphics for the Web. However, you can benefit from certain tips that universally apply to every program.

Backgrounds

Most people want their backgrounds to be perfect. However, when you design a background that you don't intend to tile, be careful not to make it too small. Otherwise, higher resolution systems whose browsers are running in a maximized state may cause it to tile, or repeat in an unintended location, and the results can be disappointing.

Thus the challenge is twofold—design sharp backgrounds that don't get tripped up by higher-resolution users. One definite way to avoid that problem is to create a "tile-able" background that looks like one complete image as it seamlessly displays in the user's browser.

The best backgrounds present a strong contrast with the foreground text. As you make some early color decisions, consider how contrast will affect the quality of your background.

TIP
Find the Free Backgrounds

Before you create your first background, be sure to look on the Web for a variety of free backgrounds available on the previously mentioned clip art sites and on various sites all over the Web that offer free backgrounds. Remember that GeoBuilder gives you dozens of images you can use as backgrounds for your site.

Part III Making an Exciting Site

Creating Sidebar Backgrounds

When a background image is so long that it ends up tiling in a stacked manner, the result is a pattern that runs exclusively down the side of a page. This is called a sidebar background as seen in Figure 9.8.

To create a sidebar background, follow these steps:

1. Start by determining how tall your background needs to be. The taller it is, the more memory it will require.

2. Set the height of your picture as needed, but set the width of your picture to 1,024 or higher. This will prevent it from appearing on the other side of the page.

3. Draw your horizontal pattern. Be sure to keep it to one-third or less of the total length of the picture on either side. Minimize the file size by keeping the image one solid color.

Save your image as a JPEG or GIF and then use it on your Website as the background.

Figure 9.8
This site uses a sidebar background to organize a page.

Creating a Seamless Background

Seams are not only unattractive, but they tip off visitors that you are far from a brilliant Web designer. You'll want to create a seamless background when you intend to tile. A seam in a graphic is any line that stands out as an edge in what otherwise should be a continuous texture.

To avoid seams, use images that tile well, such as patterns or abstract images that blend together. You can also create a process that makes seams easy to identify and fix. Some programs have built-in seamless tile processes, but fixing seams by hand produces a better result.

To do so, when you are satisfied with your design, reduce colors and size and optimize the tile to make it look as good as possible. To create a version of this tile that will illustrate how seamless it is, you need to flip both the sides of the image as shown in Figure 9.9.

Figure 9.9
Flipping both sides of your image exposes any unsightly seams.

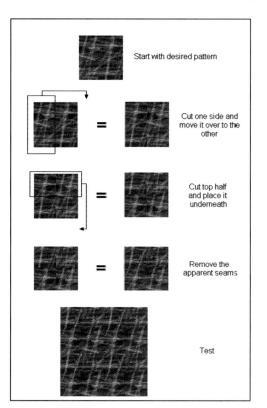

1. Start by selecting one horizontal half of your tile, place it on your Clipboard and paste it transparently into the image. Position the selection on the other side of the tile.

2. Select one vertical half of the existing tile and cut it to the Clipboard. Paste it transparently back into the image. Position the selection on the other side of the tile. This should show the seams clearly.

3. Most programs have cloning brushes, smudge tools and other features that can help you remove the seams. Once you've removed the seams without affecting the outer edges of the image, your tile should seamlessly tile in the background.

Buttons

Buttons come in all shapes and sizes. You can create them as individual images or group them together in a single image and use the image map to separate each button on your page.

A button is typically a small graphic that is either rectangular, oval, or circular, and contains text that tells the user where the button will send him or her. For example, a button labeled **HOME** might take a user to the site's home page. Sometimes text is used, or sometimes a simple picture or icon (for example, a picture of a house) is used instead. You can always use both text and pictures for the ultimate in communicative and visual design.

Horizontal Rules

Rules are used to divide sections of a Web page. In plain HTML code you can create simple rules by placing a rule tag in the code of the page using the HTML <HR> tag. Some people like to go the extra mile and create their own graphic rules for a more creative look. You need to keep a number of issues in mind when creating rules:

▶ Keep your rules narrow and roughly 400 to 600 pixels in length.

▶ Make multiple-length rules to use throughout your pages.

▶ Gradients (bars that fade from a dark color to white) make great simple rules.

▶ Use rules that reinforce your page theme (for example, a string of baseballs or a baseball bat might look good on a Mark McGwire fan page).

▶ Use drop shadows to make your rule stand out.

Animated GIFs

Animated GIFs are a special version of the GIF format that allows you to create fun animations by embedding in the same graphic files multiple images that are cycled through when loaded to create the appearance of animation—just like an old-fashioned flip book.

Many sites offer some fun animated GIF clip art you can download. However, if you plan to create your own, you will want to do two things.

▶ First, get one of the animated GIF programs mentioned in Chapter 3, "Creating Your Initial Home Page."

▶ Second, draw out the frames of your animation.

Once you've constructed your images you'll be able to assemble them in your GIF maker and then put them out on the Web. Many of the best animated GIF makers—like Animation Shop on the PC (part of Paint Shop Pro 5)—include special tools that enable you to add effects like wipes and fades to your animation. Become familiar with the tools that your animated GIF maker offers you.

Here are some tips for making good animated GIFs:

▶ Try to minimize the file size by optimizing each image in the animation, keeping them all on the same palette, and the size and number of frames to a minimum.

▶ Keep them simple, small animated GIFs that run short and loop perfectly. Animation works best when there's no discernable beginning or end.

▶ Don't put too many animated GIFs on a page or it will become too busy and turn people off.

▶ Experiment with the time delay between each frame. You can create some cool effects for your animations by using the delay appropriately.

▶ If your painting program (for example, Paint Shop Pro or Photoshop) supports layers, put each image in your animation on a different level. This lets you draw your animation and still see the previous frames underneath so you can precisely construct the animation.

Optimizing Imagery for the Web

You can approach the challenge of making your Web graphics both attractive and small in file size in any of three ways:

▶ limit the number of colors in an image;

▶ limit the size of an image;

▶ or compress an image file size.

File compression happens in relation to the different formats for Web graphics; however, you can keep your file size small by managing your image dimensions and color scheme.

Reducing Colors

By using fewer colors in your image and making the areas of solid color larger, your saved imagery will be smaller in size. When creating imagery for your site, try to keep the number of colors in each image to a minimum. Most programs offer a variety of color-reduction tools. Many of these tools offer you the chance to "dither" a small set of colors to create pictures that have few colors but appear to have millions. *Dithering* is a process in which two pixels of a different color are set side-by-side to create the appearance of a third. For example, placing a black pixel and a white pixel side-by-side in a big image tricks the eye into seeing gray. At times, you will have to use many colors in your images; but in general, fewer colors for an image of the same dimensions results in smaller files and faster loading pages. Dithering helps tremendously with this process.

Using Browser-Safe Palettes

The "browser-safe" palette is an issue that has been heavily documented but is still poorly understood. When designing graphics for optimal viewing by browsers with screens set to 256 colors, using a browser-safe palette is necessary to optimize quality.

The *browser-safe palette* is a specialized palette of 216 colors that all the major browsers for both Windows and Macintosh share. By removing the other 40 colors, you ensure that all your viewers will see your image in the same manner, whichever of the major browsers they are using.

Always test the image in the major browsers with your computer set at 256 color mode. Many people surf the Web with their machines set to this color mode so you should make sure your pages look nice at this color depth. If you are not happy with the quality, optimize the image and reapply the palette.

Image Dimensions

Always consider how big your imagery needs to be in order to effectively display on your site. The smaller you can make the dimensions of your image, the smaller your file size will be. Be critical yet conservative: As long as your image seems to maintain its detail and sharpness, keep resizing it smaller.

Consider also resizing images to create thumbnails of larger photographs. You can display a gallery of the thumbnails, which load more quickly, and let users click through to larger versions of the images they wish to view in full size.

Rather than creating a separate, smaller version of an image, you can use the auto resize tags in browsers to shrink your larger image. However, doing so can cause the thumbnail page to load more slowly since the Web browser has to initially load the larger image. Use quick-loading thumbnails for image galleries.

Getting Graphics on Your Page– A Little Code

You've collected a virtual shoebox of photographs and graphics. Now you want to take the pictures out and showcase them on your Web page. That means it's time for some code. So, open your favorite HTML editor (remember, GeoCities provides some for you). You can use drag-and-drop capabilities to place your images in an HTML editor; the editor then writes the code for you. But if you want a little more explanation about the nitty-gritty of image placement, read on (otherwise, refer to Chapter 6, which explains how to use GeoBuilder).

Entering the <IMG> Tag

If you decide to build your Website without using an HTML editor, you'll need to learn about the **<IMG>** tag. To include an image in your HTML file, you must use the **<IMG>** tag to indicate that the element is a picture file. Then, you must embed the **SRC** attribute in the **<IMG>** tag to tell browsers where to find the picture. Here's the code:

```
<IMG SRC="images/fire_eater.gif">
```

This code indicates that you want to place an image on your Web page. Furthermore, the image you want to place can be found in the images folder. Following that, the name of the image is fire_eater.gif. It's just a matter of telling your browser what you want to do, and where the browser can go to get the information.

You can add a number of attributes (special settings) to your **<IMG>** tag to control the display of your image. For example, you can use the **ALIGN** attribute to specify whether you want your image to appear along the left or right side of the page. To align the fire_eater.gif photo along the right side of the page, you will add the **ALIGN=RIGHT** attribute, like this:

```
<IMG SRC="images/fire_eater.gif" ALIGN=RIGHT>
```

Part III Making an Exciting Site

You can use a number of other attributes within the **<IMG>** tag. If you want to play around with image placement, your best resource is the Internet. For some fun and informative tutorials, visit the Webmonkey site at **http://www.hotwired.com/webmonkey** (Figure 9.10). Also, always remember to check GeoCities' guides for helpful information.

Figure 9.10
Webmonkey gives you plenty of news ideas for graphics on your site.

Ruling Your Lines

You can place rule lines on your page using standard HTML coding or by inserting a graphic as the rule line. If you use a graphic for a rule line (lots are available on free clip art Websites, and you can create your own with paint programs), simply use the **<IMG>** tag to insert the rule line on your page. Be sure to follow the rule line image with a **
** (link break) tag or enclose the image tag between paragraph tags

```
<P><IMG SRC="images/fire_eater.gif"></P>
```

to ensure that your rule line image appears on its own line. Otherwise, you may have text wrapping around your rule line, which is the result you don't want in most cases. Figure 9.11 shows several types of lines you can use on your site.

Figure 9.11
Many different types of lines are available to you when designing your page.

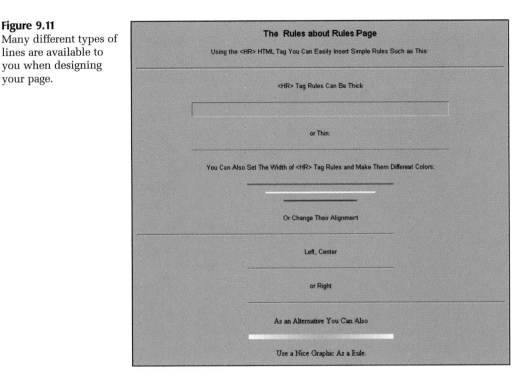

To create rule lines using just HTML, use the **<HR>** tag. You can use the **ALIGN** and **WIDTH** attributes to modify the default rule line. For example, to create a 40-pixel long rule line that appears centered within the browser window, type:

```
<HR WIDTH="40" ALIGN="CENTER">
```

You can also indicate percentages for the WIDTH attribute. For example, if you want a rule line that is centered and displays at 80 percent as wide as the browser window, enter:

```
<HR WIDTH="80%" ALIGN="CENTER">
```

Other attributes are available for the **<HR>** tag, but the basics are presented here.

> **TIP**
>
> **Learning by Viewing**
>
> A great way to learn how to use HTML code is to view the source code of pages you like. Most browsers offer a "source" option from the View menu, which enables you to view the source code for the currently displayed page.

Part III   Making an Exciting Site

Throwing in a Background

Ahh…backgrounds. As you saw earlier in this chapter (in Figure 9.3), graphics can be used as backgrounds. Background graphics can be recognizable pictures (such as helicopters) or textures. To add an image as a background, use the **BACKGROUND** attribute in the **<BODY>** tag, like this:

```
<BODY BACKGROUND="green_ripples.gif">
```

As mentioned earlier, a background image tiles, or repeats, both vertically and horizontally until the browser window is filled. Normally, background images are small, somewhat dim graphics (so any text placed over the graphic will be readable). You can find lots of background graphic samples on the Web (no surprise at this point in the chapter!). Figure 9.12 shows some sample textures from a popular background resource, The Texture Land, at **http://www.meat.com/ textures**. Another good resource is the Free GIFs and Animation Website at **http://www.fg-a.com/gifs.html.** (Click on the Backgrounds link in the left pane to view a large selection of Web page backgrounds.) You can find many more background textures by searching on the Web. Enter the terms *backgrounds* or *textures* in the GeoCities GoTo.com Search text box or in your favorite search engine.

Figure 9.12
Check out some textures offered on The Texture Land Website.

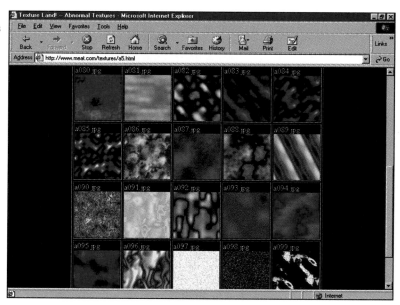

Mapping an Image

If you really want to get fancy, you can create an "image map," an image divided into clickable areas, on your page. Each clickable area links users to a different Internet resource. For example, you can put a picture of the Brady Bunch on your Web page, and then you can make each family member a clickable resource. Users can click on Marcia to visit the Out-of-Site Marcia page or click on Greg to see the Groovy Greg page.

Creating an image map is a two-part process—creating the image and using an image map editor to create the HTML code that makes the map work.

One way you can create image maps is by using one of the available image map editor programs. For example, LiveImage (**http://www.mediatec.com**) is a very popular shareware Image Mapping package. Alternatively, MapMaker (**http://tns-www.lcs.mit.edu/cgi-bin/mapmaker**) enables you to create an image map online, without downloading special software. You can also create image maps by hand, in conjunction with a paint program. Again, refer to the GeoCities Resource Guide for a lot of helpful HTML sites, online Web tutorials and HTML reference guides, and design books for creating image maps.

Moving On

As you can see, including images on your Web pages isn't so hard. After reading this chapter, you should realize that you have a practically unlimited supply of graphics; in fact, selecting which ones to include on your page may be your most difficult task! Another important consideration is keeping them small enough to work well for your visitors. The moral of the story is—keep your files small and have fun!

10

Adding Special Effects to Your Pages

In previous chapters, we first discussed planning your page and deciding what type or types of pages you wanted to create. Then, we covered what you could put on your pages, and how to enhance your pages with everything from text to audio. And in Chapter 9, "Graphics," we talked about putting graphics on your pages. Now, we're ready for the big time—adding special effects to your GeoCities site.

Now don't flip to the next chapter—this is *not* hard. In fact, almost all these special effects are surprisingly easy to add to your page. We'll start by telling you about all the effects GeoCities has already put together for you. Then we'll talk about the ultimate special effect: making money from your GeoCities page.

GeoCities Homestead Add-Ons

GeoCities calls its special effects "add-ons" and dedicates an entire page to them at **http://www.geocities.com/members/addons/**. The GeoCities Homestead Add-Ons page is shown in Figure 10.1.

Part III Making an Exciting Site

Figure 10.1
Here's the GeoCities list of various effects you can add on to your site.

Let's start from the top of the list and work our way down the options.

GeoGuide

The GeoGuide is a graphical banner that sits at the top of your page. You've probably seen these banners if you've visited other people's GeoCities sites. The banner contains a number of options that visitors to your page may want to use, such as Send This Page, Rate My Site, Pages Like Mine, and Take a Tour. It also contains links to some other GeoCities–provided effects, like a guestbook and chat.

One bonus to putting a GeoGuide banner on your page is that those pop-up ads that appear whenever someone visits your page will disappear. The ads will be integrated into the banner, which is much more low-key. A GeoGuide banner is shown in Figure 10.2.

Figure 10.2
A GeoGuide banner can give your visitors several options.

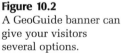

The GeoGuide can also help other people find your site. If you wish, you can participate in a Banner Exchange. This means that you submit a banner for your site to GeoCities, and it will be placed in rotation with other members' banners, as well as GeoCities' ads on banners throughout GeoCities. Then, all someone has to do is click on the banner and they'll be transported directly to your site.

TIP

No Banner Worries

You don't have to be a graphic designer to create your own banner. In fact, there are volunteers who will create one for you. Just go to **http://www.geocities.com/ members/programs/geoguide/banner_help.html** and choose a volunteer from your Neighborhood to help you out.

To install a GeoGuide, simply go to the GeoGuide Manager page within the Members' Area. Click on the **Set Up/Modify My GeoGuide** button. You'll then arrive at the GeoGuide Manager configuration page, which has a sample banner near the top of the page (see Figure 10.3). Below it is a list of the different parts of the banner from which you can choose the ones you want to appear on your page. You can have as many as nine different sections on your GeoGuide, in addition to the ad banner:

▶ Rank My Site—Visitors can rank your site for display on the GeoCities Avenues. GeoCities warns that this might not work on some framed sites.

▶ Take A Tour—Click this button to send your visitors on a guided tour of up to ten GeoCities pages that you choose.

▶ My Guestbook—A guestbook allows visitors to leave you messages, as well as comments and feedback about your site.

▶ Chat—This will send visitors to GeoCities chat, where they can interact with GeoCities Homesteaders and visitors.

▶ E-mail Me—Clicking on this button allows visitors to e-mail you directly at the e-mail address of your choice.

▶ Pages Like Mine—By clicking on this link, people can find pages that are similar to yours.

▶ Search—This link will send visitors to a GeoCities search page.

▶ Send This Page—If a visitor likes your site, he or she can click on this link and send a copy of your page to a friend.

▶ Forums—This links visitors to GeoCities' forums, where they can discuss a host of different topics.

Part III　Making an Exciting Site

Four of the sections—Chat, Pages Like Mine, Search, and Forums—are included automatically on every banner. The other five are optional. You can decide whether the optional sections appear in your banner by clicking Yes or No for each section.

Figure 10.3
The GeoGuide Manager lets you choose what your banner will include.

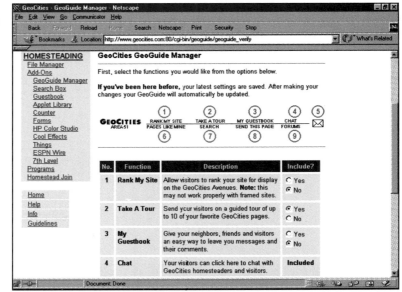

Once you've decided which items to include, you'll be taken to another page where you'll be asked to provide some information (such as the color you would like the GeoGuide to be, or a list of sites for the Take a Tour option). If you don't know what sites to enter, don't worry— GeoCities has some preloaded for you.

Once you've finished configuring your GeoGuide, you press the **Set Up My GeoGuide** button at the bottom of the second page of configuration settings. That takes you to a screen which gives you instructions on how to add the GeoGuide as designed to your pages. (Remember to add the text to every page you want the GeoGuide active on your site.)

Essentially, after you've configured your guide, GeoCities stores the profile in its internal database and you can update the settings any time. Then all you have to do is go to the GeoCities Advanced HTML Editor (click **Edit** once you've selected a page in the File Manager) and paste in the following code:

```
<!-#geoguide->
```

right after the opening <BODY> HTML tag contained on every page you want the guide to appear on.

For example:

```
<html>
<head><title>Your Title</title></head>
<body>
<!-#geoguide->
<center>This is my GeoCities homepage!</center>
</body>
</html>
```

The GeoGuide you configured will appear on your page. If you are a GeoBuilder user, GeoBuilder will automatically insert a GeoGuide for you. Figure 10.4 shows a GeoGuide on a great site (**http://www.geocities.com/Paris/3206/**).

Figure 10.4
The GeoGuide gives visitors activities to do when they visit your site.

TIP

Want to Know More?

For more information about the GeoGuide, go to the GeoGuide FAQ (Frequently Asked Questions) at **http://www.geocities.com/members/ programs/geoguide/faq.html.**

Guestbook

A *guestbook* is an easy way for you to find out who's been visiting your site, and what they think of it—sort of like the book people sign at an historical site or national park. Visitors write down their names and where they're from, and then comment on how much they like visiting the Grand Canyon (or your site!). With the electronic version, you can ask for even more information, such as the visitors' e-mail address, home page address, how they heard of your site, and more.

The guestbook actually consists of two pages: one for people to sign and another for you (and others) to view visitors' comments. To create your own guestbook, go to the GeoCities Add-Ons page (**http://www.geocities.com/members/addons/**) and click on the Guestbook link. After entering your name and password, you'll be taken to the Guestbook Set-up, shown in Figure 10.5.

Figure 10.5
The GeoCities
Guestbook Set-up page.

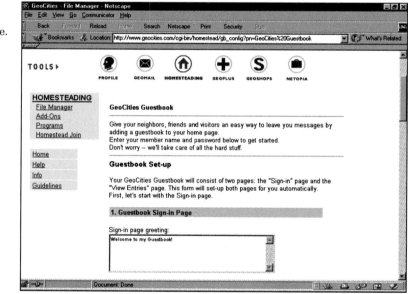

Setting up your guestbook is a simple process to follow:

1. Create a greeting for your sign-in page and decide what color the page and text will be. The default is a white page with black text, but you can choose the colors for your page and your text from seven different options.

2. In the next section you'll decide what questions to ask your guests. The default questions are Name, URL, and E-mail; you can add to these, or delete them and create all your own information boxes.

3. Then choose which of the four layouts shown in Figure 10.6 you prefer, follow a similar setup for your viewing page, and you're done.

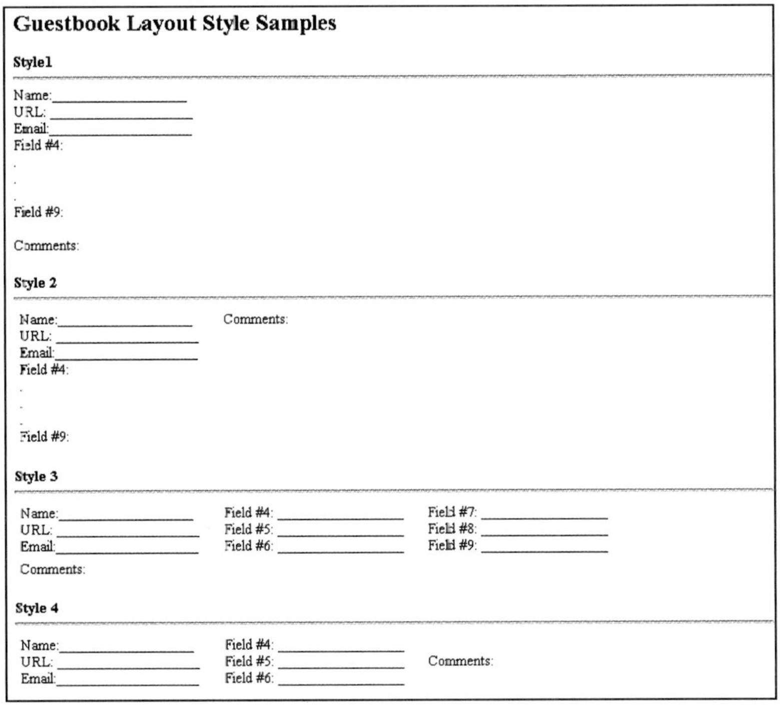

Figure 10.6
Choose from different layout options for your sign-in page.

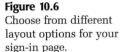

Guestbook Layout Style Samples

Style 1

Name:_____
URL: _____
Email:_____
Field #4:
.
.
Field #9:

Comments:

Style 2

Name:_____   Comments:
URL: _____
Email:_____
Field #4:
.
.
Field #9:

Style 3

Name:_____   Field #4: _____   Field #7: _____
URL: _____   Field #5: _____   Field #8: _____
Email:_____   Field #6: _____   Field #9: _____
Comments:

Style 4

Name:_____   Field #4: _____
URL: _____   Field #5: _____   Comments:
Email:_____   Field #6: _____

4. At the bottom of the Guestbook Set-up page is some HTML code that you'll want to paste into your page. This code allows you to create links for visitors to sign your guestbook and to see what other visitors have said in your guestbook. You have to add this snippet of code to your home page just like you did with the GeoGuide above.

5. Once you add the links to your guestbook to your home page, click on the button labeled **Save my Guestbook**. GeoCities saves the guestbook files in your home directory and shows you how it will appear to visitors. You can always edit the guestbook's appearance by using the Set-up guide and changing the fields of information collected, color, and style, without changing the links on your home page.

Counter

Although the guestbook gives you some feedback from visitors, it doesn't keep track of people who visit your site but don't want to be bothered with signing a guestbook. The hit counter add-on is a simple graphic that keeps track of how many visitors have been to your site. And GeoCities makes it easy to add a counter to your page—all you have to do is add this single piece of code to your site's HTML using a File Manager:

```
<img src="/cgi-bin/counter">
```

You'll then get a counter that looks like the one in Figure 10.7. It's good to add some leading text like "You're visitor number _____" before the counter, so people will know what the number means.

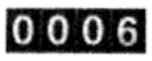

Figure 10.7
Not many visitors have seen our site yet.

`0006`

As you may have noticed from Figure 10.7, counters start at one. But, you can change your counter whenever you want by going to the Counter Manager (**http://www.geocities.com/members/tools/counter.html**). Basically, the Counter Manager allows you to track any counters you've placed on your pages in one place. And, as we implied before, you can set your counter to start wherever you want.

Forms

Forms can be so instrumental to a Website that we have dedicated an entire chapter—Chapter 12, "Developing Forms on GeoCities"—to them. Forms are a great way to gather information from your visitors and to make your site interactive. For example, visitors can rank movies, music, books, or similar interests. Forms can be used to allow visitors to leave comments on topics or simply to ask visitors to respond to certain questions by selecting and answering from multiple choices.

Cool Effects Studio

This is a place where you can really start to have fun with your pages! GeoCities' Cool Effects are simple Java applets that you can cut and paste into your page to create effects you could never do on your own (unless you're a programming wizard). GeoCities offers a rotating set of featured applets and also has applets they've featured in the past that you can consider including on your site. The Cool Effects page can be found at (**http://www.geocities.com/members/addons/cooleffects/**).

When we were writing this book, the featured applet was a horizontal image carousel. This would be a great addition to the family album site we discussed in Chapter 7, "Page Templates and Popular Designs." You could also use it in a small business site—for instance, it would be perfect for a realtor showing a number of properties. It allows you to put any number of pictures in the carousel, and it rotates on the screen. Even better, users can "grab" the carousel with their mouse and turn it at their own speed to get a better view of all your pictures. An example of the carousel is shown in Figure 10.8.

Figure 10.8
The GeoCities Carousel applet provides a great way to showcase your family pictures.

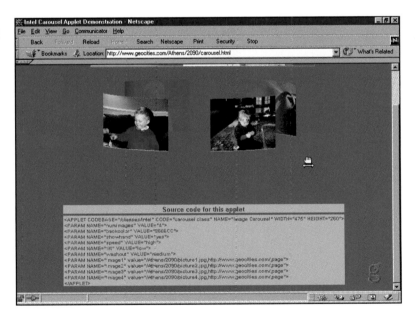

Part III Making an Exciting Site

> **TIP**
> **What's an Applet?**
>
> An *applet* is a chunk of code written in the Java programming language. But you don't need to know Java yourself to use applets. All you have to do is use HTML code that points to an applet created by someone else (like those supplied by GeoCities). At the end of this section, we'll show you where you can find even more applets.

To add any of the applets on the Cool Effects page:

1. Find the applet you want to install from the Cool Effects page. The first home page for cool effects will contain the current effect. Click on the **Past Effects** button on the right-hand side of the page to see links to the other available applets, which are labeled 3D Text, Photo Album, and 3D Photocube.

2. When clicking on a specific applets page, GeoCities provides you with the specific code to add to your page. Copy the code from your browser to your computer's Clipboard (memory).

3. Go to the GeoCities File Manager and click on the file you want to edit and choose **Edit** from the menu. This brings up the simple text editor. From here you can simply locate the area in the HTML code you want to place the applet and paste in the code.

4. All of the applets require you to modify the code a bit so that it works specifically the way you want. For example with the Image Carousel applet, you will want to change the addresses to point to pictures you've uploaded to your site. These modifications are made within the numerous <PARAM> tags that make up the basic code you paste into your page.

5. Once again, GeoCities has made it incredibly simple to add cool stuff to your site. GeoCities gives detailed instructions on how to add your own pictures and customize the Carousel or the other applets to your specifications. With the Carousel applet you can control everything from the color of the Carousel to how fast it rotates to the "tilt" of the wheel. Each applet's page has specific instructions on how to set the values in the <PARAM> tags. Just read them and make the edits in the GeoCities Advanced HTML Editor.

If you don't want to use the Carousel, other GeoCities applets are available for you try out in the Past Featured Applets section:

▶ a photo album;

▶ a 3D version of the popular 70s staple, the photo cube;

▶ and the other applet lets you create 3D swirling headlines on your page.

Two of the three are variations on the photo album theme.

> **NOTE**
>
> **More Applets to Use**
>
> You don't have to rely on GeoCities to provide cool applets for your Web page. Tons of free applets are available on the Web. Here's where to start your search.
>
> Developer.com (**http://www.developer.com/directories/pages/dir.java.fx.html**) —Formerly known as Gamelan, this site is the official directory for Java. The site contains over 1,000 different special effects applets for you to choose from in categories such as slide shows, buttons, and animation (see Figure 10.9).

Figure 10.9
A solar system applet is a pretty cool effect.

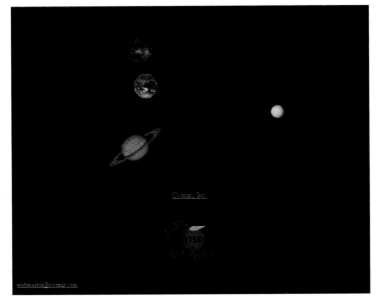

Homesteader Things

Further down the list is what GeoCities calls "Homesteader Things." These are even more multimedia effects that you can use to add pizzazz to your GeoCities Website. These extras are divided into categories ranging from animals and science fiction to sports, holidays, teens, and music.

Things are created with something called a ThingMaker, which is available free to all GeoCities Homesteaders. But what, exactly are these "Things"? Well, they're fun little animated graphics that will, for instance, jump or change color when you move your mouse over them. They don't really *do* anything, in the practical sense of the word. They just add some life to your page.

Part III Making an Exciting Site

An example of a Thing is shown in Figure 10.10. Things do activities when your mouse moves over them or clicks upon them.

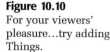

Figure 10.10
For your viewers' pleasure…try adding Things.

Adding a Multimedia Thing to Your GeoCities Page
To add a multimedia Thing from Thingworld.com to your site:

1. Locate the exact Thing you want to place on your site.

2. Right click on the Thing you want to add (things are not available for Mac users) and a menu will appear showing several options:

   Save Scene—A Save As dialog box will appear, allowing you to save the Thing to a location on your hard drive. Things are saved with a .tms extension.

   Copy Thing—Choose this option to copy the Thing to your Clipboard. This makes it easy to then simply paste the Thing to a folder on your hard drive or even your desktop.

   Place on Active Desktop—If you are running Microsoft Windows and have the Active Desktop option installed on your system, you can choose this option to place the Thing on your Active Desktop.

3. Assuming you saved the Thing or Things to a folder on your drive using the .tms file extension, simply copy them to the folder on which you want them on your GeoCities site by using the File Manager to upload the files. You must upload the Thing to your site for it to work properly. Be sure to save the Thing on your site with the correct case-sensitivity. Thing files are usually saved with the first letter of the .tms file being capitalized.

4. Now you must place the Thing on your pages using HTML code. Go to the Thing you found and right-click on the Thing to bring up the menu. Choose COPY HTML tag for the Thing. Then, using the basic editor on GeoCities (or any other manner in which you want to edit the actual HTML code of your Web pages), paste the code you copied from the Clipboard to the area where you want the Thing displayed.

5. Test your page to see if it works. If the Thing doesn't display, you might not have installed it correctly. Check to see if the Thing was uploaded and that the filename is exactly the same as the filename in the HTML code used to display the Thing on your site (remember the case sensitivity issue!). If you are a GeoBuilder user, you can add Things directly from the Insert menu bar.

Cosmo Homespace Pavilion

The final GeoCities-provided add-on is the Cosmo Homespace Pavilion. This isn't really something you add to your page; it's a whole new way of creating your site. You can use a program called HomeSpace to write VRML (Virtual Reality Modeling Language) to create virtual 3D worlds that visitors can walk through and explore by using the Cosmo Player. This is a bit more advanced than other add-ons, so we'll cover VRML in much more detail in Chapter 11, "Adding Multimedia to Your GeoCities Site." We'll leave you with a picture of what a VRML world can look like, so you can get an idea of the work involved in creating one (Figure 10.11). You can see the Cosmo Pavilion's showcase of the best GeoCities VRML sites at **http://www.geocities.com/members/addons/CosmoPavilion/showcase/**.

Figure 10.11
We're going to the chapel…

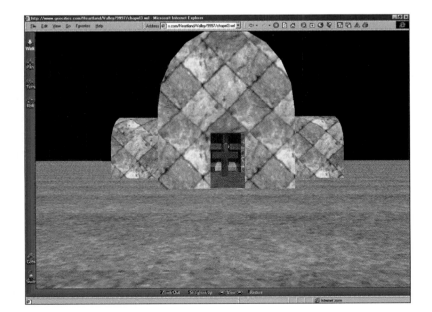

Part III Making an Exciting Site

Other Add-Ons Available

Adding ESPN.com News Wire to Your Site

GeoCities recently made it possible to add ESPN's News Wire Java applet to your site. This is an excellent addition to any news site.

The ESPN.com News Wire includes both current headlines and continuously updated scores. Be careful how you use the News Wire on a complex page because, while the width of the ESPN.com News Wire is always 428 pixels, the height will vary. According to GeoCities, depending on how many headlines are displayed at any given time, you can only be sure that the applet will be at least 182 pixels high.

To add the ESPN.com News Wire applet:

1. Insert the code <!—#snrnews —> into your page's HTML in the spot that you want to display the applet.

2. You must now activate the headline capability on your site. Go to the GeoCities' ESPN News Wire Add-On Page located at (**http://www.geocities.com/members/addons/EspnWire.html**) and click on the **<Enable Headlines>** button.

3. Return to the page(s) containing the ESPN News Wire to see if it is activated. If it isn't, check your HTML code and re-click the **<Enable Headlines>** button again. Figure 10.12 shows the news headlines in a page.

Figure 10.12
The ESPN News Wire
Add-On page.

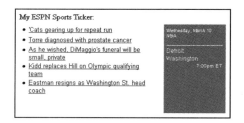

To remove the ESPN News Wire from your site, simply remove the <!—#snrnews —> comment code.

*E*TRADE Stock Quotes Installation*

GeoCities members can offer the built-in E*TRADE stock searching form. This provides a way for visitors to quickly track stock information. This simple add-on makes it possible for visitors to type in the name of a stock and get a return from the E*TRADE site.

A detailed stock quote from E*TRADE not only shows you the price, high, low, and ticker, but also the 52-week high and low, bid, ask, volume, opening price, previous trading day's close, earnings, and P/E ratio. You can also use the same tool to get quotes on options and mutual funds.

To add the E*TRADE stock form, add the following code to your page (cut and paste from the Add-On page):

```
<FORM METHOD="POST" ACTION="http://www.etrade.com/cgi-
bin/gx.cgi/AppLogic+ResearchSymbol">
<input type="hidden" name="INFOTYPE" value="DET_QUOTES">
<a href="http://www.etrade.com">
<img
src="http://pic.geocities.com/images/search/e_trade_88x31.gif"
width="88" height="31" border=0>
</a>
<br>
<font size="1" face="Arial, Helvetica, sans-serif">Company
Symbol:<br></font>
<INPUT SIZE=10 MAXLENGTH=20 NAME="SYMBOL">
<INPUT TYPE="submit" VALUE="Get"><br>
<SELECT NAME="Type">
<OPTION VALUE="S">Stock</OPTION>
<OPTION VALUE="O">Option</OPTION>
<OPTION VALUE="I">Index</OPTION>
<OPTION VALUE="F">Mutual Fund</OPTION>
<OPTION VALUE="M">Money Market</OPTION>
</SELECT>

<br>
<font size="1" face="Arial, Helvetica, sans-serif">
Quotes are delayed 20 minutes during market hours
</FORM>
```

If installed properly, the E*TRADE ticker will look like Figure 10.13.

Figure 10.13
The E*TRADE ticker.

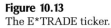

E*TRADE Portfolio Add-On

GeoCities also offers the E*TRADE Portfolio Manager Add-On. This will allow you to create multiple portfolios of stocks, options, or mutual funds that you want to track. Once you've created a customized portfolio, you can add, change, or delete entries whenever you want. Prices for stocks are updated throughout the day. Prices for mutual funds are updated each day after the close of the market.

To use this service, log on to E*TRADE (**http://www.etrade.com**), set up an account (they're free and no credit card is needed) and create a portfolio to watch. You can then place a simple button on your page to quickly log on to your portfolios or offer people a link to set up their own.

The following HTML code needs to be put in the area of your page that you want to display this button:

```
<IMG
    SRC="http://pic.geocities.com/images/members/addons/etrade/
    portfolio.gif" ALT="E*TRADE Portfolio Manager" WIDTH="175"
    HEIGHT="100" USEMAP="#etrademap" BORDER="0">
<map name="etrademap">
<area shape="rect" coords="5, 3, 172, 50"
    href="https://trading.etrade.com/cgi-
    bin/gx.cgi/AppLogic+loginpage?SOURCE=COBRA7">
<area shape="rect" coords="3, 50, 171, 93"
    href="https://trading.etrade.com/cgi-
    bin/gx.cgi/AppLogic+REGMemberCreateForm">
</map>
```

When set up, the button will look like Figure 10.14.

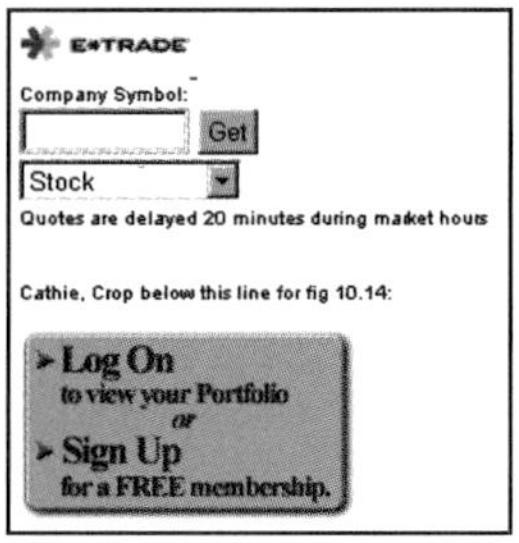

Figure 10.14
The E*TRADE Portfolio button.

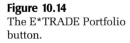

Adding HeadHunter.net to Your Page

GeoCities has partnered with Headhunter.net to offer job search help. It is also another opportunity for you to earn money from your GeoCities home page—you get $5 for every 1,000 pages viewed by visitors who go to HeadHunter.net.

According to HeadHunter.net, typical users view an average of 13 pages per session. But active job seekers view an average of 30 pages per session. So that's $5 for every:

▶ 77 users who view 13 pages per session

▶ 50 users who view 20 pages per session

▶ 33.3 users who view 30 pages per session

Depending on the nature of your site, this could be a very good opportunity for you.

To add HeadHunter.net's affiliate program to your GeoCities site, do the following:

1. Register with HeadHunter.net by completing a two-page form that asks you for vital address information and your e-mail address. Once you've filled this out, a password will arrive in your e-mail.

2. When you receive your password, proceed to (**http://back1.headhunter.net/scripts/UserLogin.asp**) and log on to HeadHunter.net.

3. Upon logging on, you will be greeted with four options (My Accounts, Make Money, My User Info, and Logout) to the left side of the screen. Choose **Make Money**.

4. This brings you to the heart of the affiliate registration process. There are three steps to this process:

   —Accept the Agreement

   —Create a Link

   —Send Traffic

   Start by accepting the agreement. This takes you to a lengthy document outlining the legal rules and how the affiliate program works. When you get to the bottom of the document, choose **I AGREE** if you want to proceed.

5. Upon agreeing to the terms of the Affiliate agreement, you are sent to a page where you open an account for referrals. This is slightly different from the overall user account you created to begin the process. Create a unique name for your account.

6. Upon entering a unique referral account name, the site will move you to a page where you can generate the proper links for your GeoCities site. Two button types are displayed. Next to these animated GIFs are buttons marked Generate HTML. Click on those buttons to generate the HTML text you need to paste into your GeoCities page. This will allow people to click through to HeadHunter.net.

7. With the code copied to the Clipboard of your computer, go back to the HTML editor you use to edit the HTML code on your site and paste the code into the area of your page in which you want to display the button.

8. You're done. Whenever you want to check the status of your affiliate account, simply log on to HeadHunter.net and choose the **My Stuff** icon at the top. Then choose **My Accounts** to view your progress.

Part III Making an Exciting Site

Adding a GeoCities Search Box

GeoCities offers an attractive Search Box for your site that lets users quickly search GeoCities member pages or the Web.

To add the GeoCities Search Box to your pages:

1. Go to the Search Box page on GeoCities (**http://www.geocities.com/ members/tools/searchbox.html**).

2. Select a search box from the different color schemes (Figure 10.15) displayed and click on the corresponding **Show me my code** button. A box will display showing the exact HTML code you need for the button.

3. Cut the HTML code from the window and paste it into your Web page's HTML code.

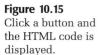

Figure 10.15
Click a button and the HTML code is displayed.

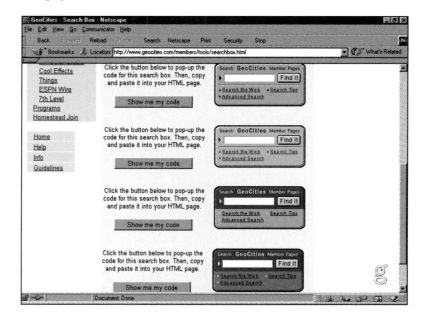

Whew! That takes us through all the add-ons that GeoCities provides. Pretty generous, huh? GeoCities makes it as easy as possible for you to make your site a cut above the rest. But don't stop here! You can find other effects out there on the Web—more applets (like the Gamelan site we mentioned earlier), animated GIFs, hit counters in a wide variety of formats, and more. Here's another great place to get more cool stuff:

▶   Web Developer's Virtual Library (**http://www.stars.com**) —A great reference for Web developers as well as a repository of resources and links to other sites' resources.

Pages that Pay–
The Ultimate Special Effect

In addition to all the great add-ons we've covered, GeoCities offers its members the ultimate special effect: the ability to make money from your home page. Through the GeoCities program called "Pages that Pay", you can become partners with many of the biggest e-commerce sites on the Web.

Here's how it works. GeoCities takes care of building large scale relationships with companies that sell products on the web – such as books, videotapes, office supplies, and much more. Through your Website you create links to participating merchants that sell items relating to your site. For example if you built an Independent Music site (like the one we created in Chapter 3) you might link to an on-line music or video store.

Once you build these links, visitors can click on each link to bring them to an on-line store where they can purchase that item. As a result of referring that customer, you receive a percentage of each item the customer purchases that session. It is that easy! A check is sent to you quarterly (as long as your commission reaches a certain amount). Figure 10.16 shows the Pages that Pay homepage.

Figure 10.16
Earn money and help your visitors at once.

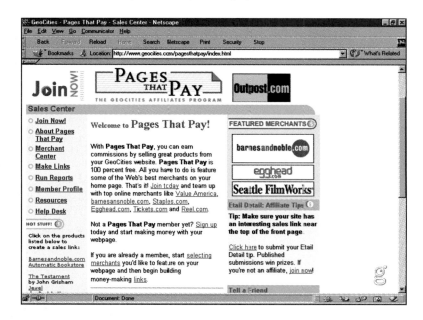

To join, visit **http://www.geocities.com/pagesthatpay/index.html** and select **Join Now**. You must go through a separate sign-up procedure for Pages that Pay to ensure that you understand the rules around this e-commerce program. The sign-up procedure lets you select which merchants you want to include on your page and then steps you through a wizard creating your own affiliate store. Figure 10.17 shows a generic store linked to **barnesandnoble.com**.

Figure 10.17
This generic store is only the beginning.

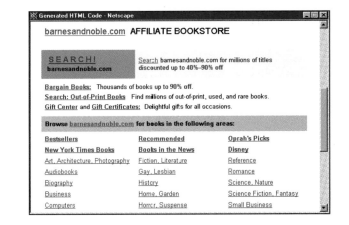

Each affiliate merchant/program lets you configure your online store differently to promote their products. You can even generate complete sales, popularity, traffic, and commission reports (Figure 10.18).

Figure 10.18
How many books sold this month?

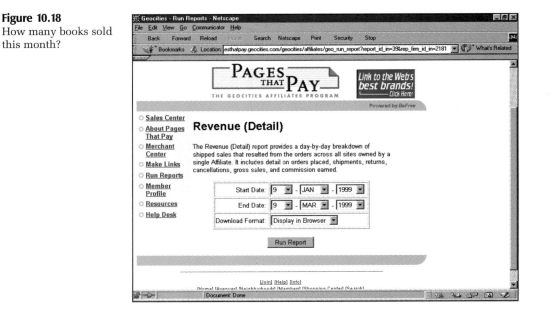

For more tips on setting up shop through GeoCities and the specific rules of the Pages that Pay program, you can visit the Online Resource Center (**http://www.geocities.com/pagesthatpay/ptp_resource.html**). This comprehensive section shows you examples of good online stores, provides tips for building a more complete affiliate network, and shows you how to generate more traffic to your site.

GeoCities partnerships are always evolving—many times you'll find that affiliate programs are added or modified to the mix for you to choose from.

Moving On

Now you have no excuses for putting up a boring Web page. GeoCities makes it easy by providing everything from a guestbook to a visitor counter. Then, you can add even more GeoCities add-ons, like applets that create rotating picture albums. Or, you can go out and surf the Web for other applets and interesting multimedia (more on this in the next chapter). Finally, you can be creative and make money at the same time through Pages that Pay, GeoCities money making affiliate program.

Well, what are you waiting for? Start making your page unique with all these special effects!

11

Adding Multimedia to Your GeoCities Site

At one point, disk space was at such a premium that GeoCities couldn't offer members enough room to include much multimedia content.

Today, with access to 11 megabytes of free space, you can offer a lot of cool content on your site. Assuming you have created a number of pages with nice graphics and interesting text, you probably have a lot of space left over. Rather than let it go to waste, why not add some multimedia? This chapter focuses on how you can fill your site with video clips, audio feeds, and cool-sounding music. Along the way we'll cover different audio and video formats as well as some specific multimedia formats such as Macromedia's Shockwave and Flash programs.

If you press your ear to this book, you still won't hear a MIDI version of "MMMBop," nor will you be able to see those adorable little Hanson brothers dancing around in RealVideo. Rather than including a bunch of largely useless screenshots, we'll offer up some of your neighboring GeoCities sites that are worth visiting.

What Is Multimedia?

Multimedia is the combination of graphics, sound, and animation into a single new form of media. In a more general sense, many people use the term "multimedia" to describe any of the more advanced media content forms—whether they are audio, video, or animation. In this chapter, we'll talk about several key products and forms of multimedia files that you can put on your GeoCities home page. These products and their uses are listed in Table 11.1.

Table 11.1
Multimedia Files and Forms

Audio in the following forms:	
.WAV files	Dominant sound format for Windows
.AU files	Major sound format for UNIX
RealAudio (.RA) files	Most popular streaming audio format
MPEG3 (MP3) files	Up and coming CD-quality music format
Active Streaming Format files	Microsoft's streaming audio format
Midi files	Format for synthesized music
Video in the following forms:	
.AVI/Active movies	Dominant movie format for Windows
MPEG movies	Open standard for digital video
QuickTime (.QT) movies	Apple's popular standard for video
RealVideo files	Most popular streaming video format
Vivo movies	Popular plug-in streaming video type
Active Streaming Format movies	Microsoft's streaming video format
Animation/multimedia in the following forms:	
Director/Shockwave files	Multimedia program technology
Flash movies	Plays back small and fast line-art animation

In many cases, you will need a special program to develop specific types of multimedia content. You may optionally need another program to convert your audio, video, or multimedia file into a specific format. For example, to create a RealVideo movie, you must capture the video and edit it with a video-editing product like Adobe's Premiere. Then you will need a program such as RealPublisher to convert the raw video file into the specific format that lets you send it out as a RealVideo file.

Chapter 4, "Building Your GeoCities Skills and Toolbox," covered some of the basic programs that you should have in your toolbox when creating your GeoCities page. We mentioned several products, including RealPublisher or RealEncoder, which lets you turn audio and video files into the RealMedia format. Also mentioned were several programs for recording sounds.

When and How to Use Multimedia Files

It is easy to misuse video, audio, music, and multimedia files on a Website. How often have you come across a page that immediately forces you to listen to some awful MIDI version of a movie theme song? You can't find the Back button fast enough! The same can be said for any low-quality or poorly timed audio effect or movie file you might impose on your visitors.

In a word, adding multimedia to your personal home page is all about positioning. If you position multimedia effects correctly so that users can understand in advance what the effects are, how long they'll take to load, and what they potentially offer, you can make far more effective use of multimedia than do most people.

Multimedia files work best when used to accentuate something. Make multimedia a real treat to your users; don't use it just for the sake of using it. For example, if you were building a site about your favorite baseball player, you could include a video clip of his first career home run or an important play he made in the World Series. Multimedia files should also be as small in size as possible without sacrificing quality. You can do this in any of several ways, including making the size of the video small, using lower quality audio (or no audio at all), or breaking long clips into smaller parts.

Previewing Your Clips

If you offer a large multimedia file for download (perhaps one megabyte or more in size), consider placing a short preview on your site. For audio files, this can be a fifteen-second sound clip of a three-minute song. For video files, you could include two or three stills from the video. This will help people decide whether or not they want to download the entire file.

If you want users to view the multimedia on your site (why else would you include it?), you need to make it as easy as possible for them to click on and enjoy the multimedia you post. For example, CDnow allows you to listen to song clips before purchasing music.

A General Note about Copyright Issues

As we mentioned in Chapter 9, "Graphics," you are responsible for *not* including material on your site that has been copyrighted by another party. The risk to you for using such material increases with multimedia files because they are easy to spot with search engines as well as special programs that look for copyrighted music, video footage, and such. There are actually special companies that work on the behalf of copyright holders, such as the record companies, movie studios, and artists, to look for copyrighted materials. Since many of the search engines such as Hotbot can search for files on the Web with specific extensions (e.g. .AVI or .WAV), you can be sure that it's a snap for people to eventually find stuff on your site that could be copyrighted.

You might just get a slap on the wrist (or no penalty at all) for posting a RealAudio file of an interview of your favorite movie star from the latest Barbara Walters special. But it's also possible that you'll have your site pulled down, or get a nasty note from an attorney. Use caution. You could even be sued and held liable for damages and incur legal expenses for copyright infringement. And if you're even the slightest bit worried about violating copyright laws, the easiest way to be safe is to not put the content up.

Although not directly responsible for material placed on their site by Homesteaders, GeoCities does have a comprehensive policy surrounding this topic area. GeoCities' content guidelines state that members are not allowed to commit acts of copyright, trademark, patent, trade secret or other intellectual property infringement. This includes, but is not limited to, providing pirated music or links to such files. To read GeoCities' FAQ concerning trademark issues, refer to **http://www.geocities.com/members/ guidelines/copyright.html.**

Creating Audio Files for Your GeoCities Site

When it comes to adding audio to your site, you can acquire the raw audio in two ways:

▶ record and digitize it yourself; or

▶ obtain it from the Web or a clip library.

However, if you have to digitize it yourself, you'll need to get digitization software and possibly some recording hardware.

Recording Hardware

When digitizing your own sounds, you can often forgo the need for recording hardware. Any CD you put in your CD-ROM player can be digitized directly from the computer (remember copyright concerns if the CD isn't music you created yourself). If you're digitizing off tape, just plug the audio output on your stereo into your microphone or auxiliary on your computer's soundcard. You may need to combine your left and right stereo channels to go from your stereo to your computer, but a simple y-cable found at an electronics shop should do the trick. Tell the salesperson what equipment you have and what you want to do, and they'll send you in the right direction.

To record your voice or some other real-world sound, you'll need a microphone. If having good sound quality is important, you should purchase a microphone from a local music store. (Most microphones that are bundled with sound cards and computers these days are very poor quality. Even an inexpensive, low-end microphone purchased from a music store should prove much better.) If you're just goofing around, the microphone that may have come with your computer is probably fine.

If you intend to record sounds from a trip or anywhere not in the presence of a computer, you'll need a tape recorder of some sort. Be sure to bring along the microphone as you'll find that the built-in microphones on most portable tape recorders are also dreadful.

The soundcard in your computer will usually be a limitation only if you plan to record high-fidelity music recordings. If you want to use a high- fidelity music card, check the soundcards made by Antex (**http://www.antex.com**). Otherwise, most standard 16-bit capable soundcards, which have been sold over the last 2-3 years, are more than fine.

Software for Digitizing Your Audio

To record your audio into a digital form, you'll need a sound editor/recorder. Several tools are available for both Macintosh and Windows users.

Shareware tools such as:

► Cool Edit (**http://www.syntrillium.com/**);
► GoldWave (**http://www.goldwave.com**)for the PC; or
► PlayerPro (which can be found on C I Net's **http://www.download.com**) for the Mac are popular.

If you want to purchase a commercial package, try

▶ Sound Forge XP from Sonic Foundry (**http://www.sonicfoundry.com**) for Windows

▶ Sound Edit 16 from Macromedia (**http://www.macromedia.com**) for Mac

For this chapter, we used GoldWave (Figure 11.1)—a great shareware program from Chris Craig. The program lets you record sound effects off CDs placed in the CD-ROM drive, and directly from the microphone attached to your soundcard. You can also open many existing sound files and manipulate them until your heart is content. When you are done, you can output your file in many different formats, including .WAV, .AIFF, .AU, and more.

Figure 11.1
To add or edit sound effects for your GeoCities site, you need a sound editor like GoldWave.

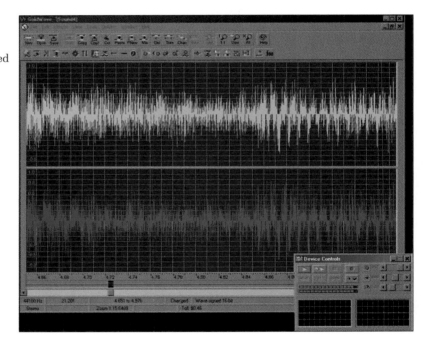

However, as is the case with many sound-editing programs, you can't output it as a RealAudio file. Fortunately, RealNetworks provides a $44.95 program called RealPublisher (Figure 11.2) that allows you to take any major sound file and convert it to RealAudio. This program makes publishing RealAudio or RealVideo a snap. By moving your audio or video files into a streaming-oriented format like RealAudio or RealVideo, you end up with a smaller sized file that begins playing almost immediately or within a few seconds upon the user requesting the file from your site.

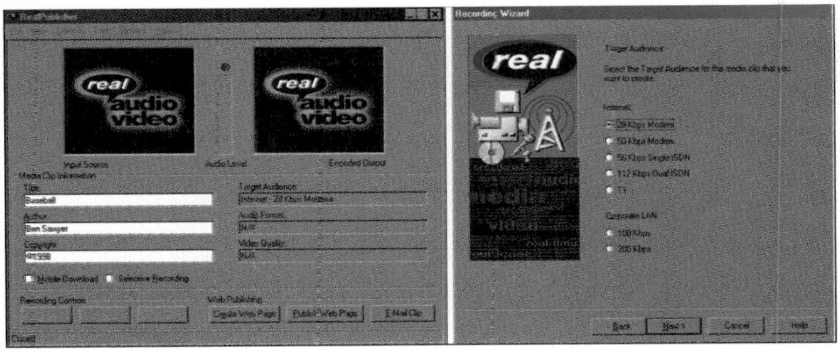

Figure 11.2
The RealPublisher
program makes creating
streaming audio and
video content easy.

You can also download for free the basic encoder product. Some of the
commercial packages, like Sound Forge XP, have built-in support for the
RealAudio format as well. Essentially the free encoder is a little less user-
friendly than the RealPublisher program. RealPublisher supports video
and compression and is less expensive than some of the more robust
sound editors that have built-in support for RealAudio. We'll discuss
RealAudio more specifically later in this chapter.

Understanding Audio Quality

When you digitize audio, you must pay particular attention to two things:
the quality of the recording and the size of the file. Unfortunately, the two
are diametrically opposed—the higher the quality of the file, the larger it
will be. However, not everything you digitize will have to be done at CD-
quality sound.

Sound quality can be easily measured in KHz (kilohertz). The range of
KHz used to reproduce a given sound determines the quality of the
digitization. Human ears can perceive differences in frequency (Hz) up to
44100 Hz. CDs are digitized at 44100 Hz, which is the best level an ear
can hear. By lowering the Hz level, you lower the quality of the sound
reproduction, but you also present the file with less data to save, thus
creating a smaller file size.

Most sound packages let you set the quality of the digitization to fit your
recording needs (see Table 11.2). For example, if you were merely
recording holiday greetings for your visitors, you could set the
digitization rate to 11025 Hz, which is perfectly fine for speech clips. If
you must have the best audio fidelity, you can record your clips at 44100
Hz. Most sound packages will also let you save your files in stereo or
mono format. While stereo will produce a better quality, it will also create
a larger file size.

Part III   Making an Exciting Site

Table 11.2.
Sound Quality
Settings in Hz

8000	Telephone quality
11025	Low-end radio quality. Good for voice.
22050	FM radio quality. Good for music and voice.
44100	CD quality. Excellent for all sounds.

TIP

Keep Your Hertz High

Record at the highest quality and then use your sound editor to resample the sound into a lower quality setting. Resampling is the process in which your sound editor takes the sound and processes it down to a sample rate of lesser quality. However, the file will now also be much smaller in size as a result.

To get the most out of your sound files, save them in the correct format. In general, the .WAV file format common to Windows will suit your needs. Since most machines (including the Mac) support this format, .WAV is among the best to use for sound clips and effects. However, if you want to offer a download of a song of your band or some other CD-quality clip, you may want to investigate the MP3 standard. MP3 can compress CD-quality audio better than any other format. The downside to this format is that the users of your site must have a sound player capable of playing back MP3 files, although a lot of people are downloading MP3 players. You can also help them by including links to the latest players.

Creating and Playing Back MP3 Files

MP3 is a relatively new file format for CD-quality audio that is spreading like wildfire through the Web. A number of unscrupulous types have been using it to illegally distribute commercial recordings. Pearl Jam, Madonna, and Alanis Morissette (among others) have all had songs illegally released on the Internet in MP3 form before the songs were available commercially. But some pioneers have been using MP3 to legitimately share the music they have created. If you are a musician, mix DJ, singer, etc., you might want to consider using your GeoCities site to share your talent with the rest of the world. And when it comes to audiophiles—and audio files—on the Web, nothing comes close to MP3.

To create an MP3 file, you'll need a special encoder program that takes a standard .WAV audio file and converts it to MP3. You'll find a list of encoders to use on MP3.com's Website (**http://www.mp3.com/software/ encoders.html**).

Start by creating the highest fidelity .WAV file you can make—44100 Hz, stereo sound (don't hold back!). Then save it to your hard drive. A three- to four-minute .WAV file of this kind can easily tip the scales at 20MB to 40MB (megabytes) of space. Run that file through your MP3 encoder and out comes a 3MB to 5MB file.

Upload the file to your GeoCities Website and offer it for download. Including a short, lower quality .WAV or .AU file for preview purposes would also be smart. You should also include links to popular MP3 player sites, including:

▶The Winamp Player (**http://www.winamp.com**)

▶The Sonique Player (**http://www.n55.com**)

▶The Macamp Player (**http://www.macamp.com**)

TIP

More about MP3

MP3 is an exciting and innovative new technology. To learn more about effective ways to use, create, and listen to MP3 files check out *MP3 Power! with Winamp* (ISBN: 0-9662889-3-9). This new title is co-authored by Justin Frankel (creator of Winamp) and the authors of this book.

A Nice Audio Benchmark

There are many sites that effectively use audio on GeoCities. One nice example of audio used on a GeoCities site is Lee Pipken's fan page for Gillian Anderson, the actress who plays Dana Scully on the *The X-Files* (**http://www.geocities.com/Hollywood/Academy/2482/index.html**). On Lee's sound page (see Figure 11.3), there are over a dozen small sound clips of famous lines uttered by Scully, which are stored in .WAV format. Clicking on a link will launch a helper application (such as the Windows Media Player), which plays back the line. Other sites feature MIDI music such as Rico's fan page to the 80's movie *Flash Gordon* (**http://www.geocities.com/Hollywood/4262/**).

Figure 11.3
On Lee Pipkin's Gillian Anderson Website, fans can hear famous lines spoken by her character Dana Scully on The X-Files.

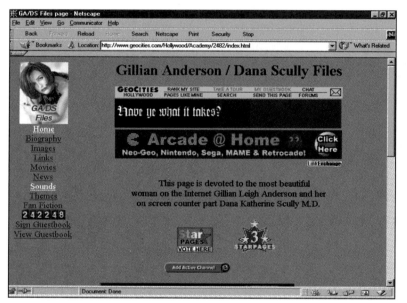

Producing MIDI Music Files for your Site

MIDI is a unique musical file format that uses your computer's built-in synthesizer card to play back songs. Instead of recording the actual audio, a MIDI file simply records the musical note, the instrument type, the duration of the note, and some other characteristics. When a MIDI file is played back, your computer reproduces the music. The files are very small in relation to a full .WAV or .MP3 recording.

The downside to MIDI is two-fold. MIDI files can't include vocals, as there is no way for a computer to reproduce singing from a text file. And, because there are so many sound cards with varying degrees of sophistication in synthesizer capabilities, the playback of MIDI songs can be extremely different from machine to machine. Frankly, most machines make MIDI files sound something akin to a kid playing on a toy keyboard. Still, with a little luck, you can create a simple MIDI melody for your page. Our tip: Keep it short and simple.

On the other hand, many fans love to collect MIDI files from other sites and the public domain that pertains to their page's interest. If done right, it can offer a nice theme for a page or it can enhance the download offerings. For example, if you made a page devoted to the old *S.W.A.T.* TV show, you might include the MIDI file found on the MIDI Farm (Figure 11.4) page (**http://www.midifarm.com**), a popular clearinghouse of MIDI files on the Web. If your page is devoted to Robin Hood or King Arthur, some old Celtic or medieval music might be a nice touch.

Figure 11.4
The MIDI Farm page is one of many MIDI archives.

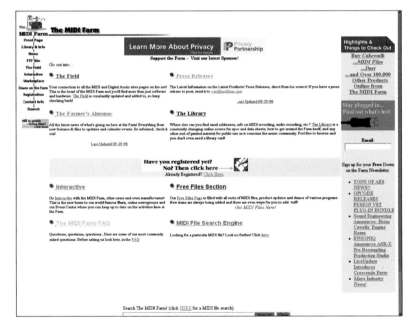

If you want to modify or create your own MIDI tunes, you'll need a program to record and modify MIDI songs. We recommend two shareware titles. For the PC, try WinJammer (Figure 11.5), which you can download from **http://www.winjammer.com**. For the Mac, try MIDIgraphy, which you can find on **http://www.download.com**.

Figure 11.5
WinJammer is one of many shareware programs you can use to modify or make your own MIDI files.

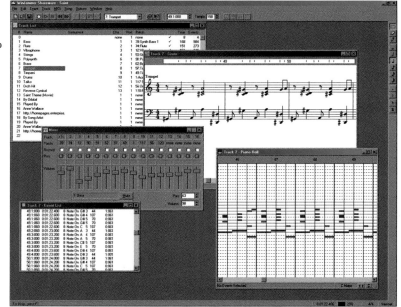

If you want to modify a file, you can load it into one of these programs and change instruments and other file characteristics. If you want to record your own files, you'll also need a synthesizer/keyboard, which is why most non-musicians turn to the major MIDI file download sites (see Table 11.4).

Table 11.3.
Major Midi Archives on the Web

House of MIDIs	**http://www.geocities.com/Hollywood/Hills/5683/**
MIDI Farm	**http://www.midifarm.com**
Shout House MIDI Archive	**http://www.shouthouse.com**
The Classical MIDI Archives	**http://www.prs.net/midi.html**

*You can also search Yahoo! for **MIDI Archives**.*

Here are a couple of GeoCities pages that include MIDI:

▶ Marie Madeleine's Home Page:
http://www.geocities.com/Wellesley/7088/

▶ Pumkin's Music:
http://www.geocities.com/Broadway/Alley/3273/music.html

Producing and Digitizing Video for Your GeoCities Site

You might even want to add video to your site to create some zip. There are a number of reasons to do so, from fun to business. You may want to offer a tour of your home if you are putting it on the market. Or, if you have a travel site, interesting video can lift an already attractive site to an even higher level. You can also add such fun items as home-movie clips for relatives to see or even clips of your own film if you are a film student or independent filmmaker.

If you want to see a professional example of what video can add to a site, just look at any good movie site like the Star Wars Official Site (**http://www.starwars.com**).

Unlike audio, to digitize video you will need a few items that you might not have around your house. Obviously, some kind of capture device is required, such as a video camera, a VCR, or a digital camera (like some of Sony's Mavica line). You'll also need a video capture card unless your capture device like many Web cams (like the Connectix Quickcam) lets you input video through another port like the serial, USB, or parallel port. Some computers are now actually coming standard with video-in ports. If not, you will need a device that allows you to connect a video source to your computer.

When you capture video, either through a camera onto tape or live at the time of digitization, the same goal that you have for creating audio holds true: You need to get the best quality possible with a manageable size. To do that, you must decide on several critical items:

▶ The content of the video you're digitizing

▶ The quality of the video and sound

▶ The dimensions of the video window

▶ The preparation for digitizing

▶ The file format to use

Video Content

If your video includes a lot of movement, the file size will be bigger. If you want to generate smaller-sized video content, such as news-style talking heads, or with slower pans, they will tend to digitize better and have smaller file sizes.

Video and Sound Quality

With a good video capture program, you can set the quality of the audio that goes with the video. You can even choose whether to include audio. The video quality can sometimes be set by choosing the number of key frames to include (fewer frames lowers quality and file size) and by setting the CODEC (the formula used to compress the video). Consult your capture software's manual for more on setting CODECs and compressing your video.

Video Window Dimensions

The dimensions you set for your video file will determine file size. Because video is so demanding, files set for a size of 120 x 80 pixels is not an uncommon sight. This "postage stamp" size may be a bit difficult to look at on a screen, but it will keep your file size much smaller than setting it to 240 x 160 pixels.

Preparation for Digitization

You can improve your video dramatically with preparation. Before you digitize, consider the following issues:

▶ **Use a quality camera to capture your video**—Simple video-conferencing cameras aren't as good as a decent video camera.

▶ **Purchase decent cabling to connect your camera to your PC; purchase quality tapes if you plan on recording first**—Always use the highest quality setting to do your taping.

▶ **Optimize your computer system**—Defragment the hard drive prior to capturing the video and stop running all programs except for the video digitization software.

▶ **Capture at the highest setting first**—The next step is to lower the final edited clip down to whatever setting produces the desired file size/quality ratio.

Choosing a File Format

You can choose from essentially six major formats for delivering video to your users (see Table 11.3). Each one offers different quality issues in return for file size. You will need to experiment to see which one works best for you. In general, the streaming formats of ASF (Active Streaming Format), RealVideo, and Vivo will compress the best, but they offer lower quality than that offered by .AVI, MPEG, and QuickTime files.

Table 11.4. Selecting which formats to use	**RealVideo (http://www.real.com)**—Widely supported because the player is so well downloaded and now comes with Netscape Communicator.
	Vivo (http://www.vivo.com)—Used quite a bit because it plays back well without a server. Plug-in is needed, but it's easy to download.
	ASF (http://www.microsoft.com/asf/)—Developed by Microsoft but it is the least supported of the streaming formats. Used mostly on the Windows platform.
	AVI—Well-supported and used extensively. Easy to download and play back.
	QuickTime (http://www.apple.com/quicktime)—Supported better on the Mac than Windows, but overall provides excellent quality on both platforms.
	MPEG-2 (http://www.mpeg.org or www.mpeg2.com)—Excellent quality, although the file size can be bigger than that of AVI or QuickTime.

Encoding RealAudio and RealVideo Files

Since RealEncoder is a very popular way to publish audio clips and video clips, it is important to include some basics about this free program. RealEncoder lets you take any captured or live audio/video and write it out as a file for playback on your GeoCities site. Here's how to take advantage of what RealEncoder offers:

1. To obtain the free shareware version of RealEncoder, you can download it from Real Networks. Go to **http://www.real.com/ products/tools/index.html,** where you will find a link to the basic free encoder. After filling out the registration form and downloading and installing the version for your machine, run the program.

Part III Making an Exciting Site

2.   RealEncoder runs in either Wizard or Advanced mode. The Wizard mode (Figure 11.6) makes it much easier to use. Once you're more familiar with RealEncoder, you can switch to Advanced mode and quickly set the parameters you need and then encode.

Figure 11.6
RealEncoder's Wizard mode makes it easier to convert a sound or video file into a streaming RealMedia file.

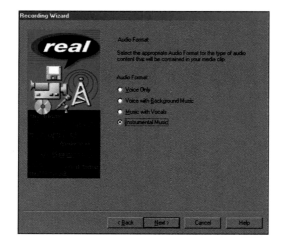

3.   Start the Wizard by choosing **New Session** from the menu. The first screen will ask you if you wish to record from a previously saved file, from an operating device (such as video camera or microphone), or a live broadcast. Disregard the live broadcast. Instead, assuming you created and saved your file, choose "from a recorded file."

4.   The Wizard will show an introduction screen and then, after you click **Next,** will ask for a filename. This is the filename of the sound or video file you created. The encoder reads in QuickTime, .AVI, .AU, and .WAV files as source files. Click the **Browse** button to bring up a file dialog box to choose the source file. Once you are done, click **Next.**

5.   Once you've chosen a file, you can set the title, author name, and copyright information. Enter this information and click **Next.**

6.   Now you must set the target audience. This allows the encoder program to determine how much it must constrain the file to work. For GeoCities, you should set this to 28.8 Kbps modem. Click **Next.**

7.   You will then be asked what the nature of the audio clip or video clip is. By choosing the item closest to your content, the encoder can employ the best method to render the highest quality file possible. After you've done that, click **Next.**

8. Now you must choose the name and location of the output file. When you've done this, click **Next** and the Encoder Wizard will show you a summary of your choices.

    If you need to change any option, back up to that step and change it. If you're satisfied, choose Finish to encode the clip. You will be returned to the main Encoder window with all of your settings applied.

9. In the lower left-hand corner of the Encoder window, press **Start** to encode the file.

Now your file is done, and you can upload it to your site and offer it for download.

> **TIP**
>
> **The Real RealPublisher**
>
> RealPublisher, which is basically an enhanced version of the free RealEncoder program, can be configured to automatically upload files to your GeoCities account.

Posting Multimedia Files on Your GeoCities Site

Once you've created your audio, MIDI, or video, you will obviously want to post it to your site. This can be done in one of two ways:

▶ You can offer it as a link, which will launch a helper application that runs outside the browser to play back the file.

▶ You can embed the file into a Web page (Figure 11.7) that integrates the file into your site much like a graphic.

It's your choice. However, we do offer a piece of advice: Think seriously before you set an embedded piece of video, audio, or MIDI to automatically play when your page is loaded.

> **TIP**
>
> Uploading any multimedia file to your site is no different than uploading a graphic or HTML file. Simply go to the GeoCities File Manager. In the Upload field(s), type in the name of your multimedia file and upload it. Sometimes using the FTP method of uploading is a bit faster, which is good for larger-sized files.

Figure 11.7
You can embed a video (as well as standard audio or MIDI) file directly into your Web page.

If you want to embed a file into your Web page, use the <u>EMBED</u> tag, which you'll need to add via straight HTML using an HTML editor or GeoCities built-in Advanced Editor. This tag works with most 3.0 or higher version browsers. The syntax is as follows:

```
<EMBED SRC="location of file here" CONTROLS=false|true
AUTOSTART=false|true VOLUME=0-100 LOOP=false|true BORDER=0-??
HEIGHT=0-?? WIDTH=0-??>
```

You can set several items to be true or false, and set a volume level, the border size, and the overall size of the window used to display. Here is a description of the options you can control with this advanced HTML tag.

▶ **AUTOSTART**—This extension to the tag determines whether the file plays as soon as the page has displayed. <u>AUTOSTART</u> can be set equal to TRUE or FALSE.

▶ **CONTROLS**—This extension determines whether the player used to play back the file will display the controls for it. The controls allow visitors to pause, stop, and rewind the video clip, but they often get in the way of the rest of your site design. <u>CONTROLS</u> can be set equal to TRUE or FALSE.

▶ **LOOP**—Determines whether the clip will play over and over (loop) or not. <u>LOOP</u> can be set equal to TRUE or FALSE.

▶ **HEIGHT and WIDTH**—Determines the size of the window displayed for the control. Normally you would use this to set the size of a video window. HEIGHT and <u>WIDTH</u> can be assigned numerical values, which correspond to pixel size on your Website. Use a height of 60 and width of about 150 to display just the controls from sound or MIDI file.

NOTE

Using MP3 Effectively.

Generally you can't use the Embed command to embed an MP3 clip on your page. Instead you must include a link to the specific MP3 file for visitors to click upon.

TIP

Posting RealAudio or RealVideo to Your Site

To get specific instructions on how to embed your RealAudio or RealVideo files and to post them on your site, read the helper documentation on Real's Web site at **http://www.real.com/devzone/library/stream/plugtest/index.html**.

You can use a compression program like WinZip or Stuffit! to create an even smaller file size to download. However, the compression often isn't worthwhile. The extra savings in file size probably won't outweigh the fact that users will have to first download and then decompress the file to view it. Although the result might be a 10 percent to 15 percent savings in file size, it will also mean fewer people will choose to look at it.

Other Types of Multimedia

In this chapter, we've talked mostly about specific forms of media, like audio and video, that are considered a part of the overall mix of media, which is often referred to as "multimedia" on the Web. However, besides specific audio and video formats, there are also formats that mix all types of media, animation, graphics, sound, music, and more into one all-encompassing file format.

These specific formats are usually larger single files that are played back using specific browser technologies or Java. While some of them take a lot of knowledge to use, it's worthwhile to know of them because they can be used on your GeoCities site.

Part III Making an Exciting Site

Adding Shockwave Programs to Your GeoCities Site

When the Web was in its infancy, multimedia development tools company, Macromedia, quickly jumped on the bandwagon and created Shockwave. Shockwave is the most popular multimedia system for the Internet. It lets developers play back inside a Web browser the applications created by Macromedia's Director development system. The Shockwave plug-in is so well installed in browsers that almost everyone with a current Web browser can browse Shockwave content.

Shockwave programs can incorporate graphics, audio, video, interactivity, and more. Incredible programs have been created with Shockwave. If you want to create your own Shockwave files for your site, you'll need to obtain Macromedia Director.

Adding Flash Animations to Your GeoCities Site

Flash animations are created using Macromedia's Flash product (Figure 11.8). The program uses mathematical information rather than raw pixel data to reproduce graphics. This allows Flash animations to remain smaller than other animation formats. Sites often use Flash to produce animated title screens as text. The Net Surfer page (**http://www.geocities.com/ Eureka/7430**) uses Flash.

Figure 11.8
Macromedia's Flash
Editor in action.

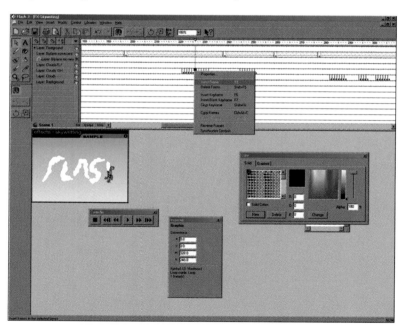

Those who can learn to use Flash (it's not terribly difficult) find it a wonderful tool. A number of Java applets are available that you can use instead of plug-ins to enable Flash playback on your visitors' machines. You can find Flash, including a trial download version, at **http://www.flash.com.**

Java and Dynamic HTML-based Multimedia

With the creation of Java and Dynamic HTML (DHTML), you have even more ways to add animation and multimedia effects to your pages. In fact, there are too many to cover in one book. You may, however, want to look into how these two technologies let you add multimedia effects to your site. Some examples that can add some pizzazz to your site—such as ThingMaker and 3D PhotoCube—were covered in Chapter 10, "Adding Special Effects to Your Pages."

If you want to explore other Java applications that will help you add multimedia effects to your site, visit **http://www.developer.com**. This site hosts an incredible index of over 800 Java applets that offer some form of multimedia for your site. The multimedia index is located specifically at **http://www.developer.com/directories/pages/dir.java.mm.html.** Intel has also been developing some multimedia Java applets you can use on your site. Download and install its photography Java applets (Figure 11.9) located at **http://www.intel.com/cpc/webapplets/.** You'll find five multimedia Java applets for displaying photos on your Web site.

Figure 11.9
Intel offers many fun multimedia Java applets for your site.

Dynamic HTML is also a good source of multimedia effects. However, due to the differences between Internet Explorer and Netscape Navigator, you must be careful about using it. Visitors to your site will also need to run version 4.0 or higher browsers. If you are still interested in what Dynamic HTML can offer, check out the Dynamic HTML Zone (Figure 11.10) located on the Web at **http://www.dhtmlzone.com**.

Figure 11.10
Macromedia's DHTML Zone is the place to find help with multimedia-oriented Dynamic HTML.

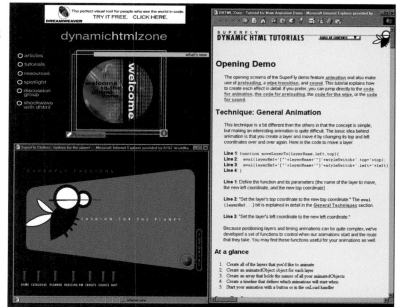

Moving On

When adding multimedia to your site, making it fun and meaningful is most important. Anybody can add a Shockwave game or a video clip that will stand out, but the best sites integrate multimedia into their overall theme.

As you develop your multimedia content, take the time to make it the right size, length, and quality. Be sure to also decide how to present it and why it makes sense to have it on your site. Once you add any form of multimedia—whether a tribute page to Clint Eastwood that opens with a sound clip of "Go ahead, make my day" or a video clip of your child's first steps—your site will stand out from the others.

12

Developing Forms on GeoCities

When you want to create an interactive site—one that receives information as well as gives it—the simplest way is to post your e-mail address on your site. However, more advanced sites use HTML forms. By using forms on your site, you can provide users with set questions and answers that allow them to interact with your site. These can be forms to leave addresses through or forms that ask people to rate your site, or give an opinion on a TV show—whatever you desire. Always remember that one of the beauties of the Web is that you can receive as well as give information. Using forms is a natural and great way to explore the interactive side of home-page building.

Developing forms on GeoCities is, for most people, a two-part process of learning

▶ The basics of developing forms; and

▶ How forms work specifically on GeoCities.

You'll find neither part particularly difficult to master and will see that forms allow you to interact with visitors to your page in a way that offers a tremendous upside.

The biggest issue you will face in developing forms is that the GeoBuilder program (or any of the popular visual editors for that matter) isn't very good at building forms. This is because form elements tend to require lots of extensions and hidden HTML codes to perform perfectly, and you can find yourself more easily hampered by a visual design tool when creating forms. The best way to create forms is to learn the HTML syntax that is used to create the forms and then use a basic HTML text editor like Homesite 4.0 (**http://www.allaire.com**) for the PC or BBEdit (**http://www.bbedit.com**) for the Macintosh. You can also use the text-based, Advanced Editor, found on GeoCities as well.

Part III Making an Exciting Site

The Basics of Developing Forms

Forms are sections of pages or entire pages that include text boxes, buttons, drop-down lists, and radio buttons which allow users to answer various questions and offer information. Figure 12.1 shows a sample form running on a GeoCities page that allows a user to tell the site operator about the user's sports-viewing habits. A form might be as simple as asking the user for his or her name and e-mail address, or it could be as extensive as asking a user about his or her ten favorite movies, along with a comment on each. When you finish editing your form and the HTML page it resides on, you simply upload it to your site just like any standard HTML page. Of course, before you upload a form, you need to learn a lot more about how forms work and are used on GeoCities. By the end of this chapter you'll know everything you need to know.

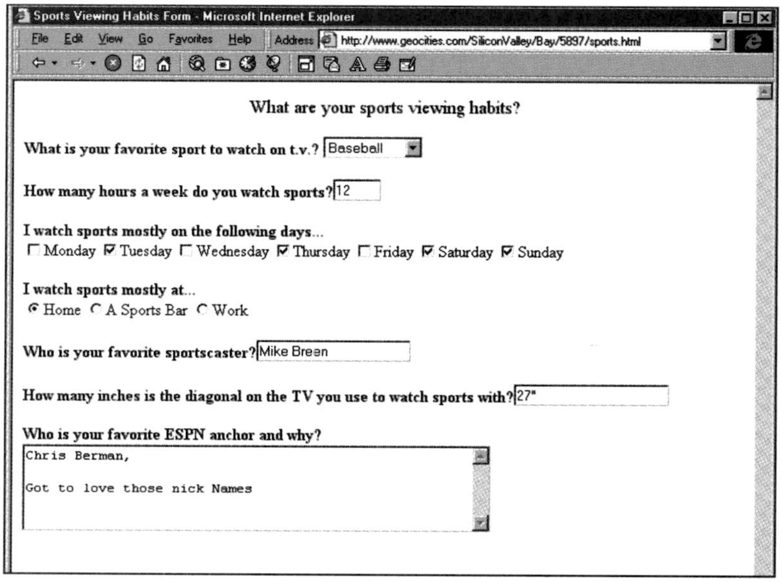

Figure 12.1
This simple form asks users about their sports-viewing habits.

Forms are designed in HTML using approximately ten tags that define the various elements of your Web form. Each form starts and ends with the <u>FORM</u> tag as follows:

```
<FORM>
          The body of the form goes here.
</FORM>
```

Within the form setting, you can add a number of critical tags that add text boxes, buttons, drop-down lists, and more to the form.

Once you've completed your forms and posted the HTML page to a site, the forms are processed by a special program that also resides on a Web server. These programs take the information that is submitted by the user and, depending on both the form's information and the specifics of the processing program, some action will take place. In the case of the main form's processor on GeoCities, the form's contents are mailed to a defined e-mail address. Once it is in the e-mail program, you are free to reply to it or just digest its contents.

How Are Forms Designed?

If you are considering adding a form to your page, think carefully about your purpose. Do you want to gain important feedback on a specific set of items, such as a survey? Will you use it to collect your visitors' e-mail addresses so you can send them updates or a newsletter? As in every other aspect of Web design, planning is crucial: When designing your form, you must decide on the type of information you hope to gain from your site's visitors, and how to design your form in such a way that the users will gladly complete them. See the next section, "What Makes a GeoCities Form Interesting," for more on building fun forms that will encourage users to interact with your Web site.

What Makes a GeoCities Form Interesting?

Let's be realistic: A form should entice people to complete it. On GeoCities that usually means coming up with fun forms that encourage people to voice their opinions. Let big companies and others create those stuffy forms that ask for every ounce of personal information. In most cases, free personal home pages are about you, your favorite topics, or a specific interest. Try to create forms that help others share their interests with you. In addition, make sure that you somehow reflect their sharing of those interests. If someone takes the time to fill out your forms, they hope to receive something in return—perhaps an e-mail reply, a posting of their comments on your site, or a site update.

What else contributes to an interesting form on GeoCities?

▶ **Snappy questions or field headings**—Instead of asking visitors to rate this movie on a scale of 1-5, use a rating system such as this: It Ruled!!, It Was Really Good, It was So-So, or This Movie Was So Hideous, I Got My Money Back!!

▶ **Short forms**—Leave the long forms for sites that want you to set up an account or order some book. A good GeoCities form should let visitors share opinions in less than three minutes.

▶ **Ask for answers that you can share with others**—Unless you are compiling a survey, don't ask for information like age and sex. Also, don't ask overly simplistic questions such as, "Who is your favorite actor?" Instead, ask questions that lead to answers that will interest other visitors. For example, "Why did you drop out of college?" or "Why is your favorite pro wrestler better than Hulk Hogan?" You can put the responses on your site to create fun reading for your visitors.

▶ **Build forms relevant to your site**—GeoCities is all about bringing together people with common interests. So if your site is all about football, don't ask visitors about their favorite television commercials—unless it's their favorite Super Bowl commercial.

▶ **Give people something fun to do**—Rather than just asking questions that require visitors to write answers, have them do something fun with your forms—vote for their favorite [fill in the blank], or rank five items from best to worst. People love the chance to do more than just type out answers on forms.

▶ **Respond to those who complete your forms**—Good forms should help you begin a dialogue with your visitor. If you ask for their e-mail addresses, be sure to send them a note, even if it is just to thank them.

There are visual page editors that can help you design forms, but designing them directly with your HTML code gives you the most control. To use this method, you should know all the ins and outs of HTML form design.

The Form Tags

As noted, you begin and end the contents of your form by enclosing all the HTML tags between the opening <FORM> tag and the closing </FORM> tag.

```
<FORM>...</FORM>
```

The opening form tag has two key extensions associated with it: <u>METHOD</u> and <u>ACTION</u>. The <u>METHOD</u> extension is used to define which method the form is performing: <u>GET</u> or <u>POST</u>. You need only use METHOD="POST" for your GeoCities forms.

The <u>ACTION</u> extension tells the form what program or script to run on the Web server hosting the page that will process the form's contents. For GeoCities, the action code to use is <u>ACTION="/cgi-bin/homestead/mail.pl?[yourmember name]"</u>. The member name is important because GeoCities uses that (rather than your GeoCities e-mail address) to locate the e-mail address to which the submitted form's contents will be sent.

The proper opening <u><FORM></u> tag to use is:

```
<FORM METHOD="POST" ACTION="/cgi-bin/homestead/mail.pl?[Your
Member Name]">
```

> **TIP**
>
> **Testing Requires a Different Tag**
>
> If you are planning to run your page from your computer for testing purposes
> before uploading it to your Web site, you must change your <u>ACTION</u> tag to
> read:
>
> ```
> ACTION=http://www.geocities.com/cgi-
> bin/homestead/mail.pl?[Your Member Name]
> ```

Text Boxes

Text boxes are used on forms to give users a place in which to enter
answers to various questions you might ask on your form. Text boxes can
also allow people to input secret passwords for your site (although
GeoCities doesn't work with passwords on forms you create).

To create a text box, use the <u><INPUT></u> tag. The <u><INPUT></u> tag actually
allows you to create several other form elements, but for now we'll
concentrate on text boxes. A text box <u><INPUT></u> tag looks like this:

```
<INPUT TYPE="TEXT" NAME="FIRSTNAME" SIZE="10" MAXLENGTH="10"
VALUE="Name Here">
```

Notice how there are several parts to this tag, called elements. Each
element allows you to control how this field on your form operates.

The <u>TYPE="TEXT"</u> extension to the tag is where you actually set the
input element to a text box. The <u>NAME</u> extension is what you use to
name the field. In this example, we used <u>FIRSTNAME</u> as the name of the
text box. You can put any words in this field to describe the contents of
the text box. When your form shows up in your e-mail, it will use the
contents of the <u>NAME</u> extension to describe the answer. For example, if
someone named "Ben" filled out this form and the results appeared in
your e-mail, it would look like this:

```
(FIRSTNAME) Ben
```

The <u>SIZE="10"</u> extension lets you set the length of the text box. In the
example, the size was set to 10 characters. Feel free to use any number
that works for your page design, although large numbers won't work
particularly well (20—60 seems to be common). <u>MAXLENGTH</u> keeps the
user from typing in more than the specified number of characters.

Part III Making an Exciting Site

The <u>VALUE</u> extension is used to place a startup value in the text box when the user first sees the form. If you don't want an initial value, don't include this extension.

Figure 12.2 shows this very simple form with a line of HTML wrapped around it to inform the reader what information I was expecting in the <u>Name</u> field. You can enter this code straight into any of your HTML pages to have the form work properly:

```
<FORM METHOD="POST" ACTION="/cgi-bin/homestead/mail.pl?[Your
    Member Name]">
<B>What's Your First Name?</B>
<INPUT TYPE="TEXT" NAME="FIRSTNAME" SIZE="10" MAXLENGTH="10"
    VALUE="Name Here">
</FORM>
```

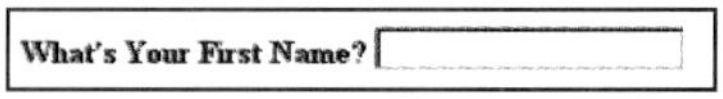

Figure 12.2
This simple form has one text box.

What's Your First Name? [   ]

Radio Buttons

A *radio button* is a form element that restricts the user from selecting many options; instead, the user must pick one answer from a group of options. As soon as the user picks one of the options, any previous setting is cleared. For example, if you wanted someone to rate a movie from "I Loved It!" to "I Hated It!" and not to be able to choose more than one response (or any other response), you would use radio buttons (Figure 12.3). A radio button tag looks as follows:

```
<INPUT TYPE="radio" VALUE="I Loved It">
```

As you notice, our friend the <u><INPUT></u> tag is here again, except this time the <u>TYPE</u> is being set to <u>RADIO</u> instead of <u>TEXT</u>. The <u>NAME</u> extension is especially important with radio buttons because all radio button inputs that share the same name act as a group. This prevents a user from choosing more than one at a time. The <u>VALUE</u> extension is what will be passed on via e-mail if the user selects that specific radio button in the group. In the case of the example given, if the user selected that radio button, your e-mail would have a line reading:

```
(MOVIERATING) I Loved It!
```

Finally, the <u>CHECKED</u> extension lets you define which of the radio buttons in a specific group are initially checked when the user first sees the form. Figure 12.3 shows a simple group of radio buttons. Here is the HTML code used for this example:

```
<INPUT TYPE="Radio" NAME="First Seen" VALUE="Theater">
    Movie Theater<BR>
<INPUT TYPE="Radio" NAME="First Seen" VALUE="Video">
    Video<BR>
<INPUT TYPE="Radio" NAME="First Seen" VALUE="Pay">
    Pay Per View<BR>
<INPUT TYPE="Radio" NAME="First Seen" VALUE="Cable">
    Cable TV<BR>
<INPUT TYPE="Radio" NAME="First Seen" VALUE="TV">
    Regular Television<BR>
```

Figure 12.3
Users can make only one choice from the radio buttons on this form.

Where Did You First See this Movie?
○ Movie Theater
○ Video
○ Pay Per View
○ Cable TV
○ Regular Television

TIP
Offer a Default Value

Use the <u>CHECKED</u> extension to initially label what you think is a most common answer for the group. If you create a radio button group that doesn't offer a most common choice, don't use the <u>CHECKED</u> extension.

Check Boxes

Check boxes are similar to radio buttons in that the user checks them on or off. The difference is that all the check boxes on a form can be checked on or off without limiting the user to one selection. So while you would use a radio button group to ask users whether they liked or hated a specific movie, you might use a series of check boxes to ask *why* they liked the movie (see Figure 12.4 for an example of this idea). A single check box tag looks like this:

```
<INPUT TYPE="CHECKBOX" VALUE="KILLER ACTION" CHECKED>
```

Part III Making an Exciting Site

A realistic example, like the one in Figure 12.4 uses several related lines of HTML code like this:

```
What Did You Like About This Movie? (Check All That Apply)<BR>
<INPUT TYPE="Checkbox" NAME="Story">The Story Was Great<BR>
<INPUT TYPE="Checkbox" NAME="Acting">It Had Great Acting<BR>
<INPUT TYPE="Checkbox" NAME="Special Effects">Awesome Special
    Effects<BR>
<INPUT TYPE="Checkbox" NAME="Action">Killer Action<BR>
<INPUT TYPE="Checkbox" NAME="Music">The Soundtrack Ruled<BR>
```

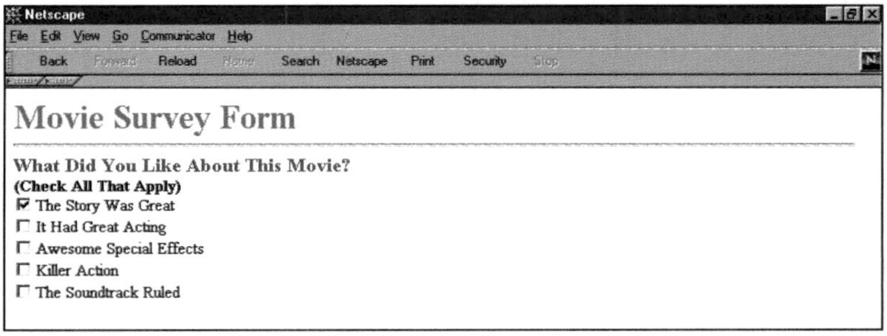

Figure 12.4

Check boxes on a form let users make multiple choices from grouped items.

Yes, it's the <u>INPUT</u> tag again. This time the <u>TYPE="CHECKBOX"</u> tag has set it to appear as a check box. The <u>VALUE</u> extension is what will be passed on via e-mail if the user selects that specific check box. Your e-mail, if the user selects the check box, will include a line that reads:

```
(KILLER ACTION) CHECKED
```

As shown in the example, you can preset the check box to the checked position by including the <u>CHECKED</u> extension.

Text Areas

Unlike a text box, a text area (Figure 12.5) lets the user enter multiple lines of information into a single element. This is great to use for inputs that require the user to give a more extensive written response to a question, such as a "comments" area on your form. You must use the <u>TEXTAREA>...</TEXTAREA</u> opening and closing tags to define this element. An example of this is:

```
<TEXTAREA NAME="Movie Comments" ROWS="5" COLS="55">
Please post your comments about this movie here:</TEXTAREA>
```

Note the three main extensions to the <u>TEXTAREA</u> tag.

▶ <u>NAME</u> is used to identify the field in the resulting e-mail.

▶ The <u>ROWS</u> and <u>COLS</u> extensions set the number of lines and the length of each line in characters of your text area.

The text that exists between the opening and closing tags will appear as the preset text in the text area. People often use this to provide a simple clue of what to type into the text area.

As with the other tags, the results of what people type in appear in your e-mail:

```
(Movie Comments) "I loved this movie, but I wish they hadn't
              killed the dog at the end."
```

> **TIP**
>
> **Wrap Your Text**
>
> Adding <u>WRAP=PHYSICAL</u> to your <u>TEXTAREA</u> tag will force the text area to word-wrap any long sentences just like your favorite word processor does.

Figure 12.5
A TextArea form element allows users to input multiple lines of text.

![Movie Survey Form in Netscape browser window]

Menus

Menus allow you to offer another way for users to select from a predefined list of options (Figure 12.6). Two sets of tags are used to create a menu. The <SELECT>...</SELECT> tags are used to define the beginning and end of a particular menu. The <OPTION> tag is used between the <SELECT> tags to set up specific options that the user can select from the menu. For example, if you want to set up a menu that allows users to select from their preferred movie genre, insert the following HTML code into your form:

```
<SELECT NAME="Favorite Type" SIZE="1">
<OPTION VALUE="Animated" CHECKED>Animated
<OPTION VALUE="Thriller">Thriller
<OPTION VALUE="Sci-Fi">Sci-Fi
<OPTION VALUE="War">War
<OPTION VALUE="Romance">Romance
</SELECT>
```

In the <SELECT> tag, the NAME extension defines the name of the menu to be used in the resulting e-mail. If the user selects the Thriller option, a line in your e-mail will read:

```
(Favorite Type) Thriller
```

The SIZE extension is used to denote the number of listings shown at one time in the menu. Set this to 1 to show only one choice at a time, 3 to show three choices at a time, and so on.

With the <OPTION> tag, the VALUE extension is what is set in the e-mail if the user makes that selection from the menu. CHECKED is used to set an initial value.

Figure 12.6

The Menu element on a form lets you offer predefined choices on a drop-down list.

Image Inputs

An image can be used as an input device (see Figure 12.7). Be warned: Sorting out the answers is difficult because of the way in which values are returned. However, when used in the right situation, image inputs can be fun to offer on your form.

To set up an image input, first create your image and save it as a GIF or JPEG. Next, use the <INPUT> tag as follows to display your form and ask for input:

```
<INPUT TYPE="image" SRC="theworld.gif" NAME="Where I Live">
```

The TYPE extension, which is on the <INPUT> tag, defines it as an image. The SRC extension is the URL of the image residing on your GeoCities Web site that should be displayed to the user. The NAME tag is used to identify the answer in your e-mail.

Answers to image inputs will be simple X, Y coordinates. This is why they're difficult to use—do you want to cross-check the image coordinates image every time someone answers your image input? You should also know that the form data will be submitted automatically and immediately when an image input is clicked, even if the rest of the form hasn't been filled out. Thus, when an image input is used, it may be wise to place it at the end or as the only element on a form.

When using an image input, the result in your e-mail will be a line that reads [NAME]=x,y, which denotes the name of the input tag and the x,y coordinates.

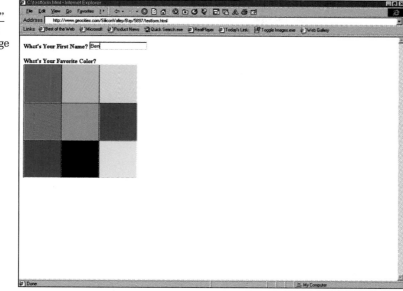

Submit & Reset Buttons

When visitors reach the end of your form, they should be offered a button that tells the server they're done and want to submit the form for processing. You can also add what is known as a Reset button. The Reset button lets visitors completely clear a form on the screen if they need to start over.

To add a Submit button, use the <INPUT> tag as follows:

```
<INPUT TYPE="SUBMIT" NAME="  Here it is . . .  ">
```

The NAME extension for the tag determines how the button will be labeled. Notice how extra spaces are used to make the button larger than what the text will force it to be.

To add a Reset button, use the <INPUT> tag as follows:

```
<INPUT TYPE="RESET" NAME="  Reset  ">
```

The only difference between these two examples is the RESET or SUBMIT label used in the TYPE=". . ." extension that tells the browser what type of button it is.

Assembling an Entire Form

Now that you know about the individual elements of a form, let's look at an entire form from top to bottom. Sticking with the example, this form lets people provide feedback on their favorite movie. To see what this form looks like on GeoCities, look at Figure 12.8:

```
<HTML>
<BODY>
<FORM METHOD="POST" ACTION="/cgi-bin/homestead/mail.pl?[Your Member Name]">
    <B>What's Your First Name? </B><INPUT TYPE="TEXT" NAME="FIRSTNAME"
        SIZE="20"><BR><BR>
    <B>Your Favorite Movie: </B><INPUT TYPE="TEXT" NAME="Movie Name"
        SIZE="30"><BR><BR>
    <B>What Kind of Movie is it?</B>
        <SELECT SIZE=1 NAME="MovieType">
                <OPTION SELECTED VALUE="Animated">Animated
                <OPTION VALUE="Thriller">Thriller
                <OPTION VALUE="Sci-Fi">Sci-Fi
                <OPTION VALUE="War">War Movie
                <OPTION VALUE="Romance">Romance
        </SELECT><BR><BR>
    <B>Where Did You First See This Movie?</B><BR>
        <INPUT TYPE="Radio" NAME="First Seen" VALUE="Theater">Movie Theater<BR>
        <INPUT TYPE="Radio" NAME="First Seen" VALUE="Video">Video<BR>
        <INPUT TYPE="Radio" NAME="First Seen" VALUE="Pay">Pay Per View<BR>
        <INPUT TYPE="Radio" NAME="First Seen" VALUE="Cable">Cable TV<BR>
        <INPUT TYPE="Radio" NAME="First Seen" VALUE="TV">Regular Television<BR><BR>
    <B>What Did You Like About This Movie? (Check All The That Apply)</B><BR>
        <INPUT TYPE="Checkbox" NAME="Story">The Story Was Great<BR>
        <INPUT TYPE="Checkbox" NAME="Acting">It Had Great Acting<BR>
        <INPUT TYPE="Checkbox" NAME="Special Effects">Awesome Special Effects<BR>
        <INPUT TYPE="Checkbox" NAME="Action">Killer Action<BR>
        <INPUT TYPE="Checkbox" NAME="Music">The Soundtrack Ruled<BR><BR>


    <B>In less than 100 Words, Tell, Why Do You Recommend This Movie:</B><BR>
        <TEXTAREA NAME="Why See It" ROWS="10" COLS="50">You should see this movie
            because...</TEXTAREA><BR><ER>
        <INPUT TYPE="Submit" Name=" Here Ya Go! ">
        <INPUT TYPE="Reset" Name=" What Was I Thinking?!?!! ">
</FORM>
</BODY>
</HTML>
```

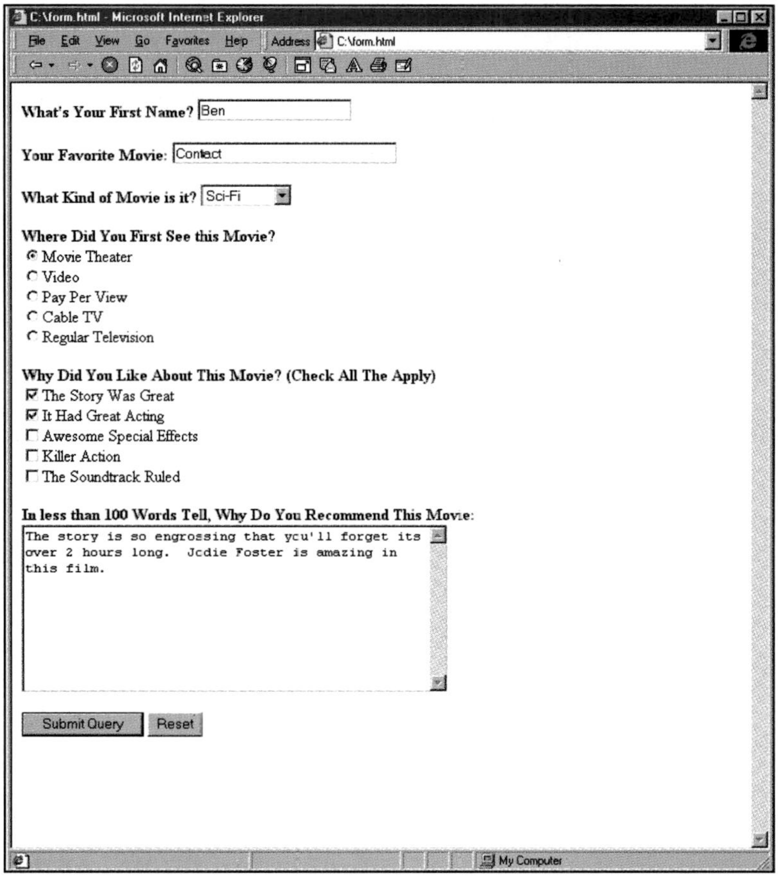

Figure 12.8
Here's the complete
movie form, as available
on a GeoCities Web site.

More Form Tricks

You've mastered the basics of form creation. However, true form artists have some tricks that make their forms better than the rest. Here are five tips about creating forms:

1. **Use tables to format your forms**—The entire example movie form was done without tables and looks like a long list of questions. Formatting the same content in a table allows you more control over the layout of the form and makes the form look a lot better, as you'll see in Figure 12.9.

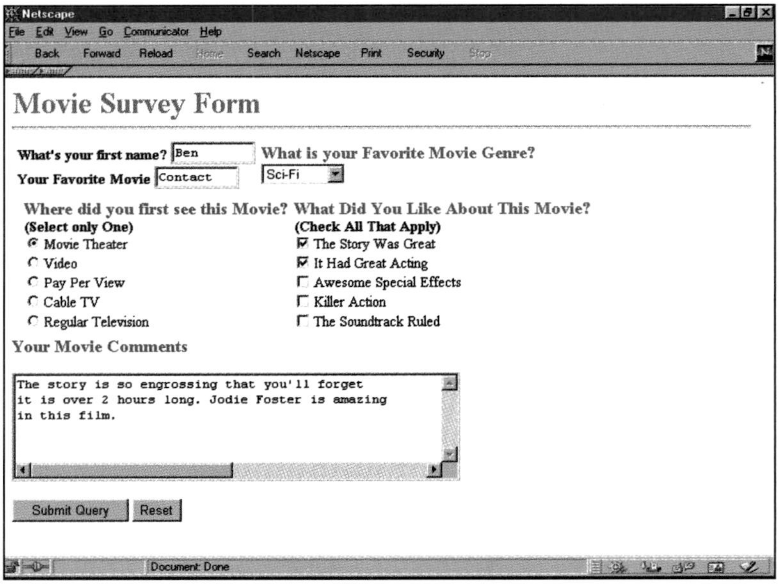

Figure 12.9
Experiment by using tables to let you do more advanced forms layout.

2. **Use <u>REQUIRED:</u> in your <u>NAME</u> extensions**—Putting <u>REQUIRED:</u> in front of your <u>NAME</u> extension in an element such as <u><INPUT TYPE="TEXT" NAME="REQUIRED:FIRST" SIZE=20></u> forces the GeoCities form handler to see whether the field has a value. The GeoCities form handler will reject a submission that doesn't have a required value and will ask the user to go back and complete the required areas.

3. **Indicate which fields are required by using some identifying text**—Some people bold the fields they require. Other people put "(required)" in small text next to the required field. Some designers use an asterisk (*). Be sure you make it clear to users which fields they are required to complete.

4. **Use JavaScript to validate your forms first**—The fact that a field is required won't stop someone from entering, for example, a letter when you want a number. While the process is too extensive to cover here, you can use JavaScript (if you've learned it) to precheck forms for valid answers before users submit their forms to the server to be mailed to you. Any good JavaScript book has a section devoted to checking forms for correct entries.

5. **Use images in place of the standard Submit button**—Some people dress up their Submit and Reset buttons by substituting a graphic for the default button style that the browser normally uses. To do this, use the image input tag discussed earlier in this chapter and make the graphic read, Submit. *Note*: You cannot use this method to create a graphical Reset button.

Hidden and Special Input Tags

Although we have come a long way, we still have a bit more to learn to properly submit the form to GeoCities. We include a few tricks that make sending the form and replying to it easier.

A form often needs to submit a value to the form handler that is constant and doesn't need the user's input. To pass values from a form without user input, the <INPUT TYPE="HIDDEN"> tag is used. This tag is important because, to properly process a form, you must include several hidden input tags in your form.

> **TIP**
>
> **Where to Hide Your Tags**
>
> It is not required, but most people list all the hidden input tags right below the opening <FORM> tag before they get to the form's input elements.

In order for your forms to work perfectly, the GeoCities forms program will require a number of <INPUT TYPE="HIDDEN"> tags.

Part III Making an Exciting Site

The Next URL Tag

The following hidden tag is used to send visitors to a specific page if they successfully complete a form:

```
<INPUT TYPE="Hidden" Name="Next-URL"
    VALUE="http://www.geocities.com/SiliconValley/Rt1244/
    thankyou.html">
```

Unlike most links, when you use the Next URL hidden input, you must set the VALUE extension to the entire URL as shown in the example, not just thankyou.html in order for this to work properly. Make sure you've built the page you are sending people to before uploading and making your form active.

The Subject Tag

A Subject tag can be hidden or you can ask people to fill it out. Most form developers use a hidden version of the tag so each form that comes in via e-mail is delivered with the e-mails possessing the same subject text. This way, an e-mail filtering process can be used.

```
<INPUT TYPE="Hidden" Name="Subject" value="Favorite Movie">
```

Filtering is especially useful when you have multiple forms on your site. By using a hidden Subject tag, you can easily see whether someone has answered a Comments form, your Movie Survey form, or some other form.

Creating a from e-mail

```
<INPUT TYPE="Text" Name="from-email">
```

Creating a text box that asks users for their e-mail address and naming that form element "from-email" will result in GeoCities mailing you the form results. The message can then be replied to directly upon receipt. Otherwise, no valid reply-to e-mail address will be included.

Creating a from-name

```
<INPUT TYPE="Text" Name="from-name">
```

Creating a text box that asks for a name and naming that form element "from-name" will result in GeoCities mailing you the form results so that the "from name" in your inbox will include the contents of that text box. This makes it easy to see who has sent you a form.

Other GeoCities Forms-Processing Tricks

A number of tricks is specific to processing forms on GeoCities. Here are the most important:

▶ Ask the user to provide his or her e-mail address in a text box. Using the <u>NAME</u> extension to <u>"from-email"</u> (for example, <u>E-mail Address <INPUT TYPE="TEXT" NAME="from-email" SIZE=30></u>).

▶ Use your e-mail program's automated filters to sort incoming subject lines.

▶ Use the <u><INPUT TYPE="Hidden" NAME="Subject" Value="Movies"></u> to automatically set the incoming message's subject to "Movies." Knowing that a form will contain the subject line "Movies" when it's mailed in lets you to set up a filter in your personal e-mail system so that a particular action will automatically occur. Check your e-mail program's documentation for information on how you can set up automated actions based on the message's subject line.

▶ Automatically subscribe and unsubscribe users to your own e-mail newsletter. Using an automated filter and the simple form code listed below, you can make it easy for someone to provide his or her e-mail address and automatically subscribe to or unsubscribe from your newsletter.

```
<FORM METHOD="POST" ACTION="/CGI-BIN/formail?[your membername]">
Subscribe/Unsubscribe To My Newsletter…
<INPUT TYPE="TEXT" NAME="Reply To" SIZE=30
    VALUE="myemail@mydomain.com">
        <SELECT NAME="Subject" SIZE="15">
        <OPTION VALUE="Subscribe" CHECKED>
        <OPTION VALUE="Unsubscribe">
</SELECT>
<INPUT TYPE="Submit" Value=" Thanks!">
</FORM>
```

g!

Part III Making an Exciting Site

> **TIP**
> **Filtering May Require More Help**
>
> For a subject-line filter to work well, you should know how to use your e-mail program's filtering system. Check the help file or manual for your favorite e-mail program and learn how to build e-mail lists and auto-replies.

▶ Use mailto: in the <u>ACTION</u> extension of the <u><FORM></u> tag to have the contents of a form automatically sent to an e-mail address other than the one specified in your user profile.

Instead of using <u><FORM METHOD="POST" ACTION="/CGI-BIN/formail?[your membername]"></u> to submit a form just to you, you can point a form's contents toward any desired e-mail address. Use the <u>Mailto:</u> option in the <u>ACTION</u> extension of a <u><INPUT TYPE="Submit"></u> tag and supply a valid e-mail address. An example is

```
<INPUT TYPE="Submit" Value=" EMail This Form"
       ACTION="mailto:myname@mydomain.com">
```

In most browsers, when the user clicks on the Submit button, a box will pop up saying that the form wants to send its contents out using the user's e-mail program (see Figure 12.10). If the user chooses Yes, then his or her e-mail program is automatically launched and the form's contents are attached and mailed out as noted. This is a good method if you want people to mail you their forms using your GeoCities e-mail account. It's also good if you want to have the contents of the form e-mailed to someone other than the owner of the site.

Figure 12.10
A user will see this warning before submitting a form that uses the <u>mailto:</u> option instead of the GeoCities forms processor.

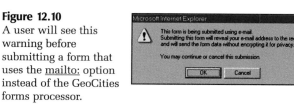

TIP
Virtual Signatures

Perhaps you are collecting "virtual signatures" to mail in an effort to bring attention to someone about something, such as a petition. You can use <u>mailto:</u> to have users of your site fill out a form and send its contents directly to the proper authority. For example, if your favorite TV show is on the brink of being cancelled, you can set up a "petition" form calling for the network to save the show. You can then use <u>mailto:</u> to have the message sent directly from the users to the network!

Moving On

The GeoCities form handler offers a great way to interact with people who visit your page. By mastering forms, you should be able to add fun surveys and other tools that let you gather information from visitors. You can use this information to spice up or increase interest in your site or to involve your readers more in the page's subject matter by reporting on the results of surveys or other information gleaned from your forms.

Part IV
Beyond Homesteading

13

Promoting Your GeoCities Home Page

Now that you've built what we're sure is a spectacular GeoCities home page, you'll certainly want to share it with the world. That world includes your GeoCities' neighbors and the World Wide Web community in general. GeoCities has a number of programs that will help you promote your site and get the hit counter spinning.

In addition to covering the GeoGuide Banner Exchange as well as the GeoCities Watermark, this chapter will discuss what search engines do for you, how to submit your page to them, and how to improve your ranking. We'll also talk about announce sites and award sites.

GeoCities is designed to help members find what they want when they want it. Obviously, choosing the right neighborhood for your site is the first step in attracting visitors. But you can do a lot more after that. So let's find some visitors.

Exchanging Banners

One of the easiest ways to get visitors to come to your site is by participating in the Banner Exchange program. The Banner Exchange program lets you build an "advertisement" for your site and through it into the general GeoCities pool of advertisements that appear to visitors.

Any member can participate and there are even volunteers who will help you build the banners for you. This section discusses the Banner Exchange program and how to participate in it.

Creating a Banner

To participate in the Banner Exchange program, you obviously must create a banner that appears on other sites around GeoCities and the Web. Banners are those rectangular promotional pieces that usually appear at the top or bottom of a site. Clicking on a banner allows someone to immediately visit the site that is promoted by the banner.

To create a banner, you will need a graphic editor like Paint Shop Pro (Windows) or Graphic Converter (Mac). You will also optionally need a way to create animated GIFs. Paint Shop Pro comes with Animation Shop, which helps you build animated GIFs for the Mac you can use a separate product like GIF Dancer 1.0 from paceworks (**http://www.animation.com**). Banners normally must be 20 kilobytes or less but GeoCities Banner exchange has special rules that you must conform your banners to:

▶ Banners must not violate any content guidelines

▶ Banners must be 468x60 pixels

▶ Banners must be no larger than 8 kilobytes (8,192 bytes)

▶ Banners can be but don't have to be animated

With this in mind you can create your banners. Start by creating a 468x80 blank image. Then using the suggested image editors (or your own personal favorite), create the main banner image. You can then save it in the .GIF format. If the size of the banner in bytes is less than 8,192 you may be able to do additional frames of the banner that will make it animated. These frames can then be assembled in a GIF animator program and if the resulting GIF animation is less than 8,192 bytes, you're in business.

TIP

Another way to create your own animated banners is to use the free service at **www.animation.com** (created by Paceworks a maker of software for creating animated GIFs). This service lets you create a few cool animated banners just by typing in some text you want to appear in the banner.

Figure 13.1
Here's a banner and the
GeoGuide that appears
on a home page.

TIP

Banner Help for the Rest of Us

Creating a banner requires a balance is design and technical skills.
Not everyone is an expert in these areas, so there are built-in self-help
programs for you. However, many of the GeoCities members who are
experts have volunteered to help create banners for the Banner Exchange
program. Volunteers in the various neighborhoods can be found at
http://www.geocities.com/members/programs/geoguide/banner_help.html.

When you send your request, provide as much information as possible,
including your e-mail address, your homestead address, and what you want
the banner to say. GeoCities requests that you not ask more than one person at
a time to create a banner for you. Since you'll end up using only one, asking
someone to do free work when you know you'll probably never use it would
be rude. Remember, too, that these people are volunteers, so ask nicely.

Most neighborhoods have at least one banner volunteer. However, if yours
doesn't, fear not. You can choose any of the volunteers listed at the address
given above.

Getting Your Banner to GeoCities

Once your banner is created, your banner needs to reside somewhere on
the GeoCities servers so your home page can refer to it. You can get it
there in either of two ways:

1. Use the EZ File Upload Utility located in the File Manager to transfer
   the banner from your computer directly to your GeoCities directory.

2. Use FTP to send it to GeoCities' FTP server.

Uploading banners is the exact same process as uploading other types of
files onto your site. We talked about the EZ File Upload Utility and the
FTP procedures in Chapter 5 if you need help remembering how to do it.

For more information on submitting your banner to the Banner Exchange,
go to **http://www.geocities.com/cgi-bin/geoguide/submit_banner**.

On this page will be a small text box at the bottom of the screen. Here
you type in the exact URL that points to the banner on your site. Make
sure it includes the entire URL with the correct capitalization and
neighborhood address. When completed, press the verify submission and
GeoCities will check to see if it's there.

When it has checked and found the banner, it will display a verification screen asking you if this is the banner you want to display and showing you the acceptable dimensions. If it is, press the **Apply** button. Once you do this your banner is submitted for approval—it may take up to a week or more to hear back from GeoCities so be patient.

Once submitted, GeoCities will review the banner and assign a rating to your banner. The rating system works as follows:

▶ **Level I**—Banners that are suitable for any viewer, including children.

▶ **Level II**—Banners that are of general interest, but aren't necessarily intended for children.

EnchantedForest Banner Exchange

There is a special GeoGuide Banner Exchange program for EnchantedForest Homesteaders. Since EnchantedForest is a neighborhood for children only and is intended as a safe place for them to build in and explore, EnchantedForest members can only accept and create Level I banners. This rating level is automatic for anyone living in EnchantedForest.

For more on the EnchantedForest Banner Exchange program, go to **http://www.geocities.com/EnchantedForest/ef_geoguide.html.**

GeoCities Watermark

As you probably know, the GeoCities Watermark (Figure 13.2) is that semi-transparent GeoCities logo that appears at the bottom of GeoCities' pages. The GeoCities Watermark is not there just for decoration.

The Watermark was developed based on feedback from members who did not want to include a link to GeoCities directly on all of their pages. GeoCities had always required a link back from member pages. The Watermark replaces this required link-back to GeoCities. It's automatic and you need not install any HTML on your pages to activate it.

So what's the point of the Watermark? It helps visitors find other sites like yours by taking them to similar Avenue pages when they click on it. And, for the benefit of GeoCities, it increases the awareness of GeoCities as a brand, which is why it's designed to always be visible on your screen.

Figure 13.2
You'll know it's a
GeoCities page when
you see one of these
two Watermarks.

Here's how it works. If, for example, you have a page about your favorite author, then the Watermark on your page will point to the Arts & Literature Avenue. If GeoCities has yet to categorize your page, the Watermark will point to the most appropriate Avenue based on the Neighborhood you've joined. If you click on the Watermark on a non-member GeoCities page (such as the GeoCities Shopping Center page), you will be delivered to the GeoCities home page.

GeoCities will continue to upgrade the Watermark to make it work better for members and users.

Search Engines

At this point everyone (at least everyone interested in building a GeoCities home page) probably knows what a search engine is. If you want to find something on the Web and haven't a clue where to find it, you probably start your search by typing in the subject at your favorite search engine. After checking out the responses, off you go in search of the best place for the desired information.

If your GeoCities home page is a good one, you too might have visitors arriving at your site via their favorite search engine. We won't bore you with all the details about how the specific search engines work. But you should know how to submit your site to a search engine and how to get it ranked higher. I mean, have you ever made it to the 1,232nd most popular nSync site? (We haven't either, and that's the point.)

GeoCities also offers the ability to search member pages at **http://www.geocities.com/search/**.

Automatic Submission

More search engines are available than you will ever use. Rather than submitting to each one individually (a time-consuming task), you might choose to submit your site once and let someone else do the work. This is called *automatic submission*.

Not surprisingly, Yahoo! (**http://www.yahoo.com**) has a list of automatic submission sites you should check. Probably the best known is SubmitIt! (**http://www.submit-it.com**). Complete one form and SubmitIt! will register your site with 15 search engines and catalogs (including many of the biggies). You can also use a more advanced fee-based version of SubmitIt! if you want to further publicize your site (Figure 13.3).

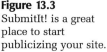

Figure 13.3
SubmitIt! is a great place to start publicizing your site.

Individual Submission

Many search engines will find your site even if you don't submit it, especially when you have outside links to it. However, most of the major search engines are easy to submit to, so why wait?

Search engines work differently. Some use information retrievers called *spiders* that index your entire site; others only index the main page. Learn as much as you can about the particular engine to which you are submitting so you can get the most recognition. While submitting your site to each desired search engine individually is time-consuming, it allows you to adjust your submission to fit the quirks of each search engine. Deciding between using an automatic submission service or doing all the work on your own will depend on how much time you have to spend on your submission.

Improving Your Site's Ranking

Search engines aren't perfect and the results they provide depend quite a bit on the skill of the searcher and tasks you can do to make your site appear closer to the top of the results lists. We'll cover a number of factors that will apply to some search engines but not others: meta tags, depth of search, keywords, title, word repetition, word placement, text and page design, and number of external links.

Meta Tags

Meta tags are placed in the head of an HTML document. The information is not displayed on your page but it can be recognized by some, though not all, search engines. One good place to go for information on meta tags is located in the Web Developer's Virtual Library. The meta tagging for the Search Engines page is **http://www.stars.com/Search/Meta/Tag.html**.

You should pay particular attention to two types of meta tags: Description and Keyword. The *Description* meta tag is just that—a brief description of your site that will appear in the search result. The keyword "meta tag" allows you to enter a number of pertinent keywords that people will likely use when searching for a site such as yours.

The structures look like this:

```
<META NAME="Keywords" CONTENT="KEYWORDS">
<META NAME="Description" CONTENT="DESCRIPTION">
```

Here is an example of meta tags that could be used for a Kobe Bryant fan site:

```
<META NAME="Keywords" CONTENT="Kobe Bryant, Los Angeles,
    Lakers, Los Angeles Lakers, NBA, basketball, pro
    basketball, dunks, Michael Jordan, hoop, young NBA stars">
<META NAME="Description" CONTENT="With his spectacular moves
    and high-flying dunks, Los Angeles Lakers guard Kobe
    Bryant is already drawing comparisons to the legendary
    Michael Jordan. Believe the hype!">
```

Remember that to add meta tag information, you must be editing a page's HTML codes. To do this, just go to the File Manager, select the page you want to edit and choose edit from the buttons below. This launches the Advanced HTML Editor, which lets you edit the direct HTML that makes up your page. Place the <Meta> tags at the top of the page after your <TITLE>. . .</TITLE> tags. In addition, place them on every page on your site.

Depth of Search

As we mentioned, some spiders dig through your entire site while some do little or no digging at all. For search engines that dig through little or nothing, you should submit each page individually, and include the hidden meta tags on each page within your site.

Keywords

Defining your site's keywords is important but not always easy. A good idea is to have a group of friends generate a list of keywords for your site. Consider the possible variations of the keywords and have your friends rank them. Use the top few keywords in your title, headings, text, and meta tags. There isn't a direct amount of how many keywords you might have for a particular page but most people tend to keep them between 10-30.

Title

Most search engines display the title of the page in the results and use the title words heavily in their ranking of sites. Having an accurate, descriptive title for all pages is essential. If you want people to find your Marilyn Manson site, don't just call it Twiggy's Music Page, call it Twiggy's Marilyn Manson Page.

Word repetition

Word repetition in your meta tags, in the description or in the text used to be an easy way to improve your site's ranking. Now some search engines penalize sites for unnecessary word repetition. However, others still use word repetition as a criterion for high ranking. Know how the various search engines that you submit your site to handle repetition.

Word Placement

Many search engines place a greater emphasis on words located near the beginning of the page, making this word selection very important.

Text and Page Design

Spiders can't read a page with no text, even if text is embedded in a graphic. You must also keep in mind that some search engines don't recognize meta tags but just use the early part of a page's text for the summary. Your text should work reasonably well as a summary should it be used in a search result.

External Links

Some search engines use the number of links to your site to determine your site's popularity and use this in their rankings. This factor makes obtaining links to your site twice as important.

Specific Search Engines

Here are a few top search engines along with some advice for submitting your site to them. Most of the search engines have an icon for adding URLs and will guide you through the process.

AltaVista
http://www.altavista.digital.com

AltaVista says its Crawler will follow links through the entire site and asks that you use meta tags. Submissions to AltaVista usually appear in a couple of days.

Excite
http://www.excite.com

Excite doesn't use meta tags. Using descriptive phrases near the top of your pages helps Excite's artificial intelligence rank your site correctly. It can take a couple of weeks for your submission to appear.

Hotbot
http://www.hotbot.com

Submit each page's URL once and limit submissions from the same domain to 50 in a 24-hour period. Hotbot (Figure 13.4) supports meta tags and focuses first on keywords in the title, followed by keywords in meta tags, and frequency of keywords in the text. Again, Hotbot can take a while to get your submission. They will send an e-mail confirmation when they do.

Figure 13.4
Hotbot is an efficient and high quality search engine.

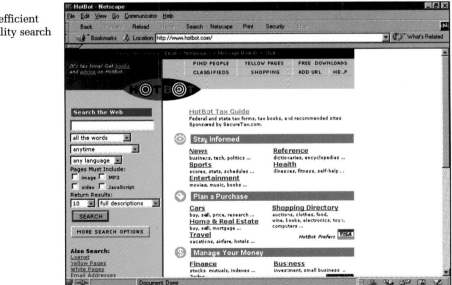

InfoSeek Ultra
http://ultra.infoseek.com

InfoSeek does not accept automatic submissions; you must submit each page of your site separately. As a GeoCities member, you must submit your site through e-mail. Include just your URL (including the http://) in the body of the message. You can submit more than one URL at a time by placing each URL on a single line.

Lycos
http://www.lycos.com

Lycos says its spider will dig through your entire site and that you will show up on a Lycos search two to four weeks after submission. You should definitely use meta tags with Lycos.

Lycos' rankings are based on keywords used in the title, in high-level headings, and in text near the top of the page. Page popularity also improves the ranking, whereas word repetition will be penalized.

WebCrawler
http://www.webcrawler.com

WebCrawler indexes every word on your site up to 1 megabyte of text. The keywords under which a page will be found in a WebCrawler search are the words on a page.

WebCrawler says it gives slightly more weight to titles than text or meta tags. Make sure the main page describes the site fully.

Yahoo!
http://www.yahoo.com

Yahoo! is actually a directory rather than a search engine, and submissions are handled by people. Before submitting, select a category and then narrow it down to subcategories. Once you have selected a specific category for your site, click on the Add URL icon.

Not all submissions are accepted, but if your site is one that is, Yahoo! will contact you via e-mail. They look for good content with a strong focus on the topic. Make sure your site is in good shape before submitting it to Yahoo! or you will likely be rejected.

Search Engine Watch

You should stay on top of search engine developments by checking Search Engine Watch at **http://searchenginewatch.com** (Figure 13.5). For GeoCities members, a particularly useful part of Search Engine Watch is the Webmaster's Guide to Search Engines (**http://searchenginewatch.com/ webmasters/index.html**). Check it all out.

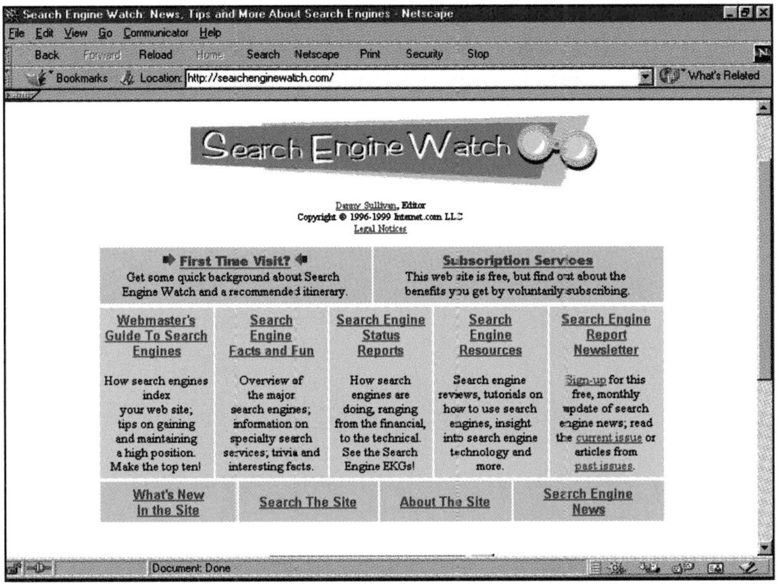

Figure 13.5
Keep your eyes here for news on registering and promoting with search engines.

Other Ways to Promote

You needn't stop there. There are even more ways to promote your site either within the GeoCities community or in the outside world. This includes being an active GeoCities member, using links, award sites, and announce sites.

Promoting within GeoCities

Aside from the Banner Exchange and its Watermark, GeoCities provides other ways to promote your home page within the GeoCities community.

▶ **Chat**—Chatting with other Homesteaders gives you an opportunity to develop connections with other people who have similar interests. That, of course, can mean more visitors to your site.

▶ **Forums**—As with chat, the forums allow you to converse with new people and possibly find new visitors.

▶ **Contests and Awards**—GeoCities is always looking for outstanding and unique home pages. The cream of the crop is featured in Best of GeoCities, or (for longtime members) the GeoCities Landmark Sites archive. These programs provide increased visibility both to GeoCities' members and the more than 10 million non-members who visit GeoCities each month. You can also enter contests held throughout the year. You can not only win prizes, but also attract visitors by becoming a contest winner. From month to month, each Neighborhood sponsors its own theme-specific contests.

▶ **Get Involved**—As with a real-world community, the more you communicate, the more people you get to know. And the more friends you have, the more visitors you have. Communicate with your Community Leader and participate in events. The more involved you are, the more visitors your site will draw.

Links

Search engines aren't the only way to draw customers to your site. You can also gain visitors who arrive at your site via a link. You can get links from similar sites within GeoCities or from the World Wide Web in general. Award sites and announce sites will link to your page as well. You can either keep your link search specific (for example, get other mountain biking sites to link to yours), or you can just try to get as many links as possible (even on sites only somewhat related to yours). Of course, you are more likely to get someone to link to your page if his or her page displays a similar interest.

Staying Specific

As you build your site, or even before you do, you'll probably visit a number of similar sites. Bookmark the best ones and, once your site looks good, contact those sites through e-mail. Tell the person what your site is about, explain why linking their site to yours would make sense, and give the person your site's URL so he or she can check it out. Assuming the person will be blown away by your spectacular site, they'll want to link to your site in exchange for a link from your site. Keep in mind that anyone providing a link to your site will want one in return. Don't approach a site about a link if you wouldn't want to offer a link in return.

If the person asks, "Why should I link to your site?" be sure you have an answer. Stress the fact that your visitors are the type of people who will want to visit his or her site and that the swapping of links will be good for both sites. If you have a large number of visitors, let the person know that. If your site is rather new and you haven't developed a huge number of visitors, explain why you think it won't be long before you do.

If you can't get the person to link to your site, you may still want to link to his or her site for the benefit of your visitors. Whatever you do, don't try to pass off an external link as part of your site. Be clear that you are directing them to a different site, not just another part of your own site.

You can also look to your friends and GeoCities neighbors, who will probably be receptive to your inquiry.

Award Sites

There are a number of award sites that can be beneficial for your site. However, only a fortunate few sites are so rewarded. Even if your site isn't honored, award sites can guide you toward some outstanding sites that might link to yours.

Here are some of the top award sites:

▶ Cool Site of the Day—**http://cool.infi.net**

▶ Lycos Top 5 Percent of the Web—
http://point.lycos.com/categories/index.html

▶ TooCool—**http://toocool.com**

▶ ProjectCool—**http://www.projectcool.com**

▶ Netscape What's Cool—
http://home.netscape.com/home/whats-cool.html

Announce Sites

Announce sites are directories of new Websites. These are only temporary listings:

▶ Netscape's What's New—
http://netscape.yahoo.com/guide/whats_new.html

▶ What's New Too—**http://newtoo.manifest.com**

▶ Nerd World What's New—
http://www.nerdworld.com/whatsnew.html

Other Helpful Hints

GeoCities has a number of helpful hints (**http://www.geocities.com/members/info/promote.html**) for its members. We've covered many of them already, but here are a few more:

▶ **Put your URL in your e-mail signature file**—That way every message you send reminds people where you live on the Web.

▶ **Put your URL on your resume.**

▶ **Send your URL to your local newspaper's technology editor—** Some newspapers regularly review, mention, or feature sites in their technology or business sections.

▶ **Join a "Web ring"—**These link people who visit a site to the next person in a circle of members and are popping up everywhere. Next time you see one on a neighbor's page, e-mail him or her and ask how to get involved.

▶ **When you're in a newsgroup, listserv, or chat room, mention your address—**Only do this when it's appropriate, however. If you barge into an online community and plaster your URL everywhere, you'll make plenty of enemies. But if you've created a site about gardening, mentioning it in a gardening-related list is fine. Just don't go spamming, which is against GeoCities guidelines.

▶ **Tell your relatives and friends—**And tell them to tell everyone they know to visit your site.

Moving On

There's nothing wrong with blowing your own horn—just do it the right way. Like any community, GeoCities frowns on spammers and has rules its members must follow. To learn what those rules are, and more on how to get the most out of GeoCities, move on to Chapter 14.

14

GeoCities Membership Benefits and Rules

Being a GeoCities member means more than just slapping up a Website; it means being a member of a community. Just like in society, there are rules we must follow and activities in which we can participate that will make us more valuable members of society.

This chapter covers the ins and outs of GeoCities membership. We'll talk about what you can and can't do (as well as what you should and shouldn't do) to be considered a valuable member of the GeoCities community.

Being a member of the GeoCities community has many benefits. You can cruise the Neighborhoods and Avenues for other members' sites. Click on the Neighborhood that interests you, turn down an Avenue, then venture onto a block until you reach the address you want. Once you're there, check out a specific site, or try the one next door.

On the home page you can get snippets of news articles from the GeoCities News Center, which will take you to more extensive news coverage at **ABCNews.com.**

Finally, this chapter will cover the GeoCities' Chat and Forum areas and how you can use them to help build a great site or just a place to shoot the breeze.

Setting Up Your GeoCities E-mail Account

Besides free home pages, the other important advantage of GeoCities is your free GeoCities e-mail account. You can use this to have a unique e-mail account just for your GeoCities home page. Perhaps you want to run your home page under a code name or Web nickname rather than the name you use for your personal e-mail. Or maybe you don't have your own e-mail account to send and receive messages from. By understanding all the specifics of your GeoCities e-mail, you can make this powerful component of the GeoCities service very useful.

First let's make sure you know your e-mail account name:

```
yourmembername@geocities.com
```

For example, if your member name is jane9, then your e-mail account name will be **jane9@geocities.com**. The password for your e-mail account is the same password that you use for your homesteading account. If you are not sure whether you signed up for the free e-mail account, then go to **http://www.geocities.com/members/help/guide_email_apply.html** and sign up.

GeoCities has set up an e-mail protocol. Before you can send any outgoing mail, you must first read all of your incoming mail. This is intended to cut down on "spammers" using the GeoCities e-mail system. If you have any question about this protocol, read the New Email Protocol FAQ at **http://www.geocities.com/main/info/system/email_faq.html**.

GeoCities suggests that, before you make any of the following changes to your e-mail, you write down all of the information you plan to replace in case you need to use the original e-mail account.

Note
GeoCities e-mail does not use capital letters. When making changes to your e-mail account, all text should be entered in lowercase letters.

It's important to know that to send and receive your GeoCities e-mail you must set up your Web browser or other e-mail client to communicate properly with the GeoCities servers.

Netscape Instructions

CAUTION

Netscape Settings Change by Version

The instructions here tell you how to set up Netscape 4.*x* to read your GeoCities mail. Older (and potentially future) versions of Netscape's e-mail client may cause changes to the location of the menu commands or have slightly different dialog boxes or field labels. In general, the instructions for setting up e-mail are the same for all versions of Netscape (and other browsers); however, the Mail Preferences option, for example, may be located in a different place depending on the version of Netscape used.

To configure Netscape to access your GeoCities mail, follow these steps:

1. Open your Netscape account and click on the Edit menu on the Netscape menu bar. From the Edit drop-down menu, choose Preferences, as shown in Figure 14.1.

Figure 14.1
Choose Preferences from the Edit menu.

2. The Preferences dialog box appears. In the category box, click on the "+" sign next to Mail & Groups. Then click on the Identity link under Mail & Groups.

3. In the Identity box, fill in your name and GeoCities e-mail address and the Reply-to address (if it is different from your e-mail address).

4. When you are finished with this page, click on the **Mail Server** link under Mail & Groups.

5. On the Mail Server page, fill out your information. In the Mail Server User Name box, type in your GeoCities member name. In the Outgoing Mail (SMTP) Server and the Incoming Mail Server box, enter **mail.geocities.com,** as shown in Figure 14.2. When you finish these fields, click on the **More Options** button to fill out more information.

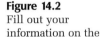

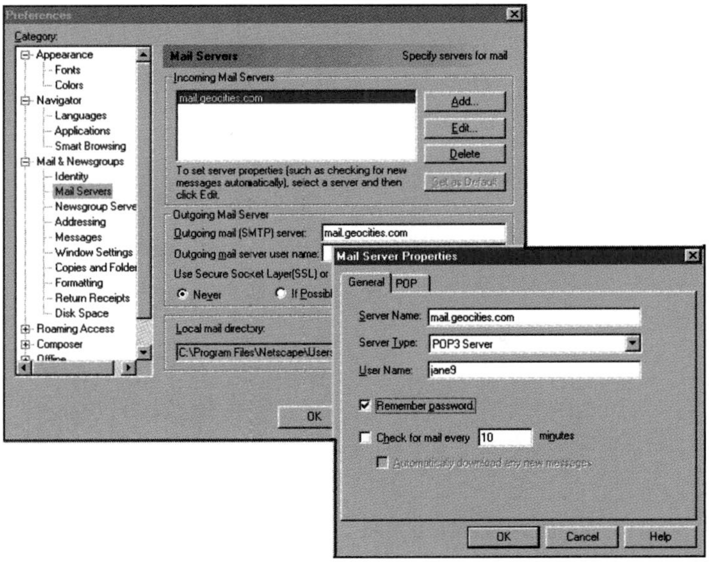

Figure 14.2
Fill out your information on the Mail Server page.

6. In the More Options box, the Local Mail Directory box can remain with the default directory from Netscape, or you can click the Choose button and enter the location where you want your mail stored. Check boxes for Mail options seem limitless. To make things easier, check the box Remember my mail password. That way you won't have to type it in every time you check your e-mail.

7. Click **OK** to enter all of these changes to your account and return to the Mail Server page. Click **OK** again when all the information is entered. Your Netscape browser is now ready.

8. To check your e-mail, click on the **Communicator** menu and choose **Messenger Mailbox**. When the Messenger Mailbox appears, click on the **Get Msg** (messages) button and the Password Entry dialog box will appear. Type your GeoCities password into the box and click **OK**. If you have new messages, they will appear.

Outlook Express Instructions

To configure Outlook Express to access your GeoCities Mail, follow these steps:

1. Start Outlook Express and click on **Tools** on the menu bar. In the drop-down menu, select **Accounts,** as shown in Figure 14.3.

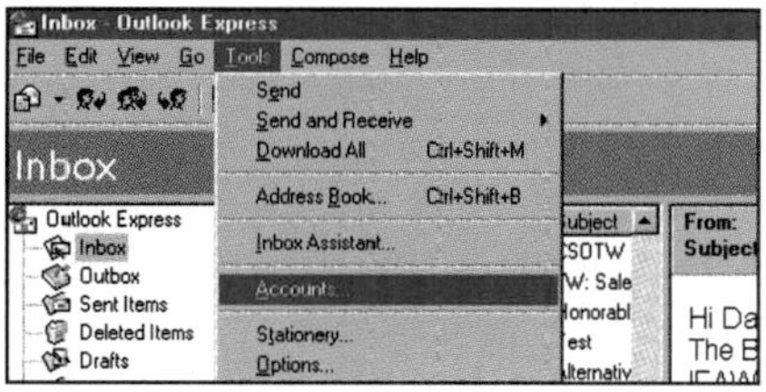

Figure 14.3
Select **Accounts**
from the Tools menu
to configure your
e-mail.

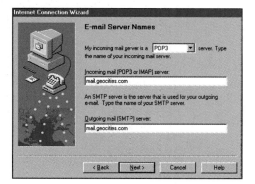

2.   The Internet Accounts dialog box opens. If the Mail tab is not
     selected, click on it now.

3.   Click on the **Add** button and select **Mail** from the drop-down menu,
     as shown in Figure 14.4.

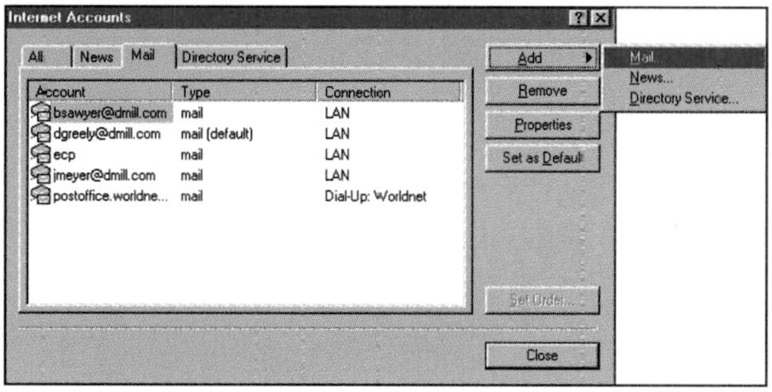

Figure 14.4
Click on the **Add**
button and select
Mail.

4.   You will be taken through a step-by-step process in the Internet
     Connection Wizard. Type your name into the Display Name box and
     then click the Next button to go to the next page.

5.   For the e-mail address, type in your GeoCities e-mail address
     (**membername@geocities.com**). Click on the **Next** button to go to the
     next page.

6.   POP3 is the choice for the first box on the E-mail Server Names page.
     Type **mail.geocities.com** into the Outgoing Mail and Incoming Mail
     boxes, as shown in Figure 14.5. Click the **Next** button to go to the
     next page.

Figure 14.5
The E-mail Server
Names page.

7. Choose **Log On,** to decide how you want to log on to the Internet. Type your member name into the POP (Point of Presence) account name box. In the Password box, enter your GeoCities password. Click the **Next** button to go to the next page.

8. The Friendly Name page should be filled out for you from the other information you have already entered. If it is not, type **mail.geocities.com** into the empty box. Click the **Next** button to go to the next page.

9. On the Choose Connection Type page, select which connection you want to use. For most people, the connection will be made using a phone line. Click the **Next** button to go to the next page.

10. The Congratulations page appears, stating that "You have successfully entered all of the information required to set up your account." To save these settings, click the **Finish** button. If you entered all the information correctly, **mail.geocities.com** should appear in your Internet Accounts dialog box, as shown in Figure 14.6.

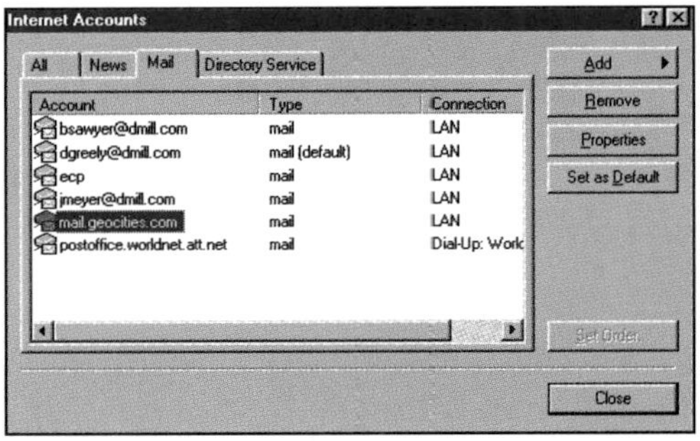

Figure 14.6
When "mail.geocities.com" appears in your Internet account box, your e-mail is set up.

Other Mail Packages

Besides Outlook Express and Netscape Mail, you can use just about any other e-mail package to read and access your GeoCities mail account. Each mail program has its own set of commands that you need to follow in order to configure your mail properly, as long as you enter your account information into it.

Here's a summary list of the important pieces of data that you'll need to configure your GeoCities mail account:

Username:	Your GeoCities member name (for example, jane9)
Password:	Your GeoCities password
E-mail Address:	membername@geocities.com
Incoming Mail Server:	mail.geocities.com
Outgoing Mail Server:	mail.geocities.com

If you have problems receiving your e-mail, your first stop should be the GeoCities e-mail troubleshooting guide, located at **http://www.geocities.com/members/help/guide_email_receive.html.**

E-mail Limitations

GeoCities free e-mail program has received an overwhelming response. Because of this, GeoCities has had to put a few limitations on its member e-mail program.

▶ **Any mail left on the server for more than seven days will be deleted.** This can be remedied by saving your important e-mail somewhere else on your computer or by configuring your e-mail client to remove the e-mail and place it somewhere else after a certain length of time.

Your GeoCities e-mail account has a 500 kilobyte maximum of mailbox space at any given time. This should be plenty if you download and remove all your e-mail from the server in a timely manner.

▶ **All incoming mail messages must be checked before you can send outgoing mail.** Recently GeoCities set up a new system for outgoing messages that is meant to help thwart spammers from using GeoCities e-mail addresses as spam servers. This limitation makes it impossible to send out an email until you first check and retrieve your mail. When you check and retrieve your mail, GeoCities activates your outgoing mail for a total of fifteen minutes. If you try to send messages before checking for mail, you will receive an error.

For more on this new e-mail protocol rule see the rules page at: **http://www.geocities.com/main/info/system/email_faq.html.**

Chats and Forums

Among the many benefits of being a GeoCities member is that you can use the GeoCities chat rooms. One advantage of chatting is that you can leave a main chat room and form a private chat room, where you can invite whomever you like by simply giving the room a name and then telling your friends to stop by that room. You are also able to send private messages to anyone in the chat room. In addition, you can create a public room at any time and invite current chatters to join you there.

While you're in public chat rooms, you can still conduct private conversations with multiple people. If you don't want to participate in the chat, but want to see what everyone else has to say, you can just sit in the room and be a silent observer. You can also be a speaker during special interest chats.

If a chat room reaches the 30-person maximum, a duplicate room will be created. You can move from room to room without having to log on repeatedly.

Unlike chat, forums aren't real-time. The advantage is that messages can go back and forth and people can log on over time to interact, trade opinions, or help each other out.

In the forums, you can get answers to questions on a wide variety of topics or just have a conversation. There are links to the forums from the GeoCities home page and from each of the Neighborhoods. Each Neighborhood has its own forums and topics that you can explore to find answers to questions or just to make new friends. If you post or reply to an article, you can list your e-mail address so others can respond directly to you.

Using Chat

Using chat is not difficult. At the bottom of the GeoCities home page, choose the **Chat** link, which takes you to the Chat page (or type in **http://www.geocities.com/cgi-bin/chat/chat_entry**). Here you must choose the chat software you want to use, pick a chat to participate in, and select a username for yourself for the session of chat (Figure 14.7).

Figure 14.7
The Chat Log-on page.

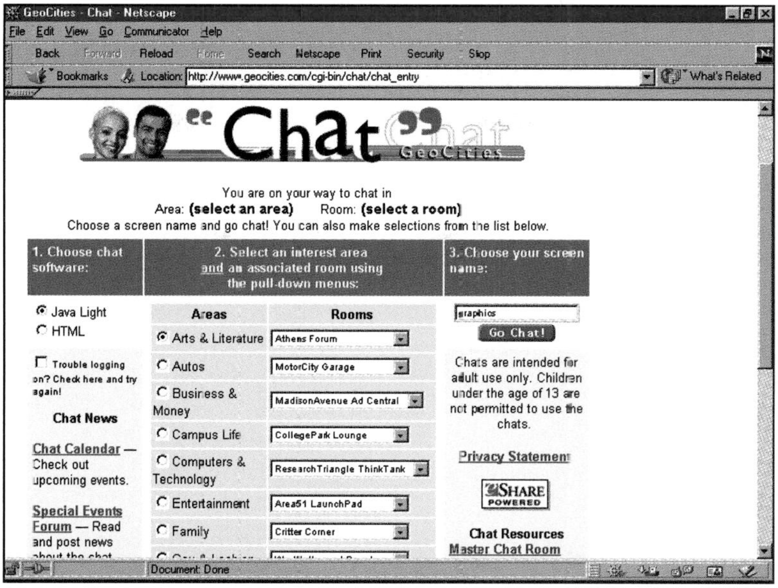

Part IV Beyond Homesteading

Most chat users choose Java Light, but if you experience problems with Java or have a lower-end machine, you can choose HTML. The Java chat is more interactive and easier to use, if your machine can support it. Select the area that interests you and the associated room. Enter your screen name and click **Go Chat,** which sends you to the selected room as shown in Figure 14.8.

Figure 14.8
Participating in a chat is a unique experience!

Once in the chat, type in what you would like to say in the box near the bottom of the screen and hit **Send** to enter your message into the conversation.

Make sure you look through the menu bar in the top right-hand corner of the chat screen. From here you can visit other chat rooms, look through a chat calendar, find a specific user, get some chat assistance, or exit chat entirely.

TIP

Private Messages Are Fine

To send a private message, click on that person's name in the box on the right-hand side of the chat box. Click on the **Users Option** button to open the User Option dialog box.

Enter the private message in the Private Message text box and click the **Submit** button to send the message.

If someone sends you a private message, it will appear in red text on your screen. Click on the **Help** button on the bottom of the chat page to go to the chat help page where you can get all sorts of chat information.

Creating a Private Chat Room

To create a private chat room, enter a specific chat room as described above. Upon reaching the chat area, select **Create Chat Room** from the menu bar in the top-right corner of your chat screen. GeoCities brings up a box titled **User Created Rooms** (Figure 14.9).

Figure 14.9
Create your own chat room.

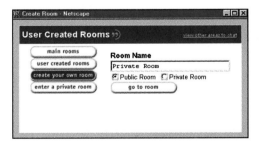

Type in a name for your private room, click on the **Private Room** radio button and then click on **go to room** from this window. Alternatively, you can also use this window to join someone else's private room or return back to the main chat room.

To invite people into your private room, pick **Users in Area** from the menu bar in the top right-hand corner of your private room. When the All Users page appears, as shown in Figure 14.10, find the person with whom you want to chat and send a private message by clicking on the **Private Message** button and telling him or her the name of the room.

Figure 14.10
Invite people to join your private chat.

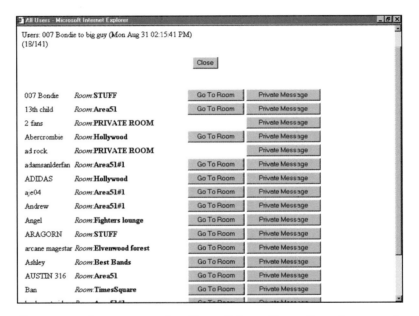

To enter a private room, select **Enter Private Room** from the menu bar in the chat area. When the Create Chat Room dialog box appears, click on the button labeled **Enter a Private Room**. In the Room Name box, type in the exact name of the desired room.

Entering Other Chats

If you want to enter a different chat, select **Other Chat Areas** from the chat menu bar and a window listing all of the available options appears. Click on the chat room you wish to join and you'll be taken there automatically.

Using Forums

Choose the **Forums** link at the bottom of the GeoCities home page, located at **http://www.geocities.com/features/forums/**. The Forums page appears and asks you to log on using a username (Figure 14.11). Click on the **Go To Forums** button to enter the Forums area. (For more information about the Forums Guidelines or Troubleshooting Help, click on the **Forums Info** link underneath the User Name.)

Figure 14.11
Forums are good for conversation.

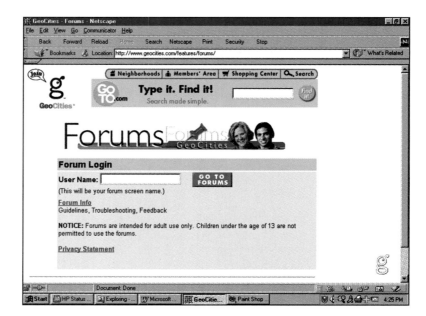

You'll find a list of options on the right side of the yellow forums bar. The first option is an X with the word "Exit" next to it; click here when you want to leave the Forums area. Below it is the Help link, which is useful when you have a question dealing with the Forums area. The bottom option allows you to turn the frames on or off.

The Search link is useful if you need help finding a particular topic. To return to the forums area from any of these links, click on the **Forums** link.

To enter or get involved with any of the forums, first check out the list of all the available forums. The list includes a brief description of each forum and the number of articles it contains. To see the topics included within the forums, click on the "+" sign beside that forum. Choose the topic that interests you by clicking on the topic title.

After you've clicked on the topic you desire, you will be presented with a list of articles, as shown in Figure 14.12.

Figure 14.12
Choose an article from the forum list.

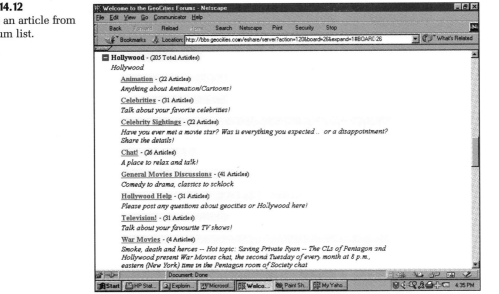

Click on the title of any article that interests you to read the messages, as shown in Figure 14.13.

Figure 14.13
Read through the forum messages.

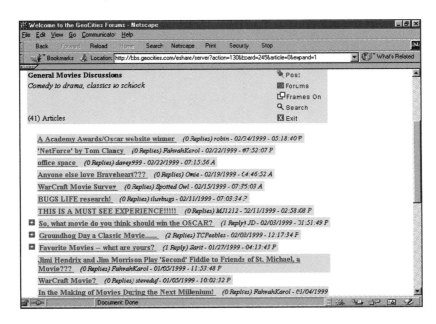

You can scroll through the messages by clicking on the Previous/Up Arrow or the Next/Down Arrow, as shown in Figure 14.14.

Figure 14.14
Scroll through the messages to read them.

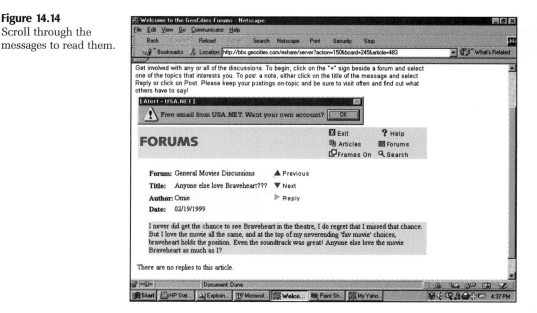

To reply to a specific message, click on the **Reply** button (a right arrow) underneath the Previous and Next arrows.

To post a note, click on the **Post** link on the menu bar above the list of articles. Once you click on a specific article, you will have to return to the previous page to post your own note. You can only reply to messages when you are at a specific article.

TIP

GeoCities asks that you "Please keep your postings on-topic." In other words, don't go to a pro-football forum to offer your thoughts on the new Marilyn Manson album.

Working with GeoTickets and GeoPoints

GeoCities offers Homesteaders chances to earn discounts on items and win online raffles. Depending on the success of your site and services you install (such as the GeoGuide), members earn GeoPoints (think frequent-flyer miles) and GeoTickets (virtual tickets to win monthly raffles).

To buy items in the GeoMarketplace, you can choose from a number of different options: You can purchase the item for the retail price, or if you are a GeoPlus member, you can purchase the item at a discount. You can also use your accumulated GeoPoints, which you can earn by having a featured page or becoming a Community Leader or Banner Volunteer.

> **TIP**
> **Double Your Pleasure**
> GeoPlus members earn double GeoPoints.

Placing a GeoGuide on your site allows you to earn GeoTickets. For each qualified impression (that is a unique visit to your page where the entire page displays) that you receive on a page containing a GeoGuide, you will earn GeoTickets.

At the end of each month, GeoTickets are removed from your account and placed in GeoCities' monthly drawings for special prizes. The prizes change each month and include anything from scanners to digital cameras to products that help you build a better GeoCities site. Don't be alarmed if you check your GeoTickets total and all your GeoTickets have disappeared. GeoCities has simply entered you into the monthly drawing.

You will be informed of your GeoTickets total by e-mail on a semi-monthly basis. If you want to check your total yourself, go to **http://www.geocities.com/members/tools/profile_editor.html** and check out the section labeled GeoCities Account Balance (Figure 14.15). You'll see a current total of GeoTickets and GeoPoints.

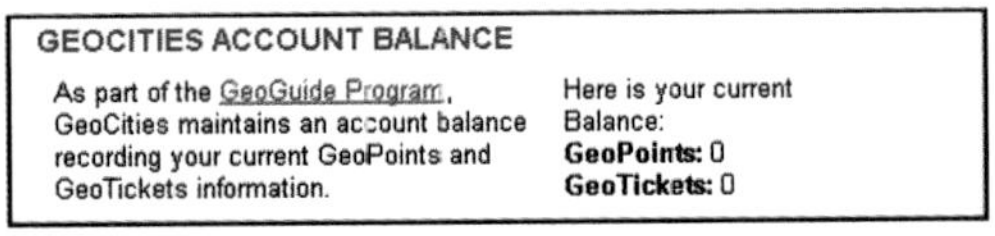

Figure 14.15
No GeoTickets or
GeoPoints this month.

GEOCITIES ACCOUNT BALANCE

As part of the GeoGuide Program, GeoCities maintains an account balance recording your current GeoPoints and GeoTickets information.

Here is your current Balance:
GeoPoints: 0
GeoTickets: 0

Shopping with Your GeoPoints

Starting at the GeoCities home page, click on the **Shopping Center** link (**http://www.geocities.com/Shopping_Center/**). Upon arriving at the Shopping Center you can shop for a variety of items through GeoCities. To use your GeoPoints, click on the button labeled **Marketplace** (**http://www.geocities.com/marketplace/**)and then **GeoStore**. Items here can be purchased with cash or through GeoPoints that you have accrued.

Upon entering the quantity of the item you want to purchase, click on the **Add to Shopping Cart** button on the bottom of the page.

GeoCities has an online shopping cart that allows you to add items to your basket and pay for them at one time. Once you are finished shopping, the shopping cart will indicate what items you have requested and the quantity of each item desired. The total should be blank if you used enough GeoPoints. However, you will have to pay shipping and handling charges, which will be calculated once you enter the shipping address. Then you'll see a grand total, which will be only the amount of the shipping and handling charges if you use your GeoPoints to pay for your purchase.

Sticking to the Rules: the Responsibilities, Dos and Don'ts of GeoCities

▶ **You are responsible for the entire contents of your site, and not infringing on others rights**—If you violate the terms of your service agreement, your site (or at least the portion of your site that is in violation) will be either removed permanently or suspended. GeoCities is not responsible for your actions and reserves the right to delete any portion of your site.

▶ **GeoCities is not responsible for any illegal use of material protected by copyright, trademark, patent, or trade secret law**—Members can be held legally liable for their sites. GeoCities does not allow any individual advertising or sponsors, or selling of products or services on any of its sites except GeoShops and its affiliated programs (to sell books and music online). The GeoGuide banners are the only banners allowed to appear on a GeoCities page.

▶ **Geocities doesn't censor sites but some things are unacceptable**— That said, let it be clear that GeoCities is not out to censor sites but has set rules that are in line with societal norms. GeoCities does not allow any of its members to display pornography or nudity, racism, prejudice, profanity, bigotry, or any material that is grossly offensive. GeoCities also does not tolerate the promotion of or instruction related to any illegal activity. Defamation of any group or individual is not allowed.

▶ **You can only engage in approved commerce opportunities. You can't run marketing schemes or collect information for illegal or marketing purposes**—GeoCities also has strict rules against its members using sites to participate in multilevel marketing or pyramid schemes on any level. Members must also refrain from using GeoCities in the capacity to gather personally identifiable information for illegal or commercial purposes.

Although only GeoShops members are allowed to sell items directly on their sites, Homesteaders can participate in Associates Programs with any affiliated store. For a list of participating affiliated stores, consult the GeoCities site. For more on Associate Programs, see Chapter 10, "Adding Special Effects to Your Pages."

▶ **You can't exploit children**—GeoCities will not allow anyone to display any kind of material that exploits children. You also cannot link to or provide pirated computer programs or cracker utilities on your site. Your site cannot be used as storage for remote loading or door signpost to another home page. You also cannot violate Internet standards in the promotion of your site.

You are also not to collect personal information from children for purposes of posting any identifiable information that belongs to children.

▶ **You can't have multiple sites**—You are not allowed to have multiple GeoCities addresses in the same Neighborhood or with the same theme. You are also not allowed to create home pages or session posts that contain hyperlinks to content which violates GeoCities standards.

> **Note**
>
> **A Note for Children and Parents**
>
> Do not put your real name, address, phone number, e-mail address, or similar information on your Website or give any of this information to a stranger.

When You Agree, You Agree

When you click "I Agree" on the Membership Application page, you are indicating that that you have read all the terms of service and guidelines and that you agree to create your site under GeoCities terms.

For a more detailed account of the members' terms of services and guidelines for all of the different aspects of GeoCities, go to the GeoCities Guideline Introduction page. Click on the link to any of the other Terms of Service or Guidelines pages in which you are interested. The address is **http://www.geocities.com/members/guidelines/**. You can also read the Terms of Service section on the Application page.

Special E-mail Rules

Your e-mail account is yours to use freely, but GeoCities asks that you not use it for "spamming" newsgroups or individuals, conducting unwanted solicitations of groups or individuals, harassing or threatening anyone, or conducting any illegal activities.

Special Chat and Forums Rules

As a member of GeoCities, you are responsible for your actions while you are in a chat or forums session and agree not to violate any of the content guidelines. You agree not to harass, embarrass, cause distress or discomfort, or threaten in any way another party using this service. You are not to use comments reflecting bigotry, racism, or hatred, or profanity.

While using the GeoCities chat or forums, you are also not to transmit any data or information that will violate the home page and chat and forum content guidelines, nor can you have anything to do with any activity that results in disruption of the chat and forums service.

GeoCities also strictly forbids the impersonation of any person, such as a GeoCities staff member or Community Leader. The chat rooms and forums are not to be used to transmit any unsolicited advertising, promotional material, and so on. Teenagers and children should never offer any personal information to strangers while using one of these services. For a more detailed version of these guidelines, go to **http://www.geocities.com/members/guidelines/guideline.html**.

Getting Help from GeoCities

GeoCities offers a help guide, located at **http://www.geocities.com/main/help/** or by clicking on the **Help** link at the bottom of the GeoCities home page. Here you can find links to other help-related topics such as Help Forum, Help Chat, and Help Guide, as shown in Figure 14.16.

Figure 14.16
Links to help topics.

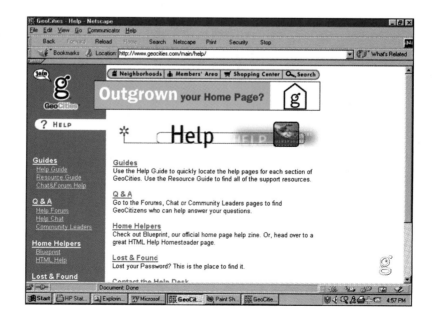

Each Neighborhood has Community Leaders—volunteers who can be found in each Neighborhood. Most of these volunteers are longtime GeoCities members who know the inner workings of their community. To reach a Community Leader, click on the **Neighborhood** link on the home page, choose your Neighborhood page, then click on the **Community Leader** link under the Getting Involved section. You can then contact your Neighborhood's leader.

You can also reach a Community Leader by going to the Ask the Experts page. GeoCities tries to have this page staffed 24 hours a day.

If you are interested in becoming a Community Leader or want more information, go to **http://www.geocities.com/join/comm_leader.html**. Although Community Leaders aren't paid, they do receive some perks, including monthly GeoPoints and additional disk space. Community Leaders are responsible for answering e-mailed questions, identifying the best sites in the Neighborhood, and making sure the Neighborhood's sites follow the GeoCities guidelines.

Forums and Chat areas each include specific sections that are dedicated to helping GeoCities members in need. In the GeoCities chat, you'll find a specific Help chat room. Its sole purpose is to answer questions from those who need help. However, if you like browsing through other people's problems to find the answer to yours, go to the Forums area and check out all the different topics available in the help forum, as shown in Figures 14.17 and 14.18.

Figure 14.17
Get help through the forum help topics.

Part IV   Beyond Homesteading

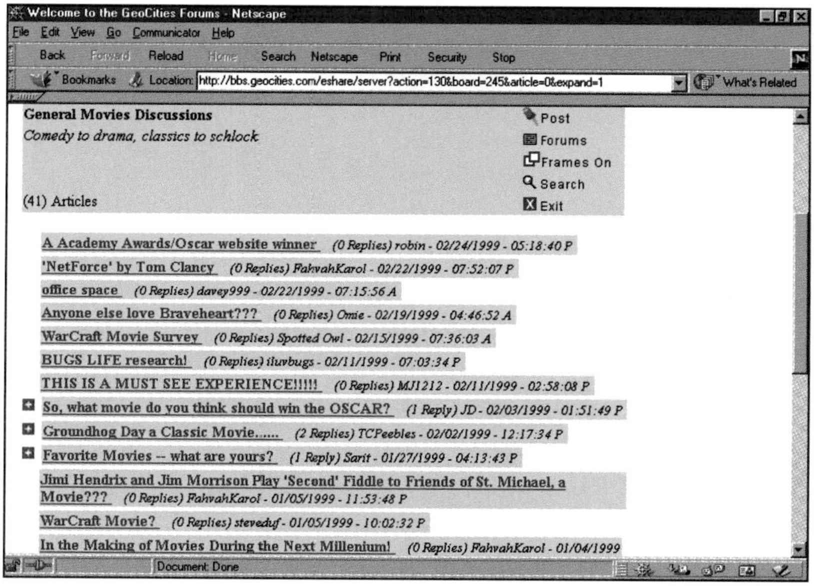

Figure 14.18
Use forum subtopics
to get more help with
forums.

GeoCities has also authored an online magazine, called *Blueprint*, that can be found at **http://www.geocities.com/main/help/Blueprint/**. This magazine is the official GeoCities home page help 'Zine. The magazine is written almost completely by GeoCities members. It offers tips to improve your site and free graphics to put on it. If you're having technical problems, *Blueprint* is a great place to find the answers.

GeoCities also provides its members with help tutorials. These can all be found in *Blueprint*, along with core columns, featured columns, and tools. Some of the Homesteaders have even used their free sites to do nothing except help other members.

Moving On

It would be easy for GeoCities to be nothing more than free home pages. GeoCities, however, has always seen itself as more than just a home page service; it really is an online community and comprehensive service. With chat, forums, e-mail, and various chances for members to earn free stuff, GeoCities goes far beyond what most people picture at first glance. Resourceful GeoCities members learn that to get the most out of GeoCities, you need to venture beyond the HTML editors and your own home page. As this chapter and the next few chapters will show you, you'll find a wealth of additional tools and services to make the most of your membership when you step out into the GeoCities world.

15

Outstanding GeoCities Sites

Make no mistake about it; not all GeoCities sites are created equal. Some people simply have more experience, more time, or more interest in creating above-average GeoCities Web sites. That isn't to say that most of them don't have something to offer—some just offer a little bit extra.

With roughly 3.5 million members, GeoCities is the home of sites that range from the good to the bad to the ugly. And, with so many sites to study, we would never claim that those mentioned in this chapter are the absolute best. In fact, we can almost guarantee that we have missed some great sites. The objective of this chapter is to provide a variety of examples from which you can learn.

Medspeak–The ER Dictionary

http://www.geocities.com/TelevisionCity/5196/

Since January 1997, Stephen Suhocki's site (shown in Figure 15.1) has made it easier for the fans of the TV series *ER* to understand what George Clooney's and Anthony Edwards' characters are talking about by defining complex medical terms mentioned in the show. For example, the site defines terms from *abduction* (moving a limb or some other body part away from the midline of the body) to *The Whipple Procedure* (a pancreaticoduodenectomy, where the distal stomach, gallbladder, and duodenum are usually also taken out during the surgery, usually leaving a little of the distal pancreas behind). And of course, the often-mentioned *CBC* and *Chem 7*.

Figure 15.1

Medspeak offers a
unique version of a
fan site.

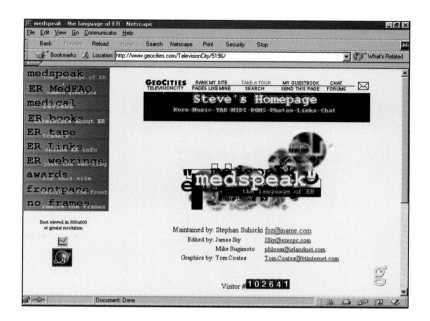

What Can We Learn from Medspeak?

This site is a good example of how focusing on unique information about a very popular topic can be successful. Sites of this nature tend to cater to hardcore fans of the material and hardcore fans want really deep information. In the case of Medspeak, it's actually an *ER* fan site; but rather than simply fighting with the rest of the typical fan sites for visitors by using photos and cast bios, this site developed a core set of information in which real fans of the show will be very interested.

Medspeak teaches that if you're looking to build a site for a passionate niche audience, a good piece of original content that complements their main interest can become the centerpiece of your site. From there you can build out, adding other information fans will typically want. In Medspeak's case, you come to the site as an ER fan looking for the dictionary, but then you stay because the site also includes links, reviews of past episodes, an *ER* bookstore, and information about watching *ER* online. Who needs four years of medical school to know what the doctors on *ER* are doing? (Just don't try to open your own practice!)

The other good thing about Medspeak is that, by offering this uniquely different approach to *ER* fan sites, it provides a useful reason for all the other *ER* fan sites to link to it. As you will learn, sites with a similar focus are more likely to link to yours when your site offers their fans something they don't have.

The Ultimate Bad Candy Web Site

http://www.geocities.com/NapaValley/2066/

"Where bad candy comes to die. . ." Since July 1997, this site (shown in Figure 15.2) has been rating bad candy and entertaining visitors with banter and colorful graphics. Ratings range from "Almost tolerable, semi-edible" to "The ultimate horror; hell on Earth."

We'll let you visit the site and get the skinny from the experts—Mark and Ben. Also check out The Hall of Stupid Letters, written to Mark and Ben by "people who make us want to stay in bed forever."

This site certainly deals with a topic that hasn't been saturated with Web coverage. It's also funny and we like to laugh.

Figure 15.2

Besides the humor and off-beat topic, getting to know the hosts makes The Ultimate Bad Candy Web Site a great idea to mimic.

What Can We Learn from The Ultimate Bad Candy Web Site?

At first glance the lesson you might take home from this site is that humor and an informative topic are a good mix. Once you dig a little deeper, however, you'll discover the real lesson you can learn from this site. Ultimate Bad Candy is a great example of how a site's creators can become central characters in the site's story. The real attraction to the site is Mark and Ben—their pictures and personal agonies while trying the bad candies—not the ultimate bad candies.

This site is like a good sitcom in which Mark and Ben are the stars you want to know more and more about. That's because the more you find out about them and their exploits, the more you laugh.

Web sites—especially personal home pages on GeoCities—are great places for people to learn about you. When you can reveal yourself in a way that is placed within an informative subject, you have a potent mix. In fact. that's how a huge Web site, The Motley Fool (**http://www.fool.com),** began. The two founders mixed financial and stock news with their own stories and irreverent humor. People flocked to their site as much because of the founders' stories as to get useful stock and financial information.

You can attract plenty of visitors to your site, too, by turning yourself into a compelling character on your site. The mistake some people make (which Mark and Ben avoid) is building the site's subject or story around themselves as well, rather than focusing on a fun topic like Bad Candy.

Stooge's NASCAR Page

http://www.geocities.com/MotorCity/1071/

Auto-racing fans (and a lot of them are out there) always complain that their sport is overlooked in favor of minor sports like football, basketball, and baseball. Since March 1996, "Stooge" (shown in Figure 15.3) has been offering racing news, driver profiles, race results, and photos.

The most popular page offers Stooge's commentary on the week's race. You'll also find a comment board, a chat room, and plenty more. So if you aren't satisfied with ESPN's NASCAR coverage, there's always Stooge.

Figure 15.3

Instead of complaining about poor media coverage of auto racing, Stooge did something about it.

What Can We Learn from Stooge's NASCAR Page?

This page is a great lesson in motivation. Building a Web site is a lot of work; you need to be motivated in order to do it right. And that motivation has to come through in some form on the site so you can connect with your visitors.

The best motivation often stems from the frustration of not finding something you wish you had. In the case of Stooge's site, we encounter a person who is deeply passionate about NASCAR racing. Only someone like Stooge could build a NASCAR site chock-full of the amount and kind of information only a truly motivated person could create and maintain. All you have to do is spend a few minutes at Stooge's site and you'll be engaged by his passion and the sheer amount of insider depth he displays.

What you learn from this site most of all is that the prettiest graphics and the coolest layout in the world won't guarantee an infectious site, but determination rooted in passion does. Think of the subjects about which you are most passionate and follow those online. Even if other sites focus on that subject, too, your exceptional motivation and passion for your subject will make good things happen.

Steve Schalchlin–Using a Web Site to Tell a Story

http://www.geocities.com/Broadway/1173/

The Steve Schalchlin site shown in Figure 15.4 is an excellent example of a page that's enthralling without being visually stunning. Steve's story of battling and conquering AIDS resulted in a special appreciation for life that pervades his music and performance art. Since March of 1996, Steve has been telling Homesteaders about his victory over AIDS, his new career, and his religion. He has an incredible story to tell and tells it well.

Figure 15.4
Steve's site shares his story with the rest of the world.

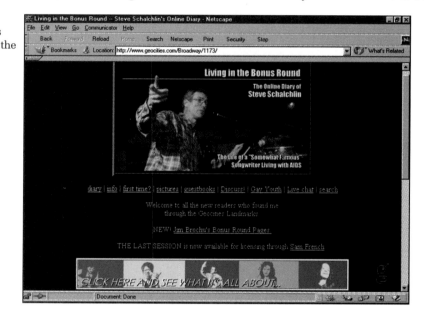

What Can We Learn from Steve Schalchlin's Site?

One compelling aspect of the Web is people and their stories. How do you go about telling your story in a compelling way, using the Web and your GeoCities site to make it entertaining and a format that makes it engaging? You can see how Steve does this by visiting his site.

Of course, Steve's site starts with a compelling story and a compelling person, but plenty of other sites that start with great people and stories don't work so well. Steve's page works because his site effectively uses the power of the Web to tell the story. His most effective tool is a daily diary chronicling his entire life with AIDS.

When creating a personal story site, a diary is a great way to use the Web. Your fans will appreciate the daily updates and the chance to watch the story unfold, page to page. In addition, as with any personal story site, the quality of the written content—what you have to say—is important.

Steve's site displays quality writing and something worth writing about. He then rounds out his site with an important counterpart to the focus on himself and his life—interactive elements. By using the guestbook, chat, and message boards, visitors who spend time learning about Steve can post information about themselves and how they relate to the content Steve created.

The Web is a good one-way medium, but it's an even better two-way medium. If you're building a site, remember that giving people a forum to respond to you creates a richer experience for them. GeoCities offers guestbooks and chat rooms that you can use to do more than just tell people about yourself.

The Web is without doubt a great place to express yourself but, as we learn from Steve Schalchlin, it is even better when people can respond to what you're expressing and share their own thoughts.

ASCII ART

http://www.geocities.com/SoHo/7373/

ASCII artwork (Figure 15.5) is created by using the symbols and characters on your keyboard—"non-graphical graphics," as the site says. You may have received some humorous examples of ASCII art through e-mail, but this site takes it to higher levels. The site includes cartoon characters, animals, season items, people/creatures, and a number of other pieces of ASCII art. Some of these pieces of art are truly impressive and may well be worth adding to your site.

Figure 15.5
It's a bird, it's a plane, it's ASCII Art!

What Can We Learn from ASCII Art?

At first you learn from ASCII Art that a great niche topic makes for a great Web site when it's done right. That's a simple lesson you probably learned a long time ago when you started spending time on the Web.

ASCII Art, however, is more than just an informative site; it's a powerful tutorial. It's also a great archive. All sites are educational to a point, but ASCII Art actually teaches you *how to do* something rather than just teaching you *about* something.

People often turn to the Web to learn how to do various things. However, not every site that claims to do this actually does a good job at it. ASCII Art succeeds by including lots of examples and well-written text that clearly explains the history, resources, and tips you'll need to become a skilled ASCII artist.

As an archive, ASCII Art includes hundreds of individual ASCII art drawings. Archives—whether they're ASCII art, sound effects, or old sayings—are a popular draw. The best archives are a source of information or items that a fan of the subject matter can use. What makes a good archive? Well, look through ASCII Art and you'll see that the archive is well organized into clear categories that make it easy to find what you want. In addition, ASCII Art's archive contains high-quality work that fans and students of ASCII Art can use. If you're planning to build an archive of some sort, you will benefit greatly by studying the way ASCII Art does it.

Myla

http://www.geocities.com/Hollywood/Hills/2844/

Myla's site is a beautiful, professional-looking home to information on actress Meryl Streep, actor/rebel James Dean, and some of Myla's favorite inspirational quotes. The site includes some wonderful photos, filmographies, and other information about both Dean and Streep. The site includes more than 600 inspirational quotes (see Figure 15.6).

Figure 15.6
Execution does count,
as visitors to Myla's fan
sites are sure to notice.

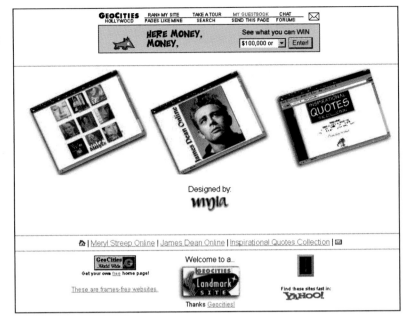

What Can We Learn from Myla's Sites?

In discussing some previous sites in this chapter, we noted how good fan sites show a passion for their subject and provide lots of worthwhile information. Myla's two fan sites on Meryl Streep and James Dean follow that formula successfully. In her other site of Quotations, we find a fun and useful archive.

The additional lesson with Myla's site, however, is that execution does count for something. As you surf through all three sites, you can see that a lot of time and care have gone into the physical design of the graphics and page layout.

Myla's site has been at GeoCities since September 1996, despite being courted by just about every site provider around. Whoever said free home pages can't be highly polished hasn't visited Myla's. As Myla's illustrates, great design, art selection, and content can really help your site. The main page is well done, with a nice graphic leading to each section. The three sections are similarly attractive and clean. You'll also notice that Myla changes the size and shade of the plain text on the site a bit to create a little variety in the design without resorting to graphics. Yet at the same time she uses some sporadic text rendered as a graphic to create headings and large quotes that stand out and help break up long batches of writing. This is a great trick that gives you variety in your Web presentation along with short download times.

Myla's art skills are excellent, but close examination of her graphics show that they're not complex creations. This should suggest to you that creating good Web design and art isn't so complex that you need a Fine Arts degree to create nice titles and appealing photography and text.

Kids' Place

http://www.geocities.com/EnchantedForest/3696/

The Kids' Place (see Figure 15.7) is a favorite of children as well as adults who have children. It's all about safe surfing for all ages, from message boards and chat to art and HTML lessons. The club has been at GeoCities since January 1997.

Figure 15.7
The Kids' Place features the online equivalent to a real children's clubhouse.

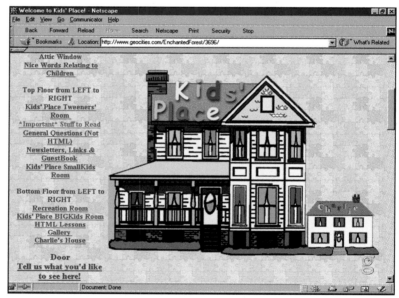

What Can We Learn from the Kids' Place Site?

A great way to organize your site is to use a motif that relates to the site's subject or audience.

Depending on the nature of your site, a cool motif-based design can be a great way to organize your site and make it easy for visitors to use. In some cases, the motif might actually help you figure out all the areas you might include on your site. For example, if you were building a fan site about a baseball team, you might choose a stadium motif. This might help you brainstorm ideas for content to match major areas of a baseball stadium. For example, you might have the team's record pop up when visitors click on the scoreboard, rosters appear when they click on the dugouts, and so on.

In the case of Kids' Place, the site is set up like a clubhouse. The main clubhouse is actually an image map that visitors click on to get to various sections of the site. For example, The Recreation Room includes links to sports, entertainment, games, books, and such. There is also an HTML Center with lessons, a message forum, and a gallery of members' work that includes stories, poems, drawings, and more.

Northern Gardening

http://www.geocities.com/RainForest/1329/

With 19 years of "hands-on" experience, Terry Yockey has provided gardeners with a practical resource guide in "Northern Gardening." This informative homestead shown in Figure 15.8 will help even those who don't exactly have a green thumb to grow beautiful plants and flowers. And Terry practices what she preaches. When asked whether she actually grows the plants she talks about, Terry says, "If a plant is mentioned in one of my articles, it has proven its hardiness in my own northern gardens."

Figure 15.8
Northern Gardening offers nice pictures and tons of gardening information.

What Can We Learn from Northern Gardening?

This is a good example of a site that provides extensive, useful information for a specific group of people. Sites like this tend to be built not only by people who have a passion for the subject matter, but who have an incredible depth of knowledge. While GeoCities doesn't allow for explicit marketing, one thing to take away from this site is how your knowledge (in this case Terry Yockey's 19+ years of gardening knowledge) can shine through implicitly on the Web. This site, while beneficial to all who visit it, is an attractive resume and brochure for people who might want to compensate you for your expertise. For example, what's to stop a publisher of gardening books, or a gardening show from coming across this site and making an offer for its author to host a show, or write a book?

By plowing (pun intended) your knowledge into a personal site like Terry has done, you create an incredible calling card for people, businesses and others searching for people with demonstrated levels of expertise.

The N-Files

http://www.geocities.com/Area51/5180/

Nicolas Stohler (Agent N) of Switzerland has constructed an attractive site (shown in Figure 15.9) that plays off the logo and feel of *The X-Files* television show. Not surprisingly, the site includes a section on the popular television drama with pictures, sounds, links, and an episode guide.

Although the entire site is not devoted to *The X-Files* (it includes pages about the creator, for example), it does stay with the dark, spooky theme of the show.

Figure 15.9
The N-Files—conveying the mood of its subject.

What Can We Learn from the N-Files?

What makes the N-Files a neat page to learn from is that instead of producing a simple "What about Me" page, Nicolas Stohler created a entertaining way to tell the world more about himself. Site designers frequently use their home pages to put up three or four pages that talk about themselves—what they like to do or read, where they've been, and so on. However, if the page isn't done with a little creative flair, even the most interesting people can seem a little boring.

Nicolas found a way to prevent his site from being nothing more than just another personal-stat-and-interest site. At the same time he's mixing in his obvious passion for *The X-Files*. The combination gives you an example of the right way to tell your personal life story.

Martin Eriksson's Destinations

http://www.geocities.com/TheTropics/3430/

Martin Eriksson's site (see Figure 15.10) includes information on such exotic destinations as Kenya, Indonesia, Malaysia, and Australia. Each country has links to more information and current weather reports.

You'll also find a section on the Wonders of the World, a page of travel tips, and some personal information about the site's creator. A wealth of information on non-conventional destinations combined with a clean, easy-to-navigate design makes this a site worth visiting and emulating.

Figure 15.10
Destinations utilizes an attractive color scheme, a consistent design, and an intriguing topic.

What Can We Learn
from Martin Eriksson's Destinations?

When you create a site of any kind, it's very easy (especially after a number of updates over time) to end up with a cluttered site. What you lose most frequently is the well-thought-out navigation structure and interface for the site that makes it work in a slick way. What you want your visitors to see instead of clutter is a clean, simple layout. This lets the information and graphics take center stage on your site.

The navigation bar on the top and bottom of Martin Eriksson's home page is an excellent piece of work. Clearly labeled buttons appear highlighted and explain what they are as the mouse rolls over them. This advanced Web-design technique is known as rollover buttons. (You can find out how to create them by getting any good JavaScript book.) While this technique isn't repeated on every page in the site, all pages here do have a similar look and feel, and all images and links are clearly displayed.

Not only are travel sites in general very popular on the Web, but Martin has a lot of good advice about traveling around the world. As you navigate his site, you'll enjoy viewing his information quickly and easily because he's used some very good navigation and interface design. (If only every site worked so smoothly!)

Scooby Doo Web O'Rama

http://www.geocities.com/TelevisionCity/1145/

Figure 15.11 shows a fan site of a different nature. Rather than a page devoted to the latest teen idol, this site takes the classic cartoon Scooby Doo to the extreme and includes a bit of everything. The Scooby Store is associated with Amazon.com. Scooby Songs and Scooby Sounds include .WAV files of the theme song and a selection of quotes from all the characters.

There's also a chat room, a discussion board, character profiles, and some unsolved mysteries to answer. There's even a recipe for Scooby Snacks and a debate over the attributes of Velma versus Daphne.

Figure 15.11
The Scooby Doo
information warehouse.

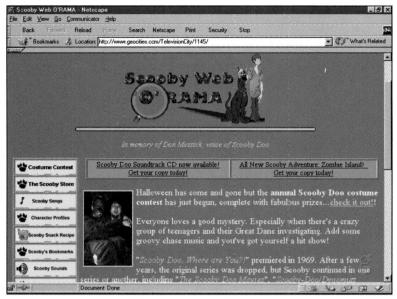

What Can We Learn
from the Scooby Doo Web O'Rama?

You have to hand it to the creators of the Scooby Doo Web O'Rama. First
they pick a site type that's popular—the fan site—but instead of making
yet another Leonardo DiCaprio site, they picked an offbeat topic—the TV
cartoon *Scooby Doo*. This kind of off-base topic thrives on the Web and
on GeoCities.

Second, the site shows some real resourcefulness on the part of the
developers to make the most of their page. You'll find a Scooby Store,
where (via GeoCities' Amazon link program) you can order the Scooby
Doo soundtrack CD and videos. On one page they use a page-counter
system to actually let you vote on your favorite Scooby Doo Valentine,
Daphne or Velma. Finally, the site makes rich use of multimedia files
offering .WAV files and RealAudio songs that were part of the long-
running series. Due to the size of the many multimedia files on the site,
the developers found a friend with a large amount of space on a server
who was willing to host the multimedia for them. They then link to that
site from their GeoCities page.

If you're looking for a page the epitomizes what building a fan site can
mean, and then uses every cool trick and content idea in the book, you
just might be inspired by this site.

Moving On

On the Web you can learn a lot about building pages just by looking at what other people have done. This is especially true on GeoCities because there is, as you've seen, something unique about a good GeoCities page. They tend to be not only good uses of the Web in general, but great uses of the community and interest oriented structure of GeoCities itself.

In a way it's one thing to build a great Web page, but it's another to build a great GeoCities Web page. So what do you do once you've done just that, built the best GeoCities Web page anyone has ever seen? Well you "upgrade the apparatus!" For the best page builders out there GeoCities has GeoPlus which gives you new features, and extra space to expand on GeoCities.

So take what you've learned here, stay on the lookout for new landmark sites, and cool uses of GeoCities, and use what you learn to be the next great GeoCities site.

16

Enhanced Service: GeoPlus

So you've built an amazing GeoCities site, mastered GeoBuilder, and tried all the homesteading tools in existence. What's a veteran free-site builder to do? Well, GeoCities doesn't stop with just free Websites. It offers an entire tier of enhanced services for the veteran Homesteader to explore.

If your site has grown to the point that you need more than the 11 megabytes of space GeoCities offers for free, that's no problem. GeoPlus is the answer. In this chapter, we'll discuss the GeoPlus program—what you get, how you sign up, and how much you'll pay.

Finally, for those of you who need to market products, GeoCities has created GeoShops (see Chapter 17, "GeoShops: E-Commerce Made Easy"), which lets you set up shop on the Web.

In this chapter, we're going to introduce you further to the GeoPlus service offered by GeoCities. It's not for everyone; but we'll teach you enough so you can make an informed decision whether these advanced services are worthwhile for you, and so you can integrate them into your current homesteading account if you wish.

Standard GeoCities versus GeoPlus

As you already know, your free GeoCities account offers 11 megabytes of space and one free e-mail account. With the GeoPlus program, which costs $4.95 per month, you will receive 25 megabytes of space—14 more than the free program offers. With GeoPlus, you can also eliminate the banner or pop-up advertising and GeoCities watermark that you're required to display on standard GeoCities pages. For more on GeoPlus, read the online brochure that you can find at **http://www.geocities.com/join/geoplus/** (see Figure 16.1).

Figure 16.1
Get details on the
GeoPlus program by
reading the online
brochure.

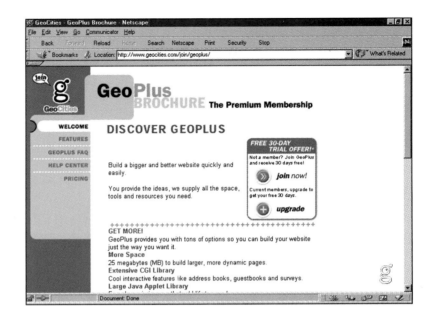

URL Options

Besides extra space and fewer requirements, GeoPlus offers you the
ability to have improved URLs to make it easier for your friends, family,
and colleagues to find you. By default, all GeoPlus members get a second
URL based on the Member ID that points to their site, in addition to their
original URL. Called the *Easy URL*, it simplifies the need for knowing
your Neighborhood, section, and address.

GeoPlus members also have the opportunity to have their own Virtual
URL—www.whatever.com, for an extra fee. To sign up for the Virtual
URL, you must decide on a name, then sign up with the InterNIC through
GeoCities. If the name you've selected is available, it's yours. If it's
already taken, you'll have to come up with a different URL. The fee paid
to InterNIC is $70 for the first two years and $35 per year thereafter. You
will also pay a $5 setup fee and $5 per month to GeoCities.

Below is a simple chart that explains the different URL options available
to GeoCities members:

Standard URL	Free Website member
http://www.geocities.com/Neighborhood/Section/yournumber	
Easy URL	GeoPlus member
http://www.geocities.com/~membername	
Virtual URL	GeoPlus member w/Virtual URL option
http://www.yourname.com	
GeoShops URL	GeoShops member
http://membername.geocities.com	

If you don't feel the need to have a Virtual URL, you can still receive the GeoPlus Easy URL for no additional charge. The new address will be **http://www.geocities.com/~yourmembername.**

If you decide you don't like your Personal URL, you can either change your member name or sign up for the Virtual URL. If you have any questions about the Virtual URL, read the FAQ in the GeoPlus area at **http://www.geocities.com/join/geoplus/bro_vurlfaq.html.** This FAQ answers a lot, if not all, the questions you may have about the Virtual URL service—from how to transfer an existing Virtual URL to canceling your Virtual URL. Since there are more questions to answer about this feature than we have room to include in this chapter, we recommend you check out the FAQ to find out more.

Cost and Payment

As we already mentioned, GeoPlus costs just $4.95 a month (plus the additional fees for the Virtual URL if you decide you need one).

If 25 megabytes just isn't enough (wow, you have a *big* site!), GeoPlus will allow you to add even more space in 5-megabyte increments for an additional $2.50 per month. (If you only use the extra space for part of a month, you will still be charged for the entire month.) You can cancel any of the 5-megabyte increments whenever you want, or you can add incremental space wherever you see the corresponding link.

You can pay for your services with a credit card (Visa and MasterCard only), GeoPoints, check, or money order. Checks or money orders must be drawn from an American bank. For more about billing and paying for GeoPlus, check out **http://www.geocities.com/join/geoplus/ price_billing.html.** This tells you where to send checks, how the credit card process works, and more.

Site-Management Features

The GeoPlus Manager is one of the site-management tools and is used as your Website control center. Here you can find account services, check out your most current Web statistics, or sign up for a Virtual URL and incremental space. You can also reach the Tools Manager inside the GeoPlus Manager. The Tools Manager gathers all the special tools and applications offered in the GeoPlus membership. You can access your File Manager to update your Website as well as all the utilities you'll need, including the Home Page Editors and EZ Upload.

To access the GeoPlus Manager, you must be a registered GeoPlus member. Then click on the **Members Area** button on the GeoCities home page. Once at the Members' Area, enter your member name and password to log on, and click the **GeoPlus** button. You'll be brought directly to the GeoPlus Manager (Figure 16.2).

Your GeoPlus Manager page will supply you with all of the information pertaining to your account and links to GeoPlus features. From here, you can go to the Tools Manager to edit your site, check out the GeoPlus Community Center to chat with other members, visit the Forums, or get the GeoPlus newsletter.

Figure 16.2
You'll find account information and links to features in the GeoPlus Manager page.

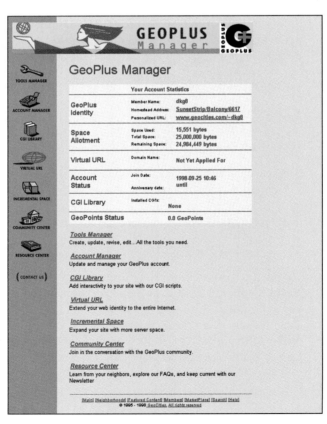

More GeoPoints

We discussed GeoPoints and their benefits in Chapter 14, "GeoCities Membership Benefits and Rules." As a reminder, members earn GeoPoints by being a banner volunteer or a Community Leader. GeoPlus members, however, earn GeoPoints at double the rate.

As a GeoPlus member, you can use GeoPoints on purchases in the GeoStore or to pay for your monthly fees from the GeoPlus program. The payment or points required for various fees are:

▶ GeoPlus service: $4.95 or 50 points

▶ Incremental space (per 5-megabyte blocks): $2.50 or 25 points

▶ Virtual URL monthly fee from GeoCities (not including the InterNIC fee): $5 or 50 points

The appropriate amount of GeoPoints must be in your account at the time payment is due or the full amount will be charged to your credit card. GeoCities will not accept any partial payments. For example, if you have the standard GeoPlus service and only 25 points in your account, you will be billed the entire one-month charge and your points will stay in your account.

You can change your billing options from credit card to GeoPoints after your first month by going to the GeoPlus Manager under "Account Manager."

The CGI Library

Do you want to boost your site's interactive capabilities? GeoPlus members have access to a special CGI Library that contains 12 CGI scripts. A *CGI script*, like the form handler, is a program that resides on the servers at GeoCities and gives you the ability to spice up your Web pages by offering new features, or processing information given to you by visitors to your page.

The CGI scripts included with GeoPlus allow you to build a guestbook, form automatic mailing lists, add a counter or clock, and include customizable surveys and forms. These CGI scripts allow you to better connect with the visitors to your site.

CGIs are self-contained programming modules that take data from your computer, run it into and through an application on the server, and return the information it collects to you.

A common reason GeoCities members upgrade to GeoPlus is that it offers a number of new CGI scripts which you can run on your page rather than just using the plain forms processor offered to basic GeoCities members.

These CGIs include:

▶ **Guestbook**—The Guestbook CGI enables members to leave messages on your site. It offers a lot more functionality than other guestbooks. For example, you can add customized imagery and backgrounds to the GeoPlus guestbook and edit posts.

▶ **Address Book**— The Address Book CGI lets visitors input and store their names and information in the address book. Think of it as a way for people to leave their contact information when they visit your site. The CGI also tells you the last CGI tool they used, such as whether they wrote you a note in the guestbook, left an answering machine message, or filled out a survey.

▶ **Answering Machine**—The Answering Machine CGI lets visitors to your site leave you notes, but unlike notes left in the guestbook, answering machine messages remain private and only you can view them.

▶ **Site Index**—This is an advanced CGI script for higher-end users. It lets you add a site index to your page. This enables people to search your pages for just the information they're looking for. You can place the script for the searching capabilities on every page. You'll have to place keywords on each page, then you can activate the indexing program so you have your own personal search engine for your site.

▶ **Clock, Countdown, and Countdown 2000**—These are three separate scripts that work in a similar fashion—all dealing with time. The Clock CGI lets you display the date and time on your page. You can set the clock to adjust for whatever time-zone you wish. The Countdown 2000 script displays how much time is left until the Year 2000. And the Countdown Clock CGI displays how much time is left until whatever date you might choose.

▶ **Counter**—Lets you add a page counter to any page on your site.

▶ **Simple Survey and Rank & Tell**—Lets you provide automatically updateable surveys to your site. You can build a survey that displays multiple-choice questions with a maximum of five answers.

Support for the CGI scripts is available to all GeoPlus members at **http://www.geocities.com/join/geoplus/bro_cgifaq.html**

Additional Java Applets

GeoPlus also includes a bunch of special Java applets you can add to your page. These include:

▶ An animated logo applet that lets you show multiple graphics on one image area (similar to an animated GIF).

▶ A rotating sign applet that rotates an image within a banner-sized graphic, like an old gas station sign.

▶ A Random Image applet that you can use to load different graphics into your page every time someone visits it (to add a bit of variety).

▶ A Gliding Image Banner applet that can be used to create interesting presentations on your site

▶ A Vertical Image Text applet that will scroll a bunch like a ticker but vertically.

The Resource Center

The Resource Center
(http://www.geocities.com/join/geoplus/bro_resource.html), shown in Figure 16.3, is where you can find a lot of the answers to your GeoPlus questions. Here the Community Center gives you the links to a special set of online tools exclusive to GeoPlus members, plus links to becoming a Community Leader, as well as Web tutorials.

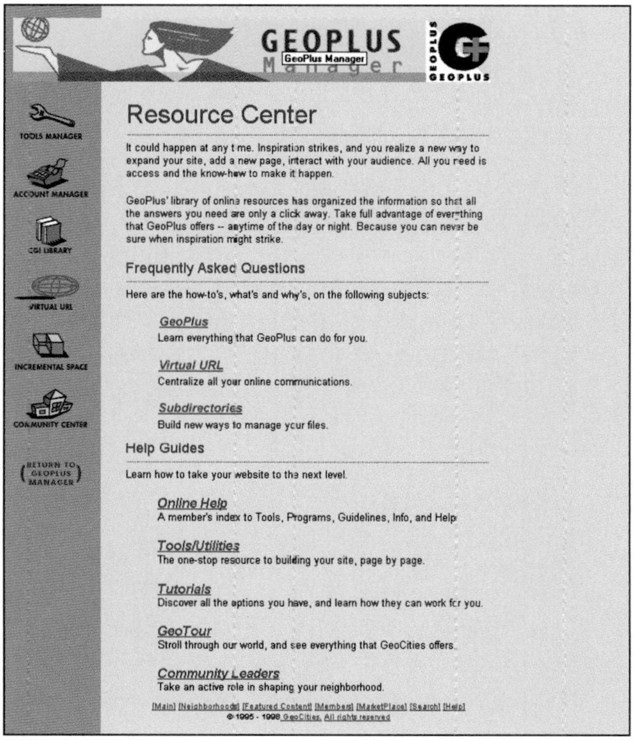

Figure 16.3
You'll find links to GeoPlus tools and Web tutorials at the Resource Center.

You will also find Frequently Asked Questions and Community Help Guides categories at the Resource Center. In addition, an online help link will give you an index to tools, guidelines, programs, and other help resources.

Signing Up for GeoPlus

GeoCities offers a free 30-day trial for GeoPlus. To sign up for the trial, you must use a credit card. If you decide you don't want or need GeoPlus, you must cancel it or GeoCities will continue to bill your credit card for $4.95 a month.

To sign up for GeoPlus, go to **http://www.geocities.com/join/geoplus/ join.html.** You can upgrade your existing GeoCities account into a GeoPlus membership or join if you are not already a member. Join GeoPlus as you would join any other GeoCities member option as described in Chapter 2, "Getting Started with GeoCities"—except that you have to figure out payment options.

An application with your original address information will appear. Make sure this information is the same as is listed for your credit-card billing address and make any necessary corrections. Add the credit-card information and click **Submit.** GeoCities will process your transaction and, assuming all is well, a page will welcome you to GeoPlus. The log-in process is explained in the Site Management Features section. A typical transaction should take just 30 to 60 seconds.

How to Upload to Your New GeoPlus Account

The upload procedure is the same for GeoPlus as it is for the free personal home page program. To learn more about uploading to these accounts, see Chapter 4, "Building Your GeoCities Skills and Toolbox." There is no separate directory for GeoPlus; the difference you will see is the 25 megabytes of space. By signing up for GeoPlus, you are not changing your site. GeoPlus just offers a lot of options to add to your site if you choose to do so.

How to Cancel GeoPlus

You can cancel your GeoPlus membership at any time. Here are some simple steps to help you along in the process:

1. Log on to GeoPlus.
2. On the GeoPlus Manager, go to the Account Manager.
3. Choose **Cancel my GeoPlus Membership**.

Checks or money orders used to pay for the GeoPlus program are nonrefundable. If your page is deleted for page-content violations (see Chapter 14), you are also not eligible for a refund.

GeoPlus pages are for non-commercial use only. They hold the same content guidelines as a free personal home page. If you want to have a commercial site on GeoCities, you can sign up for the GeoShops program (see Chapter 17).

Moving On

It's hard to outgrow GeoCities. . .even the most hardcore-site builders will be satisfied with GeoPlus. And it doesn't stop there because GeoCities also features a complete e-commerce solution, giving you the ability to sell your wares on the Web.

What once started as a simple place to build a fun Web page has quickly grown to include very powerful features. Yet GeoCities is still focused on you, giving you the power to start your own office, upgrade your site and become a storeowner. The trick is to first get the most out your free GeoCities site and then move on to the extra features of GeoPlus.

Part IV   Beyond Homesteading

17

GeoShops: E-Commerce Made Easy

So GeoPlus allows you add space and offers a number of other benefits through GeoPlus. Yet another GeoCities service—GeoShops—allows you to make money by selling your products without the help of affiliated stores.

How GeoShops Works

GeoShops lets you hop aboard the runaway train of electronic commerce. As the Internet continues to grow, so too does the opportunity to make money. That opportunity isn't limited to the Pages That Pay program. You, too, can become an online merchant (although we don't expect that you'll be challenging the e-commerce giant Amazon.com for at least a couple of years!). In this chapter, we will detail the advantages of GeoShops to help you decide whether online retailing is for you, then we'll cover the costs, show you a handful of standout GeoShops, and even give you some tips about running an online store.

With GeoShops you can sell to anyone on the Web. However, as a GeoShops proprietor, one of the advantages you have is that GeoCities helps its shops market their products. especially to the millions of GeoCities members. So while you can serve any customer, whether a GeoCities member or not, you will have an extra edge in marketing to Homesteaders because your store is part of the GeoCities community.

The Cost of GeoShops

GeoShops is not for someone who wants to slap up a catalog for fun, maybe sell something and maybe not—unless you earn some disposable income each month. GeoCities' plan for online merchants is intended for people who want to run a business on the Web. GeoCities offers two pricing plans—GeoShops with *transactional processing* and *GeoShops Basic*.

GeoShops with Transactional Processing

Transactional processing is a complete e-commerce solution for serious online merchants. The cost is $99.95 per month plus 55 cents per transaction. There is also a one-time $195 set-up fee and the optional domain name fee paid to the InterNIC ($70 for two years, $35 per year thereafter).

GeoShops Basic

GeoShops Basic is a less robust program that is also less expensive. The cost is $24.95 per month, plus the same optional domain name fees paid to the InterNIC.

Payment

GeoShops members are charged for each month in advance and payment is by Visa and MasterCard only (no checks or money orders). You won't receive an invoice; your credit card will automatically be billed. GeoPoints are not accepted as a means of payment.

You are not required to sign up for more than one month in advance; instead, you pay as you go in one-month increments. If you decide to cancel your GeoShop membership before the end of your billing cycle, you will not receive a refund for the remaining time.

If you cancel your account, you must remove all commercial material from your site.

NOTE

Signing Up

The signup process is simple, so we won't bore you with the details here. Just go to **http://www.geocities.com/join/geoshops/join.html** and follow the directions.

The Advantages of GeoShops

The price is affordable and the payment terms are acceptable, you say? You're in! So which way should you go? That depends on how serious you are about the online retailing business. Of course, it also depends on how much money you want to spend to make it work. If you want to promote your business and are trying to ease into selling products on the Web, the Basic package may be the way to go. If you've done that and are ready to go full steam ahead, you might consider adding transactional processing. We certainly don't want to tell you which option to select, since we don't know what your situation is. We will, however, provide you with the information necessary to make your decision.

The Basic package offers:

▶ An online store

▶ Residence in a GeoCities Neighborhood

▶ Three topic search engines

▶ Virtual URL (domain name fees not included). See Chapter 16, "Enhanced Service: GeoPlus," for more information on Virtual URLs.

▶ Unlimited e-mail aliases

▶ 25 megabytes of server space

▶ A library of utilities and programming modules

The transactional processing package is a complete, end-to-end e-commerce solution that offers all that's offered in the Basic package, plus:

▶ Credit-card processing capability

▶ Real-time credit-card verification and authorization

▶ SSL (Secure Sockets Layer) standard for security

▶ Instant online access to order status

▶ Online inventory manager and catalog builder

You also get:

▶ An unlimited number of **e-mail aliases** allows you to catalog your e-mail when it is sent. For example, you can have customers send customer service questions to **service@businessname.com**; Website comments to **webmaster@businessname.com**; and so on.

▶ GeoCities also provides all the tools you need to build your store. The **GeoShops Manager** allows you to revise your site, process sales, and interact with other GeoShops merchants in the members-only area. The Manager also provides instantly updated account information (such as server-space statistics).

▶ GeoShops' suite of **File Manager** tools allows you to update your store at any time. Updating product inventory or revising catalog pages is easy and doesn't require any HTML knowledge.

▶ As a GeoShops member, you also have access to the CGI library that we mentioned in Chapter 16. As an online store operator, you'll find the interactivity provided by these scripts even more valuable.

▶ But most importantly, the high-end option allows you to offer **secure credit card processing**, something that is absolutely essential for anyone hoping to sell products directly over the Internet. GeoCities has a partnership with Internet Commerce Services Corporation (ICOMS), a commerce service provider that uses the OpenMarket transaction-processing platform.

Begin Taking Orders

To begin taking orders, you will first need to set up a *merchant account* that will work with GeoCities' transaction server. For more information or to apply for a merchant account, go to **http://www.geocities.com/join/ geoshops/wellsfargo.html**.

Here's how it works. You build your inventory or list of products that you will sell from your GeoShop, then create Web pages that display and describe your products. You can offer color pictures, lively descriptions, price information, and whatever else you find necessary or helpful.

When someone chooses a product, the inventory item number and price are automatically transmitted to ICOMS transaction server. ICOMS displays a GeoShops Internet page to collect your customers' payment information. Customers can even register so the information is only collected once.

The transaction processing system then calculates shipping charges and sales tax and secures real-time credit-card authorization. When the credit card is authorized, ICOMS sends you an e-mail alerting you to the sale, posts the order to the GeoShops Manager, and sends a digital receipt to your customer.

The transaction is held until you confirm to ICOMS that the product has been shipped. Once you have confirmed the shipment, ICOMS processes the customer's payment through a credit-card processor or accounts-receivable system and credits your merchant account. Customers also have the benefit of being able to check the status of orders by using the online Smart Statement.

ICOMS also provides the following reports to merchants on a regular basis:

▶ Notice of order and shipping instructions

▶ List of orders processed

▶ List of orders reported as not shipped

▶ Number of transactions in the database, including the date of the oldest

▶ Summary of funds transferred into the merchant's account

▶ Monthly summary of sales tax accruals by state

▶ Detailed billing information

All credit-card data, purchase order information, and item and price lists are encrypted, keeping your private information and that of your customers safe. You can control site access, customize security settings, and set payment limits for specified customers. ICOMS service is based on TransAct from OpenMarket, one of the top Internet transaction-processing systems. ICOMS continually oversees its systems and operations.

Any Questions?

So that covers the basics of GeoShops' offerings. Still, we're sure you have questions and think you'll find most of the answers in GeoCities' extensive list of Frequently Asked Questions that you'll find at **http://www.geocities.com/join/geoshops/geoshops_faq.html**. While this FAQ covers any questions directly related to GeoShops, the following sections list some questions and answers about running an online store.

Can I run my GeoShop out of my house or apartment?

Depending on the nature and size of your business and the size of your home, you can operate your GeoShop without an office. In fact, budget constraints may dictate that you start your online business out of your home. Of course, if you are simply expanding an existing business to include a Web presence, you don't need to worry about this issue.

However, running your online business somewhere other than your home will help you separate your work life and your home life. Hopefully, your online store will become so successful that you will have to move it to its own space.

Do I need any employees?

You can start as a one-person operation and add employees if and when growth warrants.

Should my site have content other than product descriptions and pictures?

You'll also need to generate content for pages such as company policy, common questions, updates, and shipping information. You can also add industry news and reviews either by linking to other sources or creating it yourself. Much like a non-commercial GeoCities site, the more interesting, fresh content you can provide, the more reasons people will have to visit. And the more they visit, the more they'll buy.

What should I sell?

If you already have a traditional store, you can skip this one. But if you are building a Web store from scratch, there are a number of things to consider. Some items that sell well are CDs (music or computer-related), books, and video games. The best advice, however, is to sell things you are enthusiastic and knowledgeable about, assuming there is some kind of market for the products you know and like.

Will GeoCities help me get products to customers?

Shipping is up to you, and you'll find a number of options available. The more you offer, the better for your customers. If someone absolutely, positively needs something overnight and you don't offer overnight delivery, they'll go elsewhere. Remember, the customer pays for shipping, so you don't need to worry about losing money by shipping overnight.

So I can just open my GeoShop and the orders will start rolling in, right?

Um, no. If it were that easy, everyone would have a GeoShop. You need to draw people to your store just like you would any other GeoCities site. For more on promoting your site, check out Chapter 13, "Promoting Your GeoCities Home Page."

Are there any good references out there?

Some of the best information will come from simply visiting other established Websites. You can also get information from a number of good books out there, including the following:

▶ *Getting Hits: The Definitive Guide to Promoting Your Website* by Don Sellers (Peachpit Press)

▶ *How to Grow Your Business on the Internet* by Vince Emery (Coriolis Group Books)

▶ *Creating Stores on the Web* by Joe Cataudella, Dave Greely, and Ben Sawyer (Peachpit Press)

You should also interact with other GeoShops merchants at the members-only GeoShops Manager Area and visit some Usenet spots such as **alt.business.misc**, **comp.internet.net-happenings**, and **alt.internet.commerce**.

Ten Good Tips on Running Your Store

GeoShops gives you a lot of help in getting your store onto the Web, but running an online store still takes a lot of work. Here are some good tips to help you successfully run your GeoShop.

1. **Good design helps tremendously**

   The design of your store will be a big part of its success. Since people will navigate your store to find items and purchase them, make sure browsers can easily locate your site to find the items they want and to get information about you and your store.

   Shoppers tend to evaluate stores by how attractive the store's site is. If the site has a nice clean look and gives the impression you've worked hard to make it look good and work well, then prospective customers will be more likely to do business with you.

2. **Content is critical**

   People don't just turn to online shopping for cheap prices and simple price lists. Shoppers tend to turn to online shopping as much for the expertise the store offers as for anything else. This may be especially true on a community-oriented service like GeoCities where many of your shoppers may be coming to you for information related to the Neighborhood in which you located your store.

   Useful content, which comes from people who are interested in and knowledgeable about the topic, gives your site value. Valuable content brings shoppers. For example, a site that sells vintage music should offer plenty of information about vintage music, not just a price list of old records. This might include biographies on the groups and singers, ratings on the quality of the recordings, pictures of the album covers, and other detail that will attract customers.

   To create good store content, focus on presenting smart information and wise opinions about the products you sell. Internet shoppers tend to give their money to merchants who best provide the content they need to make informed buying decisions. Successful marketing is most likely to occur when customers perceive merchants as presenting precisely what they want. Sure, some shoppers will come to you for the information then go elsewhere for a better price or another item, but most shoppers look for good information first and are more likely to return to sites where they get it.

3. **Promote as much as possible off the Net**

   While the GeoShops service helps with submissions to search engines and other online promotional efforts, never forget the value of the public relations (PR). Put the domain name for your store everywhere you can. Look for ways to promote the store in newspapers and at various events. Although many shoppers use search engines and indexes to find stores, not everyone does.

Part IV Beyond Homesteading

This is especially true for online store counterparts to real-world stores. Put the Web address for your store on the receipts, on your boxes used for shipping, on customer bags, and anywhere it's likely to be noticed. If you run a real-world store, you'll find that many online customers will be people who at some point visited your physical store. Make sure you're doing the most you can to promote the online store to those customers.

4. **Be prepared for international orders**

    The second you go live on the Web with a store, you have a worldwide customer base. Whether or not you want international orders, you'll need to be prepared for them. The biggest issues that will crop up are trusting the orders you receive from overseas and fulfilling them.

    In terms of fulfillment, be sure you have a stack of customs forms (available at the post office) since you'll need to fill these out for international orders sent via the post office. You'll also want to know which overnight couriers service which countries, and their respective rates.

CAUTION

Beware of suspiciously large orders

If you accept credit cards, be wary of international credit-card orders, especially large orders. One store owner we know recommends that you request a faxed copy of the customer's credit card (both sides) in order to prevent fraud. This will let you know exactly who the issuing bank for the card is, which will make it easier for you to verify the card. GeoShops owners also recommend you adopt a policy limiting the size of orders from international customers until you've established a relationship with them.

5. **Be careful about fraud and crime**

    Just like in the real world, store crime is an issue for online stores. However, taking some wise precautions will minimize this problem. First and foremost, if you plan to accept orders, make sure you use GeoShops' secure ordering process to take orders from customers. This prevents hackers from stealing credit-card data as your customers transfer this information to your store.

    Be wary of large orders from customers you don't know. Not every large order is a sign of fraud, but you would be wise to dig a little deeper into the verification of cards used to pay for unusually large orders.

    Other forms of fraud to be on the lookout for are kids using their parents credit cards without permission, and customers who pay for the goods then claim they never arrived. To avoid being hurt by such

Part IV   Beyond Homesteading

deceitful practices, require some form of signature when you send your goods. If your goods appeal to kids, put a warning on the site addressed specifically to kids about using their parents' cards without permission. Some kids might not be aware of the seriousness of using a parent's credit card without permission. Spell it out for them: "Warning: Unauthorized use of a credit card, even if it is your parents', is a crime that could result in fines, jail time, and a criminal record."

Online crime is not rampant, and the secure system on GeoShops is good, but being aware and vigilant will enable you to do the best job of ensuring that you'll remain victimless.

6. **Build the most flexible shipping policy**

Getting your wares to your customers is very important in the online store business. It's the only physical link between you and your customer. Many times you'll need to have multiple shipping accounts so you can offer the widest array of pricing and service. One store we know uses the post office, UPS, FedEx, and DHL. The post office is great because they offer Priority Mail, which is a cheap way to get items to customers within 2 to 3 days.

UPS is excellent for larger items because it offers ground-shipping rates, has higher weight limits, and allows more box shapes than do other shippers. UPS also has good overnight and international rates. FedEx has excellent rates, shipping software, and package tracking. The company recently unveiled lower-priced, three-day shipping, too. DHL is known for being the leader in sending items overseas.

Another reason to have multiple accounts is that some couriers pick up later than others. In some cities, Airborne Express is known for having later pick-up times than other couriers. The post office's Express Mail is one of the only services that will deliver on Sundays and tends to be the cheapest for overnight orders for Sundays.

TIP

Have Reasonable Shipping Rates

A final tip on shipping is actually a pricing tip. Many online stores try to shave prices by having high shipping and handling costs. This tends to work for a while as you subsidize your product pricing by a few dollars while charging $8 for shipping and handling for a $3.20 priority mail package. Then customers start to see through this tactic—and you ultimately lose.

7. **Keep customers informed so they'll come back**

Ask customers for their e-mail addresses, and ask to add them to your monthly or weekly e-mail newsletter. Inform them of sales and new product offerings; otherwise, they might not come back. The secret of any small storeowner, online or otherwise, is repeat business.

With GeoShops you can create forms that customers can fill out which automatically add them to a mailing list. See Chapter 12, "Developing Forms on GeoCities," for more information on how to do this with the GeoCities Forms Processor.

8. **Don't forget about taxes and other legal issues**

One reason online stores are booming is that Web stores in the U.S. aren't required to collect sales tax for the moment (except for state sales tax). At some point this could change once the tax moratorium is over. In addition there are still laws pertaining to interstate shipping of some goods (such as wine) and other laws you might need to be aware of besides tax laws. When you open an online store, you should consider consulting with your business or personal attorney. He or she might have some advice or words of warning.

9. **Be unique in some fashion**

Just being on the Web these days is not enough. For your store to work online, you need to have some sort of unique offering that will separate your store from the others out there. You'll also want to avoid some of the big categories of stores that are being dominated by colossal online stores like Amazon.com.

Selling "different" goods or services—such as hard-to-find information, unusual goods (self-manufactured items will certainly give your store a good uniqueness!), exceptional service, or a special presentation—will make your store unique.

Another factor that will make your store distinctive is that GeoShops are integrated into the GeoCities communities. By becoming an active member through chats, link exchanges, and discussion with similar sites on GeoCities, you can help your store thrive.

10. **Offer other ways to order**

GeoShops lets you set up secure order forms for your store. However, if you can offer people a phone number they can call to order goods, do it. Even though Internet shopping is taking off, orders taken via telephone are too important to turn away.

Some Good Examples of GeoShops

Rather than just tell you about GeoShops, we thought we would show you some good examples.

Healthy Habits

http://www.geocities.com/HotSprings/Villa/3224

Healthy Habits (see Figure 17.1) sells personal care products and also offers plenty of free health-related information and reports. This site is notable for a number of reasons.

Most obvious is its attractive, clean, consistent design. The graphic that identifies each page includes a close-up photo of a sunflower—certainly a healthy image. The overall look is clean and fresh, with pale drawings of leaves and smiling sun buttons. Products are also broken down into categories such as Body Cleansing, Weight Management, and General Health Maintenance. This is a good technique so your customers don't have to search high and low to find what they want.

Healthy Habits also offers free reports, but you must fill out a response form to receive one. This is a good way to a build a voluntary database of potential customers.

Figure 17.1
The Healthy Habits home page offers free health advice and information while selling a number of personal care products.

JS-Computers

http://www.geocities.com/SiliconValley/Peaks/9376

JS-Computers is taking on the big guys by, they say, offering lower prices. The site is not spectacular to look at, but that isn't the point. JS-Computers says it offers the same warranties and technical support, not to mention custom-built systems. They also offer CPUs, motherboards, hard drives, modems, and more.

JS-Computers is an example of the other side of online retailing—minimal Website, solid product, low prices. You don't need the most spectacular Website if you can offer better deals, customer service, and such.

You won't beat your competitors in every facet of retailing, but if you can be the best in one—such as price—you will likely find a customer base. Figure 17.2 shows their order screen.

Figure 17.2
Customers use the JS-Computers online order form to purchase products.

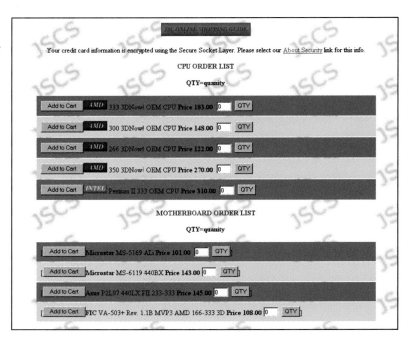

Part IV Beyond Homesteading

Maine's Finest

http://www.geocities.com/NapaValley/8967

Maine's Finest (see Figure 17.3) is a unique online store in that it offers a very specialized product—Maine lobster. Maine offers the best lobster in the world and Maine's Finest will ship it to you when you order online.

While shipped lobster is certainly expensive, Maine's Finest offers instructions for cooking lobster, other lobster-related recipes, and Fun Facts about lobsters (such as lobsters smell their food with four small antennae).

This site includes some nice photos and little touches, such as the Fun Facts and recipes, that make a store more interesting.

Figure 17.3

Maine's Finest offers Maine-grown lobster and other seafood-related products.

The Festival

http://www.geocities.com/RainForest/Canopy/5294

The Festival sells clothes and accessories for Deadheads and those with similar fashion sense—yet another specialized market, but one capable of providing products to a large customer base.

The Festival home page (see Figure 17.4) sticks with that theme with a wonderful cartoon of a Volkswagen bus (the preferred mode of hippie transportation) plastered with bumper stickers. The stickers send customers to various areas of the site—accessories, skirts, real stickers (of Dancing Bears or Jerry Garcia, for example), and links (such as to The Grateful Dead and Phish).

Figure 17.4
Hop on The Festival bus.

The site is fun, cool to look at, and well organized. All items are described and shown in full color (see Figure 17.5).

Figure 17.5
The Festival catalog
page shows and
describes fanny packs.

Moving On

Wow. That's it! Thanks for sticking with us from start to finish. We hope
we have provided you with valuable information from the basics of Web-
building and the range of tools provided by GeoCities to some tips on
e-commerce. Now you should be able to create a great Website on
GeoCities—one that will reflect your knowledge and interests while
standing out from the millions of sites on the Internet.

If you haven't yet started building a site, what are you waiting for? Even
if you have, keep this book nearby as a reference for those days when you
want to improve your site but just can't figure out how.

Index

Index

Index

Creating Paint Shop Pro
Web Graphics

Price: $44.99
ISBN: 0-9662889-0-4
Pages: 384
Author: Andy Shafran

- Full Color
- Foreword by
  Chris Anderson,
  VP of Marketing,
  Jasc Software

Highlights:
- Sixteen focused
  chapters that teach
  you how to
  understand layers,
  special effects, plug-ins,
  and other important Paint Shop Pro features
- Integrates with a comprehensive Website that
  contains updated information, complete examples,
  and frequently asked questions
- Detailed Web specific topics such as transparency,
  animation, web art, digital photography, scanners,
  and more

MP3 Power!
with Winamp

Price: $29.99
ISBN: 0-9662889-3-9
Pages: 320
Authors: Justin Frankel,
Ben Sawyer,
Dave Greely

- CD-ROM with
  software, utilities,
  and popular music

Highlights:
- Unique and complete
  coverage of MP3
  technology and Winamp
  technical specifications and
  optimizations. Ideal for casual and expert MP3 users
- Covers creating MP3 files from existing CDs, finding
  MP3 files on the Internet, and marketing MP3 files for
  others to download and use
- Discusses finding and building virtual radio stations
  on the Internet

QuicKeys Solutions
for Windows and Mac

Price: $24.99
ISBN: 0-9662889-5-5
Pages: 240
Author: Don Crabb

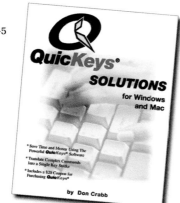

- Solution-focused
  format
- CD-ROM with
  valuable
  software
- Includes $20
  coupon towards
  QuicKeys software

Highlights:
- Teaches you how to
  get around shortcomings
  in Windows and Mac OS using QuicKeys to
  automate repetitive and complicated procedures
- Shows how to turn common or complex sets of
  commands into a single keystroke, saving you
  significant time
- Comfortable book tone for novice and power users

eBay
Online Auctions

Price: $14.99
ISBN: 0-9662889-4-7
Pages: 224
Author: Neil J. Salkind

- Glossary
- Question and Answer
  format

Highlights:
- Explains the concepts
  behind how eBay works
- Fully explains the
  bidding, buying, and
  selling process for items,
  exchanging currency, and obtaining the
  auctioned items
- Describes the different types of auctions, options
  available for bidders and sellers, and limitations of
  each format
- Shows how businesses can use eBay to buy and sell
  items affordably

MUSKA&LIPMAN

Order Form

Postal Orders:
Muska & Lipman Publishing
9525 Kenwood Road, Suite 16-372
Cincinnati, Ohio 45242

On-Line Orders or for more information visit:
http://www.muskalipman.com
Fax Orders:
(513) 794-1913

Qty.	Title	ISBN	Price	Total Cost
_____	Creating Paint Shop Pro Web Graphics	0-9662889-0-4	$44.99	_____
_____	Creating GeoCities Websites	0-9662889-1-2	$39.99	_____
_____	eBay Online Auctions	0-9662889-4-7	$14.99	_____
_____	MP3 Power! with Winamp	0-9662889-3-9	$29.99	_____
_____	QuicKeys Solutions for Windows and Mac	0-9662889-5-5	$24.99	_____

Subtotal _____

Sales Tax _____
(please add 6% for books shipped to Ohio addresses)

Shipping _____
($4.00 for the first book, $2.00 each additional book)

TOTAL PAYMENT ENCLOSED _____

Ship to:

Company _____

Name _____

Address _____

City _____ State _____ Zip _____ Country _____

Educational facilities, companies, and organizations interested in multiple copies of these books should contact the publisher for quantity discount information. Training manuals, CD-ROMs, electronic versions, and portions of these books are also available individually or can be tailored for specific needs.

Thank you for your order.